The Politics of Administrative Representation

The Politics of Administrative Representation

School Administrators and
Local Democracy

Dale Mann
Teachers College
Columbia University

Lexington Books
D.C. Heath and Company
Lexington, Massachusetts
Toronto   London

Library of Congress Cataloging in Publication Data

Mann, Dale.
    The politics of administrative representation.

    Bibliography: p.
    Includes indes.
    1. School administrators. 2. School management and organization.
I. Title.
LB2831.62.M36   371.2'01   74-25062
ISBN 0-669-97188-x

Published simultaneously in Canada.

Printed in the United States of America.

International Standard Book Number: 0-669-97188-x

Library of Congress Catalog Card Number: 74-25062

To my Father and Mother

Contents

List of Figure and Tables

Preface

Over the last fifteen years there has been remarkable growth in the use of political terms to analyze schools, schooling, and education. This book applies the political interpretation of schools to the analysis of school administrators. Many administrators may resist, or at least not understand, what it means to adopt a political interpretation of their work. The word "politics" provokes images of buying and selling influence, making "dirty" and secret deals, and compromising moral gains. For administrators, "politics" has an even less attractive personal meaning because they see themselves as the targets of unwanted political pressure. "Politics" is the force that would have them favor someone's nephew for a teaching job, the power that hamstrings their professional prerogatives, or the selfish motivation that causes an ambitious citizen to turn a critical spotlight on the administrator's school. All of those are indeed aspects of politics, but they are not the total, or even the most important part, of politics. The motives that compelled a president to disgrace the office is part of politics, but so is the moral indignation that forced him out. The privately negotiated understandings among the members of a school board are part of politics, but so is the keenly felt outer limit of responsibility to constituents beyond which individuals will not go. The rivalry and duplication among offices with overlapping missions leads to "office politics" in the bad sense, but that same competition can produce political responsiveness that we would all benefit from.

Like other systems, politics has to cope with all the human characteristics that are so easy to disdain—ambition, parochiality, ill will, misunderstanding, and on and on. The job of public policy—and of politics—is to arrange intensely human and individual characteristics so that they aggregate to more inclusive interests. The system that puts the ugly part of its political actors on such prominent display is attempting to do that. Adopting a political interpretation means moving past mere cynicism to see in people's shortcomings how the public's interest is, or can be, served. Administrators who do not go beyond their cynical rejection of "politics" cannot then engage all their responsibilities as administrators. They cannot manage the shortcomings of the people in their organizations and their environments so that the public's interests are nonetheless served.

If school/community interaction is viewed in this broader and more accurately "political" context, then no one should be surprised that administrators have been reluctant to embrace a political interpretation of their responsibilities. To the obscure and difficult task of schooling has now been added one that is even more obscure and difficult—politics. To the central social task of educating children has now been added the task of doing that with and through society's political process in the school itself.

This book argues that schools are political institutions and that administrators are political actors in ways that are not yet very widely understood. How can that understanding be enhanced? Most practicing administrators recognize that something has happened in their community relations. The fluctuations from apathy to conflict, and from allegiance to hostility, are more stressful and more uncertain than ever before. Communities expect better quality schooling, yet at the same time they expect more responsiveness to varying particular interests—all for the same or less money. And communities seek to hold administrators personally accountable for delivering on that difficult agenda. Political scientists see a common thread in such situations and in the public controversies like community control and decentralization that are the symptomatic expressions of a more general development. The dilemma faced by administrators is one of representation, that is, how can (or should!) the wishes and interest of the publics be reflected in decisions of a professional school administrator. Theories like that of representation are, or at least are supposed to be, concepts that explain. Yet the administrator who turns to the idea of representation for help will discover that virtually all the work in the area to date has been done on legislative, not administrative representation.

This book uses the idea of representation to examine the interaction between school administrators and their communities. One half of that interaction, from the administrators out to the community, is examined in the first part. The second half of the school/community whole, from the community back to the administrator, is discussed in the second part of the book.

This analysis of the school administrator's political behavior argues for a more adequate recognition on the part of school people of the political responsibilities of their jobs. Yet school people justifiably take academics to task for failing to follow their analysis through to its logical, if prescriptive, conclusion. The failure to close with the application of analysis is especially puzzling among political scientists who generally recognize the truth of what Woodrow Wilson wrote in *Leaders of Men*: "The men who act stand nearer to the mass of men than the men who write; and it is in their hands that new thought gets its translation into the crude language of deeds." Because I have wanted to do justice to those school people who must do what others write about and because I believe that prescription is a legitimate test for an applied science, the second half of this book focuses on those aspects of school/community interaction that have led to improved goal achievement. The last chapter summarizes much of the rest of the book in the format of an "operations manual," or a guide, to good practice. The "manual" can be used by those administrators who wish to move their school/community relations to a level of shared control.

As a graduate student, I was surprised to encounter people who had devoted their entire working lives to understanding a single concept, especially when they were forthright enough to admit that they had not exhausted their chosen topic. Yet it turns out that the political ideas around which the goodness of our public xiii

experience revolves are, almost without exception, so complicated, paradoxical, and ambiguous as to require at least that sort of investment. "Equality," "the public interest," and "democratic participation" are such terms. Having spent several years struggling with and puzzling about representation, I know that it belongs to that class.

Fortunately, I have had a lot of help. Charles Benson, Will Riggan, and Jim Guthrie supported the research of the first half through the New York State Commission on the Quality, Cost and Financing of Elementary and Secondary Education. A grant from the National Institute of Education and the substantive help of Tom Clemens at NIE made possible the nation-wide search on which the second half is based. Barbara Blummer and Madeline Holzer made important contributions at every level of the analysis and interpretation. Maria C. Barde-guez and Marva Harrison helped with early drafts and Darlene Sinnah-Yovonie did an outstanding job of producing the final manuscript. My colleagues in the Department of Educational Administration contributed by graciously ignoring the many idiosyncracies that appear whenever I have to try to meet the demands of scholarship and of the English language, both at the same time.

One person became involved in my research on representation as soon as I did. She critiqued the conceptual framework, contributed to the research design, helped with the data collection and analysis, all the while serving as office manager and general problem-solver. Her own convictions and professional experience directing a day care center in New York City led her to contribute to and frequently to dissent from the conclusions in the second half of this book. Even more remarkable than her unfailing good cheer while helping with my work was that fact that she could be of such varied assistance while managing a separate career of her own. It does not diminish the contribution of all the individuals named above to say that their assistance does not equal that which I have had from my wife, Sandra Rodman Mann.

Finally, I trust to the good judgment of the reader in locating the proper and only person to blame for the shortcomings of this book.

Dale Mann
October, 1975
New York City

The Politics of Administrative
Representation

1 Demands on Administrative Decisions

Introduction

School administrators are constantly presented with problems of political representation. On the one hand, they wish to make objective decisions based on the facts of an educational situation; on the other hand, they need to take account of the needs and interests of the public. Guidance from those sources is often not as consistent as either administrators or communities would want. For example, take the case of a school principal who had spent the early part of her career as a specialist in reading research. Upon becoming principal of a school, she discovers that a particular early-reading curriculum that she had previously discredited is still being used; moreover, it is very popular among the parents. What should she do? Replace it immediately with the best alternative available? Replace it and then explain to the parents what was wrong with it? Resolve to wait until she is better established in the community before making such a major change? Propose a cooperative reevaluation committee on which parents are represented? Keep it and try to improve on it? As another example, put yourself in the position of a high school principal faced with a large group of students who want to hold a protest rally in the school's cafeteria. You are confident that the rally will be a peaceful way to vent grievances, but some vocal community leaders are adamant in expressing their fear that it will spill outside the school and cause widespread damage. Would you: authorize it and hope to demonstrate to the community the soundness of your judgment? Go ahead with plans but work with student leaders to ensure that it does not get out of hand? Delay the students and hope to change the community leaders' attitudes? Negotiate with the students with the intent of stopping the rally? Or would you prohibit it?

Questions about how the community should be represented in professional decisions recur throughout school administration. Should a superintendent buck majority opinions about school integration? Which clientele should get a new principal's first attention—those served by a reform in grouping? By ethnic studies? By an emphasis on reading? How do administrators determine how much or how little of what the community says it wants will indeed be reflected in the policies and the services of the school? How do they choose among competing claims or conflicting criteria? Or, more accurately, as professionals in the public service, how do they weight those multiple criteria in arriving at a final decision?

Until the recent past the dominant, if not the exclusive, decision criterion for

1

school people was expertise. Was not education a science? Weren't educators professionals? Hadn't they been entrusted by society to make decisions instead of, or on behalf of, that society? Wasn't it to everyone's best interests to leave schools to educators? The public's satisfaction with the schools increased the confidence with which professional educators pursued their autonomous course. But the storms over school governance have pushed many decision-makers a long way off that course, and many of them are very unhappy with where they find themselves. Their desire to return "educational" decisions to "educational" foundations is understandable. Administrators *do* know more about schools and schooling than lay people do. Many areas of education require decidedly scientific approaches. Some curriculum packages are clearly preferable to others. For children with specified characteristics, some teaching practices yield more effective learning than do others. There are significant areas of education where it is possible—and desirable—that decisions be made on those grounds closest to the hearts and minds of professional educators—i.e., merit, expertise, reason, technical determination, scientific analysis.

Moreover, school people are legally responsible for those decisions. Communities expect administrators to choose the best possible course of action. Some communities strive to hold their administrators accountable for the results. Whatever the efforts of communities, the professional socialization of administrators drives home their obligation to "education" as the nearly exclusive base for schooling decisions. The tug that many administrators feel to return to the former patterns of professional autonomy is a lot more compelling than just reverie for simpler times. It reflects some painful judgments on the moral responsibility of a professional. Even for administrators who readily acknowledge an allegiance to community or citizen participation, the potential clash between professional and political criteria is a difficult reality.

Politics is, of course, the other horn of the representational dilemma, and it is a horn that most administrators try to avoid. Admitting the legitimacy of political concerns in school decisions complicates those decisions, raises the specter of moral compromise, and diminishes the autonomy of the professional educator. To avoid that, administrators must deny that the school is a political institution. If schools are only the passive reflectors of decisions made elsewhere or if the answers to all schooling questions can be determined scientifically, then the responsible school administrator has a very straightforward task. Running schools then will be like running a free public waterworks backed by an unlimited supply of water: One might simply watch the dials and pull the levers to satisfy clientele demand. What then of politics? One of the most famous formulations of politics is Harold Lasswell's "who gets what, when and how." Making such crass considerations a legitimate concern would be venal and certainly inappropriate for administrators of the equitable and munificent public waterworks just described.

But the reality of the school as a social institution is very different. There are many, many facets to the political nature of schools, but perhaps the most powerful is the fact that schools distribute very scarce resources among very needy constituents. The range of demands made on schools is as familiar as it is extraordinary. We expect schools to provide values, individual fulfillment, social enhancement, mobility, job preparation, entertainment, custodial services, and on and on. At the societal level, these expectations may seem amorphous, but at the school building level they are shrill, persistent, and highly personalized.

Schools never have enough money, teachers, relevant curriculum, or operational knowledge about the causes of teaching and learning to satisfy the demands made on them. Thus, because of scarce resources (and in spite of good intentions), school officials must decide whose interests will be served how soon and how well. Lasswell's blunt formulation of politics—"who gets what, when, and how"—turns out to be painfully relevant to the school principal who recognizes that what the seventh grade gets, the ninth grade won't; or that time devoted to reforming a science course is lost to the improvement of reading; or that a new curriculum pointed at the needs of poor black kids in an integrated urban high school is unlikely to be equally useful to the middle-class white kids in the same school. Because the demands always overwhelm the resources, the school is forced to discriminate among children by groups, by social class, by race, by behavior, by learning style, and by other aspects of perceived (and ascribed[1]) reality.

What schools do is distribute values, and that is the center of David Easton's frequently cited definition of politics, "the authoritative allocation of values for a society."[2] There are three main types of values that schools make differentially available. The first is *social mobility*. Despite their critics, the schools remain society's foremost institution by which poor people *may* bootstrap themselves into different circumstances. It is not necessary to ignore the revisionist critics to recognize the school's role in mobility. We have all learned a more useful modesty about the boosting power of schooling. Certification does not overcome racism. Credentials are less powerful than discrimination. Course work does not equal connections. But for poor people who want out of that circumstance, although its sufficiency has been quite properly challenged, formal school-based education is still the main chance. Similarly, the more we learn about the family as educator, the more important the school becomes. If the attributes of the middle-class nuclear family determine later achievement, then what about those people who do not happen to be born into such families? The importance of the school is increased in direct proportion to the unavailability of other sources of education.

Mobility is like stratification, and stratification is similar to discrimination. That harsh word simply directs attention to the fact that schools are supposed to sort some kids up and others out. Schools are supposed to differentiate among those who will and won't fit into bureaucracies, who will and won't accept societally determined roles, who will and won't endorse the previous culture.

The usually prosaic decisions about which programs to emphasize, which texts to adopt, which teaching practices to sanction are really decisions about the rungs on the mobility ladder. No decision has exactly the same impact on the children in a school or a system, and thus all decisions have distributive effects. We have been arguing that social mobility is the first of the values distributed by schools, and the functional (although not rhetorical) reality of the school reveals that it plays an important part in allocating mobility to some and denying it to others.

The second of the values allocated by schools is that of *norms*. Schools inculcate children with differing versions of a wide range of societal norms: competition over cooperation, individual effort over collective work, cognitive over affective responses, science over art. In addition, schools transmit norms about good citizenship, racism, sexism, agism, and the acceptance of authority.

The third area of values distributed by the schools is perhaps the most obvious: *Schooling is big business.* It has been estimated that there are 100 million people in the United States engaged in some sort of formal educational experience.[3] Elementary and secondary education costs 68 billion dollars a year.[4] Teaching jobs, paraprofessional and clerical positions, access to facilities, contracts for textbooks, insurance, and construction—are all very large prizes.

Whether the actions of the school are labeled "allocation" or not makes little difference because it is clear that schools either determine or play a very significant role in sorting children, depressing or enhancing social mobility, stratifying opportunity, and in general awarding to some but not to others the scarce resources available in the school. The schools allocate values, but the Eastonian formulation of politics has another necessary element: The allocation must be done authoritatively. There is little doubt that the school's distribution of values is done legitimately. In the first place, by compelling attendance, the state delivers a daily audience of captive children. Next it provides tax money to process those children. School people of all sorts are licensed and certificated and credentialed by state agencies so that they may act with the formal power of the state. The decisions of such authorized people are consistently upheld when they conflict with other, less formally legitimated people (parents, for example). School administrators who sit at, or at least near, the top of the hierarchy of schooling are making authoritative allocations of values for the society.

Yet many school people struggle to avoid the complications and the dilemmas of admitting that there is a portion of their professional role that is legitimately political. Some seek to argue that they only take orders, and thus the responsibility for political consequences lies elsewhere; others argue that education is a scientific field, and thus unscientific concerns are irrelevant in school administration. The authority structure of education is often invoked as a defense against accepting personal political responsibility. The existence of school boards as the representatives of the people is supposed, somehow, to absolve administrators of representational responsibilities. Unfortunately for that defense, school administrators must contend with their own past political successes. There was a time when citizen boards of education did, in fact, run schools, determine curriculum, hire teachers, and so on. But as the power of professional school administrators grew, that arrangement became more and more unsatisfactory, and administrators seized more and more de facto autonomy in *both* policy determination and implementation. The consensus of the last decade is well summarized by the title of Norman Kerr's article, "The School Board as an Agency of Legitimation." Several powerful traditions such as local control, academic freedom, and the autonomy of the classroom reinforce the dominant position of administrators vis-à-vis those above them on the organization chart. As those nominally superordinate policy-makers have discovered, the power of the school administrator is nearly sufficient in many areas such as school prayer, integration, and innovation. Laws and regulations get routinely rewritten in the thousands of daily, delivery-level administrative determinations about how (if at all) they should be implemented in particular and remote districts and schools. Thus it is more than a little difficult for school administrators to maintain that they are only taking orders. They are not and they cannot be exempted from scrutiny as political actors.

It is also difficult to argue that education is only, or even mainly, a field of scientific decision making. Whether the search has been for an educational production function, or a successful curriculum reform, or a sufficient behavioral intervention, or an effective compensatory education strategy, the conclusion has always been the same where the search has been honestly conducted. The fact of the matter is that there is no technology of teaching and learning that is even vaguely adequate to the demands of schooling. After an exhaustive search of the empirical literatures, Harvey Averch *et al.*, concluded that:

Research has not identified a variant of the existing system that is consistently related to students' educational outcomes. . . . Research has found nothing that consistently and unambiguously makes a difference in student outcomes.[5]

Science is a skimpy shield against the intrusion of politics.

None of this is to argue the abandonment of reason or the dissolution of the authority structure. In the course of examining the interaction of political with educational concerns, we will have occasion to argue for modifying aspects of the authority structure, but the present purpose is simply to demonstrate the unavoidability and the legitimacy of considering the political dimensions of administrative decisions. The extreme de facto decentralization of decision-making authority to administrators, combined with great uncertainty about the causes of effective teaching and learning, mean that school administrators make decisions that authoritatively allocate values for the society. And because they do, they are political as well as educational decision-makers.

The demands of a community may persuade more administrators than the logic of a functional analysis. As we shall demonstrate, many administrators are acknowledging the political dimensions of their roles for no other reason than that they have to. Pressures toward the political are apparent in many contemporary educational forces. New York City's first guidelines to decentralization stated:

A major goal is to reduce the gap between the source of important decisions and the place of impact. Decentralization should result in making all administrative and supervisory services more readily responsive to the needs of the children, and to the ability of the schools to cope with these needs. It is to be hoped therefore that as much authority as possible will be delegated by local school boards to the schools, so as to make it possible for them to operate more independently and thus more efficiently and more responsively to local needs.[6]

The reality of administrative decentralization has been to increase the competition for the scarce resources of the school by having added or enhanced the number of relevant clientele constituencies. A major goal of decentralization has been to redirect attention to immediate constituencies. There is a clear expectation that administrators will represent the proximate people in a particular fashion, one that is more responsive to them and less responsive to bureaucratic superiors. That expectation is even more vivid among proponents of community control.

The push for accountability is fueled by some related desires. From the community viewpoint, the purpose of accountability is to compel the school to produce the kind of outputs desired by the community. From the point of view of most educators, accountability means working to someone else's schedule. That prospect becomes a specter if the educator is left with the personal and professional responsibility (and consequences) for something with which he or she cannot agree or cannot deliver. As with decentralization, the congruence between what the constituents want and what the administrator does, is the sticking point. That is a question of representation. Administrative representation deals with how the community's wishes and interests are reflected in the decisions of a professional. The more communities press for responsiveness and the more administrators strive to satisfy the demands made on them, the more salient the question of representation becomes.

Representational Theory and Analysis

Even in usual times, people are acutely aware of their schools. Neighborhoods are in more intimate contact with their schools than with any other government institution. The principal of the neighborhood school gets asked questions that are more frequent, more direct, more persistent, and sometimes more embarrassing than those asked of other public officials. And because the school is physically "around the corner" and conversationally as accessible as the children over the dinner table, people expect to monitor, criticize, and affect the school in a direct personal fashion. By and large, school administrators respond to those expectations. The process that moves school people into management positions places great emphasis on interpersonal relations, thus role theory is a promising tool for the exploration of administrative behavior.

Jacob Getzels and Egon Guba define a role as "the set of complementary expectations regarding the actor in his interaction with other individuals. . . . Broadly conceived, [role] theory holds that an actor's behavior may best be understood as a function of role and personality."[7] But social behavior is interaction between an original actor ("ego" in role theory terms) and others ("alter"). Thus to the original actor is added

a second individual who has it within his power to hinder or help the original actor (ego) in the attainment of desired goals. Now whenever ego acts, he must take into account the possible reactions of the other actor (alter). He builds up a set of expectations regarding alter's reactions, and he will modify his own proposed activity in terms of these expectations in order to assure himself of alter's approval or at least to avoid his active disapproval.[8]

The mutual modification of behavior explicit in role theory is neatly paralleled in the theory of political representation. We expect public officials to modify their behavior in relation to public interests and desires. When citizens demand that the schools be decentralized, made more responsive to their desires, made better instruments to prepare children for "relevant" futures, etc., those demands carry an explicit assumption that the school's administrator will be bound by them. In short, the attempt is to prescribe the administrator's representational role orientation.

What is it that representatives do? On a superficial level, the answer is very simple. Practically everyone has a useful grasp of the meaning of representation. But immediately below that surface agreement is a very murky world of competing and inconsistent definitions. Because representation is one of the central ideas in the process of government, we should be as clear as possible about its meaning.

Common language definitions of representation usually run as follows: representation is, "acting for someone else," "doing something instead of someone else," or "acting on behalf of someone else." The shared thread is that of "re-presenting," or making present again something that is not, in fact, available. Thus someone acting as a political representative brings the wishes, interests, demands, and opinions of the constituents to the attention of decision-makers when those constituents are not themselves present. A good deal of the importance of representation comes from the fact that the constituents can virtually never be present themselves. The number of people in almost any constituency, the number of different decision-making bodies that affect them, and the complexity of the decisions that must be made, combine with the disinterest of most people in civic affairs to make representation the standard vehicle of what we loosely call, self-government. Emmette Redford has put it bluntly but well: "The first characteristic of the great body of men subject to the administrative state is that they are dormant regarding most of the decisions being made with respect to them."[9]

Thus the quality of representation determines a lot about the quality of what happens to us. The outstanding analysis of representation is Hannah Pitkin's *The Concept of Representation*.[10] Pitkin identifies four types, or ways, in which representation occurs.

Formalistic Representation

Here the focus is on the arrangements through which the representation takes place, not on the acts of representation themselves. Formalistic representation deals with the way the representative is authorized to act for the represented. That can happen either before the act of representation when the representative is being chosen, ordained, or authorized to act (e.g., through election, appointment, or certification) or after the act of representation when the representative is being held accountable for those actions (e.g., reelection, reappointment, or termination). When administrators maintain that their certifications by a state agency and their appointments by school boards authorize them to represent the community, they are defining representation in the formalistic sense. When people complain that appointed school board members are less representative than elected members, they are referring to formalistic representation. Changing entrance requirements for jobs so that a group of incumbents with new characteristics may now be eligible is a strategy to increase formalistic representation. Finally, those few accountability proposals that make rewards or sanctions contingent on performance are designed to increase formalistic representation. [Note: formalistic representation, strictly speaking, does not deal with the act of representation, but only with that which precedes/initiates it or follows/terminates it. As Pitkin says, this type of representation is "formalistic in the sense that [its] defining criterion for representation lies outside the activity of representing itself—before it begins or after it ends."[11]]

Descriptive Representation

In this type of representation the critical feature is the congruence between descriptive characteristics of the representative and the represented. Thus, if a council of penguins were to be constituted according to descriptive representation, it would need the same proportion of emperor penguins, jackass penguins, and rock hopper penguins as in the overall penguin population. Whatever features of the constituency are thought to be significant must be represented among the composite of decision-makers. The rationale commonly used for elections by proportional representation (such as those by which community school boards in New York City are selected) is that it gives numerically small minorities a better chance to elect a candidate. That part of its justification rests on its supposed ability to deliver descriptive representation. Moving from a composite to an individual basis, people who argue that black administrators should run schools for black children, Italians for Italians, and so on solely because of the sharing of racial or ethnic characteristics are arguing the salience of descriptive representation. Many people question the ability of bourgeois bureaucrats to relate to the needs of an under-class clientele. If they believe that the interests of the under-classes would be better served simply by replacing bourgeois with indigenous bureaucrats, they are making an argument for descriptive representation. It is important to note that in this type of representation as in the previous type, the key is not the actions taken by the representative. Instead, to achieve descriptive representation, it is enough that the representative reflects, resembles, or is connected to certain characteristics of the represented. (It is ordinarily assumed that the simple fact of sharing those features will result in closer congruence between what those being represented want or need and what the representative does. That assumption will be examined in the following discussion.)

Symbolic Representation

Symbolic representation is even less concerned with the substantive congruence between the representative's acts and the represented's wishes than the previous types have been. This type of representation refers mainly to the way people feel about representatives or a representative body. Thus symbolic representation can come about either because the representative stands as a point of identification or because the representative enacts ceremonials or rituals that evoke an identification. Those people who support a representative regardless of the nature of the representative's actions but because "he's one of us" are satisfied with symbolic representation. Those who object to the tokenism that often characterizes minority-group employment practices are not satisfied with symbolic representation.

Substantive Representation

This category is the heart of the matter because it deals with the actions of the representative, not the method of choice or the sharing of descriptive features or the responses evoked by façades. Pitkin's root definition of substantive representation is, "acting in the interest of the represented, in a manner responsive to them."[12] The central notion here is that there must ordinarily be some sort of correspondence between the things that representatives actually do and that which their constituents would have them do.

There are two more key ideas in substantive representation. The first is that the representative's acts should be in the interest of the community, that is, what is done must be to the benefit of those being represented. Second, the actions should be responsive to the community. The idea of responsiveness is sometimes used as a synonym for representation. Here it means that the representative's actions must relate to what the community wants or needs. Those actions do not have to be precisely or continually congruent with what the community would have done. Responsiveness does not mean replication; it means only acting with general reference to something. Thus a representative who on occasion understands that the constituency desires *X* but who believes that they would be better served by *NOT-X* and who then endorses *NOT-X* is still being responsive.

As with so many political phenomena, conflict both illuminates and complicates the analysis. What happens when the representative and the represented disagree as they did in the preceding paragraph? When the representative thinks the constituency is foolish, poorly informed, and/or just plain wrong about its identification of its own best interests, should the representative's actions be guided by personal judgment or by constituency judgment? Or what if, as sometimes happens, the community passionately desires something which is not, in fact, in its best interests *and* clearly communicates that misguided passion to its representative? (Corporal punishment, for example, is strongly supported by many parents and few educators.) If the job of the representative is to make present again something that is not literally there, then there can be little mistaking what the community would have done. Yet many representatives, analysts, theorists, and pundits argue vehemently against that action.

When the representative and the represented agree about what should be done, then both are happy, and the process of government moves smoothly. But instances of disagreement are so critical for our expectations about democratic government that they have been used as the major classifying principle for the analysis of representational behavior. In the remaining chapters, the ideas of formalistic, descriptive, and symbolic representation will be used wherever they can be helpful. But our main interest is in representational behavior, in what officials do in the act of representation, and thus substantive representation is the more revealing category.

Any person who undertakes to represent another is faced with a number of practical and ethical dilemmas. Essentially, he must choose a style of representation. The major choices and their normative rationalizations have been expressed nicely by Pitkin.

The majority of theorists argue that the representative must do what is best for those in his charge, but that he must do what he thinks best, using his own judgment and wisdom, since he is chosen to make decisions for (that is, instead of) his constituents. But a vocal minority maintain that the representative's duty is to reflect accurately the wishes and opinions of those he represents. Anything else they consider a mockery of true representation.[13]

These two choices for a representational style are called "trustee" and "delegate." Briefly, a trustee is someone whose decisions are based on his own values, even though the represented may disagree. A delegate reverses the priority and is guided by expressed citizen preferences even at the expense of his own best judgment. A third position, somewhat between the trustee and delegate decision-making styles, is usually called a "politico." A politico borrows from either the trustee or delegate styles as dictated by situations but has some internally consistent rationale for doing so. The politico does not merely waffle but rather enacts a trustee or a delegate orientation according to the dictates of circumstances.

Why is the trustee/delegate/politico distinction important to public policy? It is important because it captures the essence of people's expectations. People want to know how what is done on their behalf accords with what they wanted done. The trustee/delegate/politico representational role orientation deals with a problem—the relations between the governors and the governed—that despite its centrality, has no clear guides. Consequently, this is an area where there is a great deal of dissension between communities and their officials.

For example, when a community demands a particular discipline policy that its administrator feels to be ill advised, should she implement it? A trustee may not and justify her refusal on grounds that she knows better than they what is good for them. A delegate would probably implement the policy and although she may hope to change it eventually, defend her decision on essentially democratic grounds. Or to take another example, is an administrator justified in stacking a parents' advisory group with those who support existing policies? In fact, should citizens have any role beyond that of offering advice? Trustee decision-makers generally want to weaken the role of nonprofessionals; delegates will generally prefer to strengthen it.

What can a community expect of administrators who do not share their racial, ethnic, or class characteristics? Do such discrepancies make a difference? Where the community and the administrator differ in characteristics linked to social class, should the administrator act to make the children more like him or them? How can these questions be decided? Again, trustees, delegates, and politicos will have characteristically different resolutions to such problems. And over time those resolutions affect the school's policies, the services it delivers, and the community's relations with it.

Trustee/delegate/politico role orientations to the community also have ramifications for other administrative decisions. When a local board and the local community are in disagreement, where does the administrator's allegiance lie? When, as often happens, the demands and interests of the teaching staff conflict with those of the community, how can a building principal decide the issue?

Methodology

The next three chapters describe the representational roles of a large sample of school administrators. Chapters 5 and 6 report the evidence gathered during a nation-wide search for mechanisms of successful school/community involvement.

The process of analyzing representational roles began with an investigation of the relevant literature, especially John Wahlke, Heinz Eulau, William Buchanan, and Leroy Ferguson, *The Legislative System: Explorations in Legislative Behavior.*[14] Although useful, the book deals with legislative, not administrative, representation. The procedures used by Wahlke *et al.*, were combined with those from some earlier research by this author. A free-response interview schedule was constructed and administered to 165 school administrators in New York State.[15]

The sampling strategy was designed to support generalizations about school administrators at all levels of the hierarchy, in both public and private schools, and in the entire range of demographic situations. The ten research sites included four urban places, three suburbs, and three rural areas. District size ranged from a high of 32,000 pupil enrollment to 1,300. Respondents ranged from acting principals to school superintendents. Per district, the sample was stratified to include the superintendent, other headquarters' personnel with significant community-related responsibilities, all high school principals, almost all junior high and intermediate school principals, and usually about 50 percent of the elementary school principals. In the smallest districts all administrators were included. Finally, we sought access to both public and private schools in each of the sites. The final sample includes data on administrators of 15 private schools (yeshivas, Catholic schools, and nonaffiliated independent schools).

The interviews were conducted in the schools and lasted an average of two hours. Interview data were then coded and the respondents were assigned to one of the three representational role orientations—trustee, delegate, or politico. Verifying the accuracy of those categorizations was a major interest. Therefore, in each district we tried to do one follow-up case study of school principal-community interaction for each of the representational types. Because the full panoply of types did not occur in the smaller sites, we ended up with 17 cases.

The research assistants who did the case studies were aware of the purposes of the research but unaware of how the administrator they were studying had been categorized from the interview data. The week-long case study typically began with a reinterview of the principal to identify the most salient individuals both inside and outside the school. That list provided a basis for first round interviews with those people. To ensure that we talked with all relevant people (foes as well as friends), we got from the first-round interviewees additional names of people who knew about the school. This second circle of interviews usually took the researcher outside the school and into the community. To increase comparability among the cases, research assistants were provided with a guide to case development including a sample interview schedule for use with informants and an outline for preparation of the draft report which was then edited with the principal investigator. To ensure the accuracy of the facts reported (but not their interpretation), these drafts were returned to the school principals for comments. With one exception the responses commended the validity of the case study. And again with one exception, the case analyses independently documented the accuracy (93 percent) of the representational role characterizations made from the survey data.

Four of the case studies are presented in the next chapter. They demonstrate the decisions and problem solutions characteristic of trustee, delegate, and politico representatives. The cases should introduce the reader to representational roles in their community and institutional contexts. The following chapters discuss the various correlates and factors which impact administrative representation.

Notes

1. Murray Edelman, "The Political Language of the Helping Professions," *Politics and Society* v. 4, n. 3, 1974, pp. 295-310.

2. David Easton, *A Framework for Political Analysis*, (Englewood Cliffs, N.J.: Prentice-Hall, 1965), p. 50.

3. Wilbur J. Cohen, "Education and Learning," *The Annals of the American Academy of Political and Social Science*, v. 378 (September, 1967), p. 84.

4. U.S. Department of Health, Education and Welfare, National Center for Education Statistics, W. Vance Grant and C. George Lind, *Digest of Educational Statistics* (Washington, D.C.: Government Printing Office, 1975), p. 22.

5. Harvey A. Averch, *et al., How Effective is Schooling: A Critical Review and Synthesis of Research Findings* (Santa Monica, Calif.: The Rand Corp., March, 1972), R956-PCSF/RC, p. X.

6. Board of Education of the City of New York, "Guidelines to Decentralization for the Period Ending June 30, 1969: Prepared for the Use of Local School Boards and Local (District) Superintendents" (Brooklyn, N.Y.: Board of Education, December, 1968), p. 5.

7. Jacob W. Getzels and Egon G. Guba, "Role, Role Conflict, and Effectiveness," *American Sociological Review*, v. XIX (1954), pp. 164-175.

8. *Ibid.*, p. 164.

9. Emmette S. Redford, *Democracy in the Administrative State* (New York: Oxford, 1969), p. 66.

10. Hannah F. Pitkin, *The Concept of Representation* (Berkeley, Calif.: University of California Press, 1967). In addition to Pitkin, the sections which follow have profited from the careful analysis of Richard Guttenberg, "The Dilemma of School Board Representation" (New York: Teachers College, Columbia University, unpublished doctoral dissertation, 1975).

11. Pitkin, *The Concept of Representation*, p. 59.

12. The passage is worth quoting at length: Pitkin continues,

The representative must act independently; his action must involve discretion and judgment; he must be the one who acts. The represented must also be (conceived as) capable of independent action and judgment, not merely being taken care of. And, despite the resulting potential for conflict between representative and represented about what is to be done, that conflict must not normally take place. The representative must act in such a way that there is no conflict, or if it occurs an explanation is called for. He must not be found persistently at odds with the wishes of the represented without good reason in terms of their interest, without a good explanation of why their wishes are not in accord with their interest.

In Pitkin, *The Concept of Representation*, pp. 209-210.

13. *Ibid.*, p. 4.

14. John Wahlke, Heinz Eulau, William Buchanan, and Leroy Ferguson, *The Legislative System: Explorations in Legislative Behavior*, (New York: John Wiley & Sons, 1962).

15. The research was supported by a grant to the author from the New York State Commission on the Quality, Cost and Financing of Elementary and Secondary Education (The Fleischmann Commission). The complete report is available in Dale Mann, "Administrator/Community/School Relationships in New York State" (New York: New York State Commission on the Quality, Cost and Financing of Elementary and Secondary Education, 1972).

2 Representational Types in Action

Trustee Representatives

Trustee decision-making is dominated by the trustee's personal judgment and professional experience. The trustee does what the trustee thinks is best for the children, community, clientele, and constituents. In addition, and this is crucial, the trustee will persist in following his own judgment even when he knows that that action is contrary to the expressed wishes and interests of the people being represented. The trustee believes that he has been chosen for the office he holds precisely to make decisions for, or instead of, the people he represents.

One way in which communities participate in educational decisions is through their elected or appointed school boards. Boards of education are the traditional and most formal representatives of the people. An administrator's reactions to the orders and directives of the board is thus indicative of his reaction to citizen participation at its most legitimate. All representational types are somewhat reluctant to override directives that are backed with electoral sanctions, but trustees are the least reluctant to do so. One of the principals interviewed said, "Elections don't sanctify anyone: they're not my bosses." (Although, in fact, that board was his employer.) Another said, "We can't gear everything to parents' votes." The predominant rationalization for contravening orders from a duly constituted board was the same used to rationalize exclusion of the community in general—a lack of expertise on the part of the layman. An elementary school principal in New York City said, "You want to be responsive to community boards, but not on education matters. There the professional has to decide free of pressures." But what should a board of education deal with if not education? In any case, the point is that the trustee administrators' drive for autonomy is strong enough to allow them on occasion to substitute their own opinions for those of their legal superiors.

Trustees will move quickly to override the expressed preferences of citizens when those preferences are not channeled through boards of education. One urban school principal said that lay people should have an opportunity for input and should offer advice. But anything more definitive than advice was ridiculous because decisions themselves are "the prerogative and domain of professionally trained educators." Another principal talked about how she had avoided having even to listen to parents: "Principals used to be able to be professionals and experts in curriculum for children. I have used the demands of running a school all day long to avoid going to meetings at night." Another principal summarized

15

his attitude toward parent participation by paraphrasing Spiro Agnew: "People should be heard but that does not mean they should be heeded."

The same combination of elements is generally present in trustee responses—a low evaluation of all nonprofessionals and a high evaluation of one's own contribution. As one administrator put it: "People who aren't paid to think about education simply won't function. They're all hobbyists and dabblers." A principal in Ring City[a] had told us that she thought that parent participation in the school's budget and finance decisions was a good and appropriate thing. On inquiry, it turned out that parent participation in budget matters really meant that she deigned to allow the PTA officers to have temporary custody of the petty cash proceeds from their cake sales. In addition, to protect those parents from frivolity, the principal provided them with a yearly list of approved items that she would permit them to buy for "her" school.

The question of what goals to pursue is also a way to discriminate among the various representational roles. It sometimes happens that people want a thing that is not in their best interests. (The possible conflict between wishes and interests is called the "focus of representation.") In these cases of mistaken desires, the political actor, for us the school administrator, has a dilemma. Should he act on that which the constituents have clearly said they want, or should he substitute his own estimation of what is in their "true" or best interest? Not surprisingly, the trustee takes the latter course without hesitation. One woman principal answered a question about the focus of representation with an analogy, "Spinach! You make children eat it because it's good for them." Another principal felt convinced that it was his duty to force people to do what he felt was correct and discounted the consequences. He said it was his "ultimate responsibility" to decide what other people needed; "If I agree with what they want, I'll do it. If not, I don't," and besides, "they have a short memory."

The use of parent input is the final distinguishing characteristic of trustee decision-makers. Many trustees maintained the trappings of citizen and especially parent involvement but did so in a manipulative or inauthentic manner. We have already mentioned the principal for whom parent participation in budget and finance decisions meant temporary and constrained custody of the cake-sale proceeds. Another principal maintained that he had "fully involved" parents in "curriculum decisions," but when pressed the only instance he could recall was an advisory opinion from a mother's club on which museums their children might visit. Trustee representatives are careful to restrict the participation of noneducators to symbolic or ceremonial occasions. The preferred type of PTA is one in which the officers are hand-picked supporters of the school's regime. The existence of such captive PTA's allows people to feel they have been consulted; it may direct dissent into manageable channels, and in the short run it will not threaten the professional's control of the school.[1]

The management of participation for purposes with which the participants do

---

[a]Place names are pseudonyms. The pseudonyms, "Travis Flats" and "Hession Hills" are in fact two of New York City's thirty-two community school districts.

not agree is called "manipulation." But manipulation is often in the eye of the beholder. The principal of an urban elementary school provided a good example of managed participation if not of manipulation. He had set up a parents curriculum advisory committee. The parents strongly wanted to change the school's reading-readiness curriculum and invited a speaker from a textbook company to discuss with them the merits of the Initial Teaching Alphabet (ITA) at a public meeting. The parents were impressed with the presentation, wanted to switch to ITA, and enthusiastically expressed that wish to the principal. He thought the speaker's proposal was "too commercial" and the parents "too naive and untutored to make such decisions." So, in a process he described as "ridiculously simple," he talked them out of changing the reading curriculum. He did the same thing with teaching machines and the New Math, both of which the community had wanted to adopt but which he "successfully" resisted.

Actions such as these may seem familiar and unobjectionable to many people. The trustee style has a long tradition, a strong normative defense as a desirable and functional way for society to provide itself with schooling, and a great many adherents. Those adherents include (as we shall document) a majority of educators. The fact that the trustee style should be congenial to school people is readily understandable. Self-confidence is almost a necessary prerequisite for success in a complex and demanding field like educational administration. The more self-confidence an administrator has, the less likely he is to value the participation of those from outside his sphere of competence. The tenacity with which some school people cling to the mistaken analogy between themselves and medical doctors is one sign of that. A Hessian Hills principal discounted parent advice because, "A chief of surgery doesn't allow the patients to vote about their operations, does he?"

Many communities either seek out or acquiesce in trustee behavior on the part of their administrators. Their acquiescence may signal apathy about the schools or confidence in them. Either way the administrator-as-representative has a problem. In the absence of expressed preferences, in the absence of representational cues from his constituents, the administrator may have no choice but to be a reluctant trustee.

Conclusions about how functional or desirable trustee representation is are premature. Yet two things should be noted. First, communities have a right to employ the type of administrator they believe will be best for them. And second, the definition of the trustee type, and the way in which that role is enacted, means that sooner or later, over some issue, trustees must seek to do that which the community does not want done. The frequency, severity, and consequences of those sorts of collisions are important to the determination of educational policy and the support of the public for schooling as an institution. Two trustee representatives, operating in two very different community contexts, are described in the brief cases that follow.

Mrs. Behrman[b] is the principal of a kindergarten-through-sixth-grade elementary school in Travis Flats, one of New York City's decentralized

[b]Names in the case studies are pseudonyms.

"community" school districts. But as a community, Travis Flats is a representational nightmare. Although the neighborhood immediately surrounding Mrs. Behrman's school is quite straightforward (95 percent Puerto Rican and 80 percent nonworking poor), the district as a whole is not. It is about evenly balanced between whites at one end of the district and blacks at the other end. In between, in every sense, are the Puerto Ricans and a large representation from a religious sect. Travis Flats is one of those places that emphatically disprove the idea of the melting pot. The persistence of ethnic and religious associations is more than quaint—it is political leverage of a very real sort. Elections have been dominated by the cohesive and effectively mobilized whites. A white-dominated school board replaced the previous appointed board that had many more minority members. This has had three effects. The new board serves as a visible focus for the discontent and alienation of those who had expected descriptive representation. Second, it drives its few black and Puerto Rican members to a frenzy of militancy because they feel the entire representational burden. And third, it decreases the already small stock of apparent legitimacy with which the board must try to govern.

Much of this spills down to Mrs. Behrman's school. The previous board had been dominated by militants, and the unprofessional hubbub surrounding its meetings further discredited community participation. But for the parents, the lack of an effective forum at the level of the current district board increases their sense of desperation. Without a school board that they trust to serve as a forum or a court of appeals, every battle is concentrated on the neighborhood school and its administration.

That school is a new one, and for Mrs. Behrman so is the world in which she finds herself. She had been the principal of an overcrowded, ancient, and dingy school in a nearby neighborhood and had known some of the leaders of her present community from that time. The opening of the new school coincided with the arrival of several federally funded community action projects. Parent leaders were among those enrolled in "leadership courses" where the parents discovered what their legal rights were in the school. They decided on an aggressive pursuit of their prerogatives under the decentralization law. For her part, Mrs. Behrman decries the unsuitability of many of the parents to take part in educational decisions. She says that the PTA officers seldom think of all of the children, but rather try to use their positions to interfere in the school on behalf of their own children. She also says that the school has become a punching bag for community agitators more interested in their own careers than those of the children. In general, the school's relations with the community have deteriorated to mutual apprehension and mistrust. Mrs. Behrman's conclusion about the unsuitability of many community members to take part in school decisions is hotly reciprocated by people who feel that she is unsuitable to be the principal of their school.

The principal's experience with black and Spanish-speaking children began about 1955. However, despite her best efforts, the techniques and procedures that worked then are no longer successful. Her decisions are heavily focused on her own ideas about the needs and interests of her school's neighborhood. For example, she verbalized a desire to have parents make suggestions about textbooks and curriculum matters, but in fact, she has not acted on their repeated requests to participate in just those decisions. She feels that she is a professional and therefore competent to decide about educational matters. She is confident that she is "representing" them when she makes a decision, but in the absence of any evidence that her decisions reflect what they have asked for, the community does not share that confidence. On occasion, when she has failed to be overtly responsive, the community activists have escalated their pressure. In a few cases, Mrs. Behrman has yielded. The parents are then confirmed in having couched otherwise praiseworthy criticisms as demands, and they resort to confrontations more quickly than might otherwise be the case. The principal's reaction is to discount demands because of the way they are presented, which leads to a new escalation and a further tear in the fabric of school/community relations.

The principal maintained that only a minority of the community is in opposition to her. It seemed literally true that she never saw "the good parents" as she called them. It seems also true that many of the most concerned lay people are solidly opposed to her. Mrs. Behrman's school has fifteen hundred children and the total parent population is probably more than two thousand. The activists claimed about two hundred involved supporters. In general, community/school interaction meant the fairly frequent interaction of perhaps a hundred or so people with another few hundred being mobilized sporadically on an issue basis in the course of a year. The remainder is a very large, silent group. How should their silence be interpreted? Mrs. Behrman says that many parents are happy with the school, support her, but never express their support. Her opponents claim to speak for exactly the same people. But in the end, unless that silent group can be mobilized on one side or the other, their allegiance will be moot. Mrs. Behrman says that "the 'real parents' could stop all this trouble if they would just come out." But in conflicts, what counts is the number, intensity, and skill of those in the arena, not those who only watch from the sidelines.

Architects at the central board of education had originally designed Mrs. Behrman's school as an experimental facility, rather than as a conventional K-6 school. The space now used by six hundred children as a cafeteria was not designed for that. When Mrs. Behrman pointed out the oversight during the design phase, the architects acknowledged the mistake, said they would never build another school that way, and then proceeded with the construction of their admittedly mistaken plan. The result is daily chaos in the "lunchroom." Because their union contract exempts teachers from lunch duties, the supervision of six hundred children must be done on an ad hoc basis by a team including the school's administrators. Several of the Puerto Rican mothers mistrust what is to them unfamiliar food. Because the food service staff does not speak Spanish, there has not been any way to break down that mistrust. The response of those parents who are the most fearful for their children's well-being has been to come to the school every day and feed their children food that they prepare themselves. Mrs. Behrman resisted the practice. During our interview, she made derisive remarks about the welfare parents showing no reluctance with "free lunch." Mrs. Behrman objected to the practice citing the safety problem involved in having parents feeding their children in the stairwells of the school. But only when they became angry and confronted her did she set aside a single room where those parents who wished could feed their own children. She still resists the practice on grounds that now the room is "unsanitary." Maternal concern for children is widely regarded as a valuable trait. Mrs. Behrman's unwillingness to give credence to, or cooperate with, the legitimate concern of these mothers is a clear example of her attitude toward parent participation.

The principal's relations with the PTA are another source of constant contention. The executive board is composed of the most activist parents who are in the school daily and who meet frequently. Mrs. Behrman tries to keep informed of what the board is doing but since all of its officers are Puerto Rican, they conduct their meetings in Spanish, and, because Mrs. Behrman does not speak Spanish, keeping up is rather difficult. The PTA is linked through the training of its leaders, through the local poverty corporations, and through mutual interests to a number of other activist parent groups in the city. Mrs. Behrman has forbidden parents to distribute any circulars, pamphlets, and meeting notices not strictly related to her school's PTA on the school's property. Parents and local community-action agencies see this as "censorship" and as an attempt to stifle dissent. On one occasion the principal sent a notice to the parents canceling a PTA meeting. The notice was ostensibly signed by the PTA executive board, but Mrs. Behrman had neither consulted them nor asked their permission before she sent it.

Earlier this year, relations between the two had deteriorated to such an extent that the PTA asked for a meeting with the district superintendent. At that meeting they presented a list of demands including the following:

1. that parents be hired as school aides to keep order in the lunchroom and in the corridors;
2. that the principal improve her supervision and evaluation of teachers;
3. that reading levels be improved through a more comprehensive bilingual program;
4. that Puerto Rican ethnic studies be included in the curriculum; and
5. that the principal be required to respond to PTA questions and be enjoined from issuing orders in its name without its consent.

In public, the superintendent supported the principal on all demands except the last. In private, he is alleged to have asked Mrs. Behrman to be more conscious of community demands and attempt to meet them wherever possible. Since that time the parents have put together a second list of demands including that they be informed each semester of the school's curriculum and goals so that they can better evaluate its effectiveness. They also have several demands about one of the school's central tasks—the education of bilingual, bicultural children.

Part of the explanation for the appearance of rather understandable and widely shared parent concerns in the form of "demands" can be traced to the militant and confrontational style of the parent activists. A larger part of the explanation is Mrs. Behrman's increasing unwillingness to share decisions that she believes are her's to make. The school's administrators are fearful of the parents. Many parents are undeniably out to remove the principal. Many teachers think the whole situation will explode soon. Mrs. Behrman who is at the center of all this maintains that the agitation is *not* a constant background for her decisions. She says she has to follow "the rules of education" according to professional competence. She says she tries to be flexible but that she is not, after all, "Miss Democracy."

The Behrman case displays a trustee operating in rather consistent opposition to the wishes and interests of the community. But where the administrator's decisions are made against the background of a quiet, apathetic, or allegiant community, the trustee characterization takes on a more subtle meaning. The following case shows a trustee in just such an environment.

Joe Pollaci is a 38-year-old elementary school principal with the eyes and mannerisms of an educational Paul Newman. He runs a 650-student, K-6 elementary school in a new building serving two adjoining neighborhoods. The school's enrollment is 60 percent Italian and 40 percent black. Many of the Italians are recent immigrants with little or no knowledge of English. A majority of all the families are from the working-class poor (50 percent), some are on welfare (19 percent), while the remainder are from the lower-middle class (35 percent). Black and white families are on the same economic level; in many families, both parents are employed. Most of the parents are high school graduates, a few have college degrees. Children from the higher socioeconomic families attend two all-white parochial schools.

The Italians hold the public school in an esteem that in some instances borders on awe. Complaints about the school are rarely voiced. The Italian families live in the immediate school neighborhood while many but not all the blacks live down a large hill and as far as one and a quarter miles away. The children of these families are bussed to the school. All segments of the community defer to Pollaci as the educational leader. The allegiance of the people who support him, combined with the apathy of the rest of the parents, leaves the principal with a lot of autonomy. In the absence of any more visible signals from his clientele/constituency, Pollaci uses his own ideas about their needs and interests as a reference for his decisions.

Everyone decries the fact that the PTA has been unable to stimulate participation greater than the maximum turn-out of about 40 percent (generally white parents). The PTA executive board provides a forum for the principal. The board consists of fifteen mothers, only one of whom is black. At their meetings, the principal will announce new programs or changes in policy. He asks the board's opinion, listens to their advice, and will occasionally allow an informal vote, although the vote is not binding. His next step is usually to send a flier home to the parents and then present the change personally at the next PTA meeting. If some individuals oppose a policy change, the principal probably would remain unaware of it unless he directly solicited the opinion because at these meetings very few parents actually speak out and no organized groups attend. As is the case everywhere, the school's best-attended PTA functions are those in which parents' own children perform.

It is especially difficult to involve the black parents, although this year the vice-president is an articulate, aggressive woman who is black. The PTA's officers who are white claim that, by sending fliers and issuing personal invitations, they have done all they can do to convince the black parents they are welcome. Black community leaders emphasize that black parents don't become involved because they feel the school "belongs" to the Italians and that the PTA is a white man's organization. These feelings are reinforced by the fact that most of the blacks live a considerable distance from the school, many wage earners moonlight, many do not have cars, and the evening bus service is very irregular. The PTA has never scheduled any of its meetings in the black neighborhood in which more than one third of the children live. In addition, there is the feeling that teachers should make more visits to black homes, that the principal should hire more black teachers, and that the school should teach black history. Although those sentiments are strongly held, they are confined to a very small group, only a handful, even of the black parents.

Despite the alienation of a few, the community is still a basically allegiant one. Although there is very little expressed preference, the fact that Pollaci consistently tries to anticipate or imagine the (unvoiced) needs and interests of the parents has already resulted in a form of community control. Still, some would prefer to achieve from participation what is now done from benevolence.

Two incidents provide good examples of Pollaci's trustee representation. At present, Old Exurbia children are allowed eighty minutes at noontime to walk home, eat lunch, and return to school. Instead, they rush to their homes or to mom-and-pop grocery stores in the neighborhood and then return quickly to the school where they run around for nearly an hour, become overly excited, require a great deal of supervision, and are difficult to manage in afternoon classes. The principal wants to have all the children bring their lunches and eat in the school's cafeteria in staggered half-hour periods. As a result of the shorter lunch hours, all children (and teachers!) would be dismissed early. Some parents would benefit because they wouldn't have to disrupt their day to pick up the kids or make their lunches, but some teachers oppose the idea because it would shorten their own contract-mandated lunch period.

The principal first discussed the proposal at a faculty meeting. He promised to adjust some teaching schedules. Teachers who remained opposed muted their objections because a majority of their colleagues were in favor and the principal was quite enthusiastic. The principal then brought the proposal before the executive board of the PTA where no opposition was expressed. The principal next sent an announcement home with the children. Since that time, he has not heard from one parent, either for or against the change. He has concluded that the parents must be in favor of the proposed change. If the union approves it, he will institute the program as soon as possible.

In this instance, the principal is implementing a major change in the school's scheduling without parental participation except for the white-dominated PTA executive board. Pollaci knows that many of the fliers don't reach their destinations. The only black parent he discussed the change with is the PTA vice-president who was present at the first meeting. A black community leader observed that this is the usual process—the principal is generally able to make an autonomous decision affecting the schooling of all the children without much active involvement or feedback from the community. The question here is not the substantive educational adequacy of the decision (the community's trust in Pollaci seems well placed), but rather whether it might be useful, in the long run, to build a more actively involved parental community by habitually and aggressively stimulating their participation in decisions such as this one.

The other incident revolves around Pollaci's apprehension that programs that depend solely upon teachers will always be limited by the quality of the teachers. For a long time he has wanted to adopt some program that would depend upon the child for its success. After a Title I summer program, some of Pollaci's teachers began thinking about a child-centered school. One teacher began individualizing instruction with the principal's support. The following summer, impressed with her success and the interest of other teachers, Mr. Pollaci applied for and received permission to run a summer school program called the "Open Corridor Program" and patterned it after the British Infant School.

At the beginning of the next academic year, a group of teachers initiated their own open-corridor program in four classes, grades 1-4. The program began with the principal's support but without consultation with the parents. Children normally assigned to those four teachers' classes were automatically included. No announcements were sent to the homes. The principal was confident that he acted correctly, although he acknowledges that he acted arbitrarily. He believed that because he knew what they needed and that because the community trusts his professional judgment, he was justified in acting as he did. More importantly, he was afraid that parents might oppose the program merely because it was new or "experimental."

Once the program had begun, the parents were called in for a "Meet the Teacher" night where the program was explained. The principal assured the concerned parents that, if their children weren't doing well, they could remove them from the program, but he asked that they wait four months before judging success or failure.

Later, parents representing both pro and con positions were placed on a newly created (if post hoc) "Open Corridor Advisory Committee." Parent workshops were begun. Not all parents were convinced their children would benefit from the program's freedom. They were concerned about the lack of books, homework, reading scores, achievement tests, and ostensible, that is, aversive, discipline. Mrs. King, the PTA vice-president who had been extremely vocal in her opposition, was given a job as an aide so that she might evaluate the program first-hand. She soon became an enthusiastic supporter.

The second year the principal decided to expand the program from four to ten teachers. Parents were neither told that the program was expanding nor that their children would be included. Again, whatever children were assigned to participating teachers became ipso facto open-corridor participants. After the school year had begun, parents were called in for a meeting like the previous year's. Almost all the parents were enthusiastic about the program. The Advisory Board wrote a letter to the superintendent of schools asking for continued financial support for the program. Several more teachers have volunteered for next year, and none has asked to be dropped.

Nevertheless, some people in the black community remain concerned that while the program may be accepted by the black parents, it might not be the best thing for their children. They doubt that the program will help the children catch up in reading and math; they wonder if the teachers really know what happens in the classroom; they think the program may be too permissive for some of the children; and, most important, they question the black parents' sophistication in being able to monitor the program's operation and evaluate its success. Pollaci appears to agree because he has consistently acted to preempt or foreclose parent participation at a meaningful stage (that is, *before* implementation) on grounds that the parents would be most likely to mistakenly oppose that which is really in their own interests.

There is no question that the needs and interests of the community are a constant referent for Pollaci's professional decision-making even though most often Pollaci provides his own definition of those needs and interests rather than risk compromising the quality of the school's program by stimulating authentic parental involvement. Pollaci's trustee behavior is matched by his community's expectations of him.

Delegate Representatives

In representing the community, delegates reverse the trustee priority in balancing their own ideas against those of their constituents. Delegates believe that they have been chosen to reflect accurately (not to interpret and not to replace) what the represented say they want and need. Delegates believe that the trustee style of representing their constituents mocks the idea of representation. There are fewer delegate than trustee representatives among school administrators. (The politico group is smaller still.)

Yet, the delegate concept has some powerful and topical arguments in its favor. Chief among these is the expectation of many communities that their schools should be responsive to them. This demand is sometimes expressed as community control, sometimes as a drive for accountability. It is the basic idea behind decentralization. To the extent, however, that following the expressed wishes of the community may lead an educator in directions not endorsed by himself or his profession, the delegate orientation can be difficult to maintain.

Delegates had no problem indicating their support for directives from the board of education even though they might not personally agree with them. The delegate administrators in the sample often stressed the legitimate authoritative aspect of boards of education in explaining why they felt required to enact board policies. In Travis Flats, a principal who was confronted with the possibility of being asked to implement a "bad" order, immediately began to describe the number of community-based committees and groups with which he interacted, the nominating and selection procedures for membership on those groups, and his own extensive interaction with them. If bad orders had been so "democratically" determined, he believed that the greater part of morality lay in meeting the community's wishes. At the time this part of the data was collected, New York City had recently experienced a shift in its chain of command from the old appointed boards—which had really been far more advisory than supervisory—to the newly elected "community school boards." Many New York City principals thought of themselves as being controlled in military terms. As one woman in Travis Flats said, "There is a point in everyone's career when you have to decide who is The Boss. Now it's the elected board."

Delegate administrators have to orient themselves to nonelectoral citizen input just as do others. In general, they welcome such input, regard them as an important source of assistance, and are willing to be guided by them. They also do not reflexively discount citizen input simply because citizens are not educators. A principal of a ghetto school said that he had twenty years of working with people who billed themselves as "educational experts," and as a result, he preferred the advice of his community. Another administrator, when asked if he would override the expressed preferences of the community replied,

"What am I, God?" More than one delegate administrator made remarks such as "these are their children," and "they pay for this place." The attitude is perhaps best summarized by the inner-city principal in Oleola who said, " 'public education,' that's two words, and the emphasis has been for too long on the second one!" In one case study site, a Puerto Rican community had quickly become supportive of a new principal because she was "humble and not arrogant, despite her advanced education." (This was in strong contrast to some of the trustee schools we visited in which the *only* courtesy title afforded was "Doctor," and that was used with great pretension).

Another dilemma posed for the delegate administrator is what to do with the focus of representation—those situations in which the community's expressed interests are at odds with what the administrator thinks should be done. This is a clear problem for the delegate because professional training and personal conviction conflict with the constituency's expressions on the same subject. One principal who had become acutely conscious of this area of professional responsibility after having been forced out of his former post on charges of insensitivity said that he would now accept his new community's definitions of what was in its own interests even though that meant suppressing his learned tendencies to be "professional and centralized and expert." Other delegates talked about what were essentially power questions and indicated that, although they might professionally disagree with a given preference, they believed that it was untenable to force their ideas on a group.

A delegate in upstate Oleola complained that his community was "not very sophisticated," but by that he meant that they did not oppose all that he felt they should. He welcomed any complaints as signs of life and even encouraged parents to let teachers know how they (the parents) would like situations handled in that educator's inner sanctum, the classroom. Such encouragement would be regarded by most educators as a transgression of "professional" boundaries, but this man felt it was a useful way for parents and teachers to come together on one of the few grounds that were familiar and important to both.

In summary, the delegate group is one in which school administrators who by training and experience might want to make solitary and autonomous decisions, nonetheless accept the added strain of consciously incorporating lay demands and interests into their own decisions. The following case shows a delegate administrator doing just that.

Principal Tony Gunn is a 34-year-old, very active, confident and assertive elementary school principal in an integrated neighborhood of Ring City. The area had been leaning toward a homogeneously black residence but has now stabilized. Gunn is white; 55 percent of the school enrollment is black. Gunn is an ambitious principal (he is enrolled in a doctoral program at night), who tries to be guided consistently by the expressed demands and interests of his school's community.

That community, which is both racially and economically integrated, has a substantial history of racial difficulties, but today all parents, including the white militants and the black militants seem to be working together. The easing of racial tensions can be attributed to both groups and to the principal. No one has forgotten the bitter experiences of the past, but all find it more practical to look to the future.

The penetration of community concerns in Gunn's decision-making seems to have three sources. First, he took over a school in which there was already dysfunctional community participation so he never had a choice not to involve parents. He was put into the school specifically to reconstitute its relations with the community. Second, Gunn believes in community involvement on grounds of ideology (democracy in the schools) and on grounds of educational achievement (he hopes parental involvement will diffuse to student achievement). Third, Gunn feels that an involved community is more likely to be a supportive community, and thus it is to his advantage to encourage such involvement. A fourth factor might be the fact that to date, Gunn's responsiveness to the community has not cost him very heavily in terms of his own goals.

When Gunn took over the school, relations between racial factions in the community and the school were very poor. Changing residential patterns had focused racial antagonism on the school. Some white parents demanded ability grouping in the school because they believed that would preserve all-white classes for their children. The principal refused to comply. An extreme incident occurred when one of the school's PTA officers invited black children to her apartment house to swim in its pool. The children were bombarded with racial epithets. The response of some of the whites was to have the pool closed. Frequent fights between children of different races also contributed to tensions. While most of the fights were not racially motivated, the white parents tended to see them in exactly the opposite way.

Last year, a white woman who was nominated for PTA president was publicly accused of racial intolerance by another white woman at the school's initial PTA meeting. The meeting became so fiercely antagonistic that the principal was forced to disband the PTA and organize a new one with a new slate of officers, including two black men with prior leadership experience. These men have helped white parents to respect or at least understand positions taken by black parents.

Several factors have reduced tension recently: (1) Many of the more bigoted parents have moved away; (2) the parents who have replaced them accept the neighborhood's integration; (3) as blacks increased in numbers, they have developed (and been encouraged to develop) effective leadership; and (4) the PTA has evolved as an integrated organization that provides a realistic and authentic forum for discussion. Thus, partly due to Gunn's having played the active community role for which he was hired, black/white relations in the community seem to have stabilized at an acceptable level.

The community leadership problem remains. Few parents wish to be PTA officers. This is a particularly acute problem for the black community because many black parents feel they lack the education and verbal skills to become effective leaders, and their economic struggles preclude the sort of effective access that might otherwise come from everyday involvement with the school. Gunn has done several things to counteract this. First, he initiated "dialogue groups," small, informal meetings where participation would be less threatening. Second, he convened meetings of parents from single grades hoping that the smaller numbers and more apparently relevant focus would increase participation. Third, he was careful to make very specific delegations and assignments to parents and to solicit volunteers for very carefully identified tasks to ensure that they would be carried through in what might otherwise be an apathetic situation.

Gunn's relation to the PTA may be his most important contribution to school/community interaction. The PTA is encouraged to hold frequent meetings that are somewhat informally conducted so that all parents might feel comfortable. The PTA deals with sex education (on several occasions) and with open classrooms as well as with school bazaars and cake sales. When the parents are clearly in favor of something, there is no question about the decision. If, however, some parents are opposed, the principal endeavors to win over key parents. If that fails, he will compromise. He is not afraid to present an unpopular idea, but he would never arbitrarily impose anything on the community. The availability of the PTA as a legitimate conflict-mediating device has had an important effect on parental confidence in school decision-making. Because Gunn allows dissent and conflict to be expressed within the PTA, many more parents trust the organization and use it to channel their preferences than would be the case if the PTA were confined to a false consensus on trivial issues.

Finally, it should be noted that Gunn is a fervent practitioner of that old standby of school public relations, the "open-door policy," except that in Gunn's case his door is open to everyone—parents, community people, salesmen, teachers, *and* all the school's children. Even more remarkably, Gunn makes home visits and concentrates those visits on the parents that he thinks are least likely to come to the school!

Gunn has recently moved some of his classes to an open-classroom plan. Not all teachers were in favor of allowing children as much freedom as they have in the new plan. Parents too differed. Some parents opposed the program because they felt the children would have too much freedom and too little directed instruction. Black parents were concerned about the amount of specific preparation the school's teachers had for managing children in the open-class situation. Some felt that more emphasis should be given to an overtly structured reading curriculum. Parent opinion was also split on the proper role of the PTA. Although Gunn has encouraged its participation in program decisions, many PTA members were reluctant to usurp what they felt should be the professionals' prerogatives. (This seems to be a case of freedom and participation increasing responsibility.) Despite the fact that he regards himself as an expert in curriculum matters, Gunn still took time to get staff and community acceptance of the innovation. His style of inviting participation, even when he thinks he already has solutions, has resulted in some criticism that he is slow to change and that his ideas, when they do arrive in practice, are watered down. Gunn persists in his belief that having excluded, or not having honored, the participation of either the parent or the staff group would have doomed the innovation.

A second example of Gunn's delegate style with respect to community participation concerned the adoption of a new reading curriculum that had been used on an experimental basis in the school for a couple of years. Some children had and others had not completed the entire sequence. Gunn thought that those who had not should be homogeneously grouped the following year. Although Gunn felt that the professionally indicated solution was clear, he nonetheless encouraged a meeting of the involved parents, explained the matter to them, asked for their decision, and agreed in advance to be bound by the results of a consensually derived plebiscite.

The community respects Gunn's opinion as an educator and generally accedes to his judgment, although most parents want to be consulted on matters they feel are significant. It is doubtful that the parents would either choose to or be able to prevent the principal from unilaterally enacting an educational decision if he so desired. Still, Gunn does not take advantage of this latitude by acting unilaterally, and he will generally compromise even when he might override his opposition. His success in stabilizing a volatile and racially agitated community is probably related to his choice of the delegate style of representation.

Politico Representatives

Some cynics will be surprised to find that there are fewer politicos among the administrator population than any other representational type. Politicos respond to representational issues on some occasions as delegates and on other occasions as trustees. Their choice of orientation is dominated by the issues to be resolved or by the context of the decision. Politicos are not simply indecisive—being blown from one representational pole to the other by the force of events—rather they are enacting a conscious, patterned choice in their constituent relations. Although situational factors figure prominently in that choice, the politico representative maintains some independence or autonomy such that the choice and the subsequent acts of representation may be attributed properly to him or her.

Politicos characteristically want to have more information, to reserve their options, and to reject either the delegate or the trustee type as a premature constriction of their role. In the absence of specific information about particular issues, they refused to identify a uniform delegate or trustee pattern for their own behavior. School administrators often feel like their offices are pressure cookers. One way to respond to those pressures is by adopting a consistent pattern of behavior and using that singular pattern for guidance through varying situations. Both trustees and delegates use their role choices as such stable references. But politicos do not. They are oriented instead to the problems or difficulties themselves and appear to be resolving the representational dimensions of each problem on its own merits and as a discrete case. This basic difference between politicos and the other representational types raises several questions to which we will return in considering the evidence from later chapters. Do politicos not feel the need for a consistent style of representation? Is the environment in which trustees and delegates work perhaps more forgiving than that of politicos? How is it that one group feels compelled to pay painstaking attention to their situations while others seem to have more freedom?

It was characteristic of the politico administrators that when they were faced with accepting an ill-considered directive from a duly-constituted board, they had an immediate need to know more about the substance of the directive. Where the other types were able to orient themselves with little effort to either accepting or rejecting such a hypothetical directive, the politicos wanted to know—what exactly did it require? Who supported it? How long had it been in development? How drastically might it alter what situations? Beyond that, politicos were ingenious about the extent to which the board's orders might be enacted. For the most part, they did not propose the actual subvention of such orders, a response that contributed to the trustee categorization of those few individuals who chose it. Instead they searched for ways to satisfy some amount of the directive's intent without damaging their own integrity. A characteristic politico response came from a man who verbally calculated how much "bad" education he would accept from a board because the alternative would be dysfunctional antagonism. Similarly, although he said that "by law I have to obey the board," he explained procedures by which he thought he could get them around to his way of thinking (mainly by use of leaks to the parents' association).

Perhaps the best example of the politico response to citizen participation that was not mediated by electoral devices came from the Hessian Hills (New York City) elementary school principal who refused to admit the possibility of an unresolvable conflict. In every circumstance, he broke the issue down into different protagonists with different goals and tactics and tried to show how his moves would be oriented to theirs. For example, although he thought a militant youth organization operating in his neighborhood was not especially useful, he had invited them into the school's affairs because "conflict is better located inside the school than out in the open." He also talked about how he had acted to "weed out" those people who wanted to use education issues as bases for purely personal power. He was determined to mobilize people to build community support, which he saw as essential to the maintenance of the school's high achievement *and* to his school's ability to pressure the central board for extra resources. Another principal said that he wasn't "like a politician," yet he admitted that he had not suspended a single student in two years because he felt it cost him more in community support than it was worth in classroom peace. Although he had reservations about the overall probity of citizen participation, he had been a leader in a march on the local police station because it gained him support among parents. Almost every example of a policy decision that he offered showed clearly how he worked to balance one side, group, or facet against the other for rather ultimate goals (about which he tried disingenuously to be cynical).

Politicos were as cautious about the focus of representation as they were on most other matters. One administrator rejected the idea of an irreconcilable gulf between needs and interests, and proposed a sort of sliding scale to guide his actions that would depend on the gravity of the issue and how it effected the transmission of "learning skills." He was prepared, he said, to lose on some issues in order to win others. Other principals gave examples in which they had reluctantly compromised and adopted some educational programs they knew to be unsound because they believed the effect to be only temporary or small, and substantially outweighed by the gains in community support. Several politicos spoke of the necessity of communities having the "freedom to fail." Politico responses are obviously united when it comes to less emotionally charged, less authoritative aspects of community relations. With respect to their responsiveness to frequent informal requests, the politicos were keenly aware of the exchange of small favors for larger goodwill and support.

Later chapters will demonstrate the extent to which the politico orientation is positively related to conflict. The inconsistencies and compromises that characterize the politico orientation do not recommend it to very many administrators (although we found some individuals for whom it was congenial and functional). Politicos may be making an adaptive reaction to extremely difficult situations rather than conscious prior choices about the relations with their communities. The politico case that follows demonstrates many of these points.

John Gannon is the principal of Old Exurbia's only and enormous high school. Gannon, who is black and in his late thirties, came up through the ranks in Old Exurbia and is in his second year of coping with the race, class, and ethnic conflicts of Old Exurbia High. In the 1930s and 1940s, Old Exurbia had been a classic suburban sanctuary from the ills of the big city. But, because Old Exurbia's booster philosophy worked so well and because problems are at least as mobile as populations, Old Exurbia is now a virtual microcosm of that which many of its inhabitants fled. The result is not community but coexistence. The largest group in the school is Jewish and middle class; they are the most active group in school/community relations. They are both liberal and conservative; liberal on most matters of curriculum reform and conservative on matters of race. Blacks, some of whom are very affluent, represent about 20 percent of the student body. Another 20 percent of the population is Italian. The socio-economic breakdown for the high school is 5 percent nonworking poor, 20 percent low income, 35 percent middle income, and approximately 40 percent high income. The various community factions have had ample opportunity to refine their positions in the last twenty years because Old Exurbia has had a major legal battle, usually pursued to the Supreme Court, over the schooling consequences of *each* of the phases of the civil rights movement. Although it later was attributed to a disturbed child, many people regarded the destruction of most of the high school building by arson as a sad but somewhat symbolic event in the history of Old Exurban public schools. Old Exurbia has also exhausted its constitutionally accessible tax base. People in Gannon's position feel that pinch acutely. Somehow, they must do more for everyone with the same (or fewer) resources. That increases the pressure to discontinue ineffective programs, but there are never adequate resources to begin new ones.

Gannon's decision-making is complicated by several things. First, his students are organized into several contentious and diametrically opposed factions, many of which reflect the antagonisms of the community at large. Second, Gannon's teachers mistrust him because he is young and finding his way in the job, and also because his office is still under the shadow of his vividly disliked predecessor. Third, the school's size (3000 kids, 135 teachers) precludes many face-to-face bids for support but guarantees the extreme visibility of all he does. And finally, Gannon's own drive to reform the school (which really means to force changes in the practices with which his teachers have become comfortable) would create conflict under any circumstance. On top of all that, Gannon would like to survive in this principalship for a reasonable period of time (at least until he finishes his doctorate and is qualified for a higher post). Thus he seems to feel that he cannot afford the luxury of consistently enacting either the trustee or the delegate style; he has to be a politico.

Gannon had hoped to revolutionize the school's program; he wanted to change the length of the school day, declare the state-mandated pupil achievement exams optional, do away with present rules forbidding smoking, and most importantly, move toward flexible or modular scheduling and independent study. Originally, he had thought to achieve that by articulating principles of change—a philosophy of reform and innovation—and then letting his administrators and teachers take it from there. It has not been so simple. He now thinks that some of his teachers are "defensive," "insensitive," "lip-service innovators." For support, he relies on a small but highly influential group of teachers affiliated with the local union chapter. By and large, the staff has not been enthusiastic about his proposed reforms. Instead of waiting for widespread support, Gannon abandoned his comprehensive goals and concentrated on a single change.

Despite his commitment to the more lofty areas of curriculum reform, his first move as principal was in the area of discipline. He asked several ministers to serve on an advisory committee. The group provided effective support for Gannon (at least in part because the ministers are opinion leaders for a critical part of Gannon's constituency). But when disciplinary problems waned, Gannon allowed the advisory group to flounder. Gannon has nothing but disdain for PTA's and other milk-and-cookies "do-good" groups.

Most of Gannon's community work is now done directly with the "representatives" of the racial and ethnic segments of the community. Gannon deals with the local NAACP chairman, the leader of the Italian-American association, the PTA activists, but generally as individuals not as groups, and generally on specific matters, not school policy. The ministers' advisory group served its purpose and left a residue of support; further encouragement might have stimulated it to intervene in what Gannon considers his own domain. In its place is a mosaic of relationships that include Gannon's low-profile attendance at parties, receptions, testimonials, weddings, bar mitzvahs, confirmations, and any place else where Old Exurbia politicians and would-be politicians do their business. Time spent this way allows Gannon to soft-sell the school's program, build support *prior* to crises, and especially to read community demands early enough to be able to anticipate them. This advance intelligence keeps most of the community satisfied while it keeps most of the control in Gannon's office.

Despite his careful pruning of advisory committee prerogatives and despite his disdain for traditional school groups, Gannon is sensitive to the need to mobilize support for his proposals, or at least to head off opposition. Like most places, Old Exurbia is amorphous until galvanized by events. (By that point, of course, it is too late to build support which is one reason Gannon tends his fences so assiduously.) Among the active, almost daily school visitors to his office, none are so prominent as several Jewish women presidents and past presidents of area PTA's. They alone of the lay community seem informed of changes in the school and around the city. For the most part liberal, they remain highly critical—if not outspoken—in their assessment of educational development in the high school.

While the PTA and the advisory council have legitimate and quasi-independent existences, they really depend on the needs and initiative of the principal. Gannon uses them as sounding boards, but attendance at advisory council meetings has slipped significantly since the discipline issue subsided. The PTA seems quiescent. Should Gannon seek the advice and consent of either of these bodies, attendance at their meetings would jump. While the community is not really well organized to pursue its own educational interests, Gannon is aware of its felt needs and perceived wants. He takes these into account in his decision-making, even though they may not always be reflected very directly in the outcome.

Recently the high school dropped all of its regular programs for one day a week (Tuesdays) and replaced them with "minicourses" and independent study. Two task forces of teachers had prepared materials for the program, and, despite some opposition (but more apathy) among the teaching staff, the principal had pushed it. At the same time, the principal made no effort to involve the community in planning the program. Gannon's superiors feel that the community would have agonized indefinitely over a change as radical as the Tuesday minicourses. (They may have been following the dictates of one of the few laws of bureaucracy—if you don't ask permission, you won't prematurely be told no.) It was thought that the program would be at first chaotic. If it could be implemented quickly, then there would be time to straighten out the early difficulties. Also, Gannon maintained, he had promised the students to implement this program as quickly as possible. (He regards students as his first responsibility. He is more concerned with them than with teachers.)

The students now avail themselves of the freedom inherent in the program. Some leave school Tuesday afternoons, some roam the streets or hang around the junior high schools. Some parents feel the program has little educational merit. Others feel that the program has been sloppily administered. The community reacted swiftly, both in condemnation and in defense. Criticism came from several quarters, but most from those outside the advisory group or the educational experts. Gannon met his critics by asking them to compare the principles they thought they held with those of the new system. Problems that are real—i.e., students hanging out at nearby schools—are dismissed as insignificant compared to the merits of the on-going program. But more often, students and teachers are challenged to produce "their own answers," "save the program" and so on. In all of this, one gets the sense that no one really knows what is going on except Gannon. Others are off-balance while Gannon reserves his options. People may resent such treatment—yet it is and can be interpreted as leadership and as administration. It is what Gannon believes he has been hired to do and after all, the program is muddling through. If a referendum were taken tomorrow, or better still, if he were attacked, Gannon could probably put together a very large group of supporters, none of whom would have been very much personally involved in the decisions (although Gannon had them in mind), but all of whom trust him to deliver whatever it is he thinks they should need.

None of the principal's multiple constituencies is completely happy, but all have had something that Gannon can cite as evidence of his concern for them. The conservatives are relieved to see that Gannon has abandoned his revolutionary intentions. For those who seek change, there is the minicourse program. Those who wanted tighter control can be shown a new discipline code (supported by local opinion leaders). The students have the freedom of the new program. Mostly though, Old Exurbia students are like their colleagues in high schools everywhere—a little apathetic, a little restless, and very bored. The school itself is just too big for effective influence in each classroom, in the halls, in the library, and in the cafeteria. Attempts are made to reach the students, to reach the recalcitrant teachers, but they have been only partially successful.

At present, Gannon seems to be managing a truce with his constituencies.

They had expected that he would calm the school's student body and he has—partly because black students are hesitant about embarrassing a black principal and partly because he is trusted by the students. In return for a little peace and quiet, teachers have muted their opposition to his drive for change. The problem now is for Gannon to make the size of the group that supports him grow faster than his school's problems. Before long, whatever slight "honeymoon" from criticism he may have enjoyed as a new principal will be over.

Note

1. Cf Joseph Falkson and Marc Grainer, "Neighborhood School Politics and Constituency Organizations," *The School Review*, v. 81, n. 1 (November, 1972), pp. 35-61.

3

Correlates of Administrative Representation

Trusteeness—The Basic Measure

The trustee orientation is the key to the interpretation of representational roles. The phenomenon of representation relates what is done by the official to the wishes and interests of the citizenry. Although both trustees and delegates are representatives, they come to virtually opposite conclusions about how that should be done. Because of that opposition, they are often thought of as occupying polar positions on the same continuum. Politicos borrow from the two other orientations as warranted by particular circumstances and are often thought of as occupying an intermediate position. That conceptualization is accurate and even helpful for descriptive purposes, but operationalizing it creates problems in interpretation.[1] To avoid those difficulties, the distributions presented here usually follow the form, percent trustee *of the group taking either trustee or delegate responses.* Evidence about the politico group is presented separately.

(Of the 165 administrators interviewed, four were so insular and removed from consideration of their communities that the concept of representation simply did not apply to them. They did not recognize the ideas of representation, responsiveness to a constituency, and/or school/community relations in any form or at any level. Three of the four were central staff people. All of them saw their jobs solely in terms of bureaucratic and internal duties; they believed themselves responsible to their bureaucratic superiors only. The irrelevance of community aspects of their work had no overt or malevolent aspects; it was simply not a part of their own or others' definition of their jobs. This "insular" group has been excluded from the following analysis.)

There are substantive reasons for concentrating on the trustee role. The delegate is committed to honoring the community's expressed preferences—the trustee is not. Those communities that have delegate administrators have what they want: Some of those communities that have trustee administrators are likely over time to find that they have what they do not want—an administrator who honors his own judgment over theirs. Administrative trusteeness can also indicate the responsiveness of the school to the community. It is closely related to the kind of access citizens have to their schools, the amount of participation they have in important decisions, and the general congruence between the school's output and their desires. These and associated ideas are all closely linked to the representational role orientation.

37

Using trusteeness as our basic measure does not ignore the fact that some communities seek, and value, trustee behavior on the part of their administrators. Some trustee administrators who risk their community's displeasure by overriding their wishes are only doing what people want them to do. Trusteeness does not necessarily imply a lack of responsiveness—but only *if* that orientation rests on the continued passive acquiescence of the community. The more involved people become, the more likely the trustee orientation will be a serious liability. (The eventual discrepancy between popular opinion and the national government's pursuit of the Indo-China war is a good case in point.) The trustee behavior that is valued today may be a serious liability tomorrow.

The final reason for concentrating on the trustee role is the most direct: The majority of school administrators are best described as trustee representatives. The summary representational role orientations of the sample were as follows: 61 percent trustee; 30 percent delegate; and 9 percent politico ($n = 161 + 4$ "insular" administrators = 165). Two previous studies have also found the trustee type to be predominant among public officials. The evidence from a study of United States and Canadian public administrators by Friedman *et al.*, "suggests the predominance of a trustee style among those interviewed."[2] The results from the Wahlke *et al.* study of legislators in four states are roughly comparable with those of the current research. (See Table 3-1).

Trustees are the representational type most likely to be encountered. To what extent does the summary characterization of say, Administrator McClelland as a trustee, really account for his community representational behavior? The summary trustee (or delegate, or politico) characterization does not mean that at every juncture every individual will fully enact every aspect of that role. The world of school administration is more subtle and complex than that. Rather, the summary characterization means that over time, and in most cases, the

Table 3-1
School Administrators and State Legislators by Representational Role Orientation

Representational Role Orientation	School Administrators ($n = 161$)		State Legislators ($n = 295$)[a]	
	%	n	%	n
Trustee	61	(98)	63	(186)
Delegate	30	(49)	15	(44)
Politico	9	(14)	22	(65)

[a]Percentages computed by converting the Wahlke *et al.* state-by-state reporting to a single mean score distribution.

Source: Adapted from Wahlke, *et al.*, *The Legislative System*, p. 281.

burden of an individual's representational role orientation will best fit the category assigned.

In the following section, the data on a number of personal characteristics are examined. Are black or white administrators more likely to be responsive to the communities they serve? Does ethnicity make a difference? Does trusteeness vary by age? Is it affected by the amount, recency, or kind of graduate preparation an individual has had?

Administrator Characteristics

For the group of administrators who took trustee or delegate role orientations, the tendency to choose the trustee relation increases steadily as the age of the group increases. [Of the 30-40 year olds, 56 percent were trustees ($n = 25$); of the 41-50 year olds, 65 percent ($n = 65$); of the 51-60 group, 71 percent ($n = 42$); and, of those over 61 years of age, 80 percent were trustees ($n = 15$).] Older administrators who were trustees almost invariably defended their positions on grounds of greater job experience ("I have been doing this for twenty-two years!") and community familiarity ("I *know* these people—I've been here for eighteen years!"). Yet data on those factors failed to contribute to the tendency to be a trustee. Increased experience on the job was not associated with increased trusteeness, nor was increased duration in a location. Age alone remained associated with the propensity to be a trustee. The finding may reflect the solidification of opinion generally associated with increasing age, but in the absence of longitudinal data we can make no conclusions about the impact of age on these attitudes. Although the youngest generational group is now the most heavily delegate, as that group gets older, more of them may become trustees. It has sometimes been proposed that administrators should rotate fairly frequently through new posts to reduce the feathering of nests and presumably to increase responsiveness. But the general lack of association between these chronological factors about job performance and representational style makes it difficult to believe that responsiveness can be increased that way. There are other arguments in favor of the practice, but this is not one of them.

Proportionately fewer female than male administrators are trustees. Of all women choosing trustee or delegate roles, 60 percent chose trustee roles; 70 percent of the men did so. One in twelve administrators took a politico orientation, and thus there might have been four politicos among the female administrators: in fact, there were none. If the politico orientation seems to be produced by conflict and ambiguity, why is it that the extra pressures attendant on women working in traditionally male-dominated positions do not lead to politico behavior? Although we do not have persuasive evidence, it is possible to speculate that exactly that sort of pressure forces female administrators into consistent—and especially delegate—role orientations.

The race of an administrator is of considerable topical interest. Table 3-2 shows the distribution by race on the three representational orientations.

Because not even 10 percent of our sample was from the various minority groups, the only confident generalization is that they are seriously underrepresented in administrative and leadership positions in education. Still, their small proportion of this sample is realistic.

Administrators from minority groups go about the business of incorporating community interests and desires into their decisions in a fashion distinctly different from the dominant group. Fewer than half as many take trustee orientations; many more are delegates; and a *much* greater proportion are politicos. Their overrepresentation in the politico group reflects the practice of attempting to calm conflict-laden situations by appointing a principal from one of the minority groups. When the trustees and delegates were ranked according to a rough index reflecting how established their ethnic group was, those from the more established groups (e.g., Irish, WASP, Jewish, and Italian) were decidedly more trustee than those from the less established groups (Black, Eastern European, Spanish-surnamed).

One of the common paths to civil service reform has been to change descriptive variables about people's careers. What difference does it make for an individual's responsiveness where they come from, how they were recruited, what their aspirations are, etc. For example, an individual who wants to use her

Table 3-2
Representational Role Orientation and Ethnicity of Administrator

		Representational Role		
Ethnicity	Trustee (%)	Delegate (%)	Politico (%)	Totals (%)
(Minority/Majority Groups)				
Black & Spanish Surnamed[a]				
(Minority Groups)	29	43	29	101[b] (14)
Other (Majority Groups)	65	30	5	100 (144)

Note: $N = 14 + 144 + 7 = 165$. Seven individuals have been excluded from this table: the four insular nonrepresentational decision-makers all of whom were white; two individuals whose racial background could not be determined, one of whom was a trustee and the other, a politico; and one Oriental who was a politico.

[a]Of these fourteen individuals, two were Spanish surnamed, and both had delegate orientations.

[b]Error due to rounding.

current job as principal as a stepping stone to the superintendency may, in theory, be exceptionally attentive to neighborhood preferences.

The first of these career factors is the question of the fate of the predecessor of a newly appointed administrator. Most new incumbents in a position are careful to inquire about what happened to the person before them. If a new principal follows one who has just been forced out, we can expect that this event will affect the new principal's disposition toward the community. Our data indicate that an administrator succeeding someone who suffered an unfavorable fate (such as an involuntary transfer or controversial discharge) is 20 percent more likely to be a delegate.

The active involvement of communities in the dispositions of their administrators' careers has a double effect; it not only sanctions the particular individuals at whom it is aimed, but it also tends to create a climate of responsiveness on the part of succeeding administrators, whoever they may be. (Almost half the politico group assumed their positions in the wake of an incumbent who had been in some fashion involuntarily removed. Again, this adds to the picture of the politico style as a response to stress.)

Some systems use examinations to recruit or promote their administrators, others use peer selection, others emphasize achievement in the particular community per se. We distinguished between promotion procedures dominated by professionals (examinations, peer selection) and those that seemed to be dominated by the community that was to employ or receive the person selected. As expected, the bureaucratic patterns were associated with a group that was more heavily trustee than was the promotion pattern that was community dominated. Trustees were more apt to have achieved their current position because of what their colleagues thought of them; delegates were more apt to have achieved their current position because of what their communities thought of them. Thus every time a community can participate in determining the career success or failure of its administrators, it is increasing the probability of those administrators' subsequent responsiveness.

We were also curious to know whether it made a difference that a new administrator had been recruited from outside the district or brought up from within the ranks. We had thought someone brought in from outside would, by virtue of unfamiliarity, pay more attention to the expressed preferences of a newly adopted community. That was not the case; both "insiders" and "outsiders" took trustee attitudes with about the same frequency.

The effect of tenure is intriguing. Of the 165 administrators in our sample, 97 were tenured. Surprisingly enough, more administrators thought tenure was *undesirable* rather than desirable. The group that disliked tenure generally did so on grounds that tenure was unnecessary for the competent administrator and protection for the incompetent ones. We tested the proposition that one effect of tenure is to insulate those administrators who have it. If tenure is acting as an insulator, a higher proportion of trustees should have tenure than delegates. The interview coding allowed us to differentiate representational role orientations according to the strength or tenacity with which they were held. Someone who strongly endorsed delegate notions of representation and who consistently enacted them would be distinguished from a less emphatic or doctrinaire delegate. Of the strong trustees 75 percent were tenured; of the "only" trustee group 66 percent were tenured. Of the delegates 59 percent were tenured, but only 50 percent of the strong delegates were tenured. Of course, tenure was designed to do exactly this; but at the same time, its effectiveness as an insulator is what many people object to most. The way in which one interprets the evidence depends on one's evaluation of the wisdom of lay participation in educational decisions and the desirability of educational accountability. If the lay community makes generally prudent, just, and desirable decisions, then tenure is undesirable. If it does not, then tenure is desirable. If accountability means that the material well-being of professionals should depend on their ability to cause (or facilitate) teaching and learning, then tenure is not desirable. If accountability is only another toothless rhetorical fad, then tenure is unobjectionable.

One of the norms of American public life is that our officials must not seem to be ambitious. We like to think of public officials as disinterested and selfless people who are reluctantly drafted into office or who serve from motivations far more lofty than personal gain or advancement. What is true for public life in general is especially true for education where the prevailing expressed motivations are almost always related to the interests of little children and never to a more personal drive to control a key social institution. Relatively few educators will admit that they aspire to an office higher than the one they currently—and "selflessly"—hold.

Yet the very fact that an administrator may want to move up to greater responsibility can be an important determinant of his behavior if that promotion is controlled by or affected by the people currently served. There is evidence to indicate that elected city officials who have ambitions beyond their present positions are more responsive to the public than those who are indifferent to a higher position and thus often indifferent as well to that public who can grant or withhold it.[3] In reality if not in ideology, the ambition of public officials is one of the factors keeping them responsive to their constituents. When asked, fewer than half of our respondents said they had any ambitions beyond the job they then held. Of course, ambition is related to age—a much higher proportion of younger administrators are ambitious than are older administrators. As ambition decreases, the willingness to override the constituents increases. Thus in education as in many other areas of public policy, the ambition of the public official is an important element in ensuring the responsiveness of the institution. A community seeking an administrator who will be sensitive to its expressed needs and interests may be better off recruiting someone who, because he or she may be on the way up, will be in the position only for a limited period than another person who settles contentedly into a particular job. It is both interesting and predictable that 75 percent of the politicos are ambitious for higher position. Politicos are generally located in the situations with the highest conflict; saying they are ambitious for a higher position may be the same as saying they want out of the one they have.

The question of an administrator's mobility is another aspect of personal demography considered. We used the two types of mobility patterns that Richard Carlson of the University of Oregon developed, place-bound and career-bound. The place-bound administrator values geographic location over career opportunities and will accept a promotion only within the present district. The career-bound individual wants greater responsibility and will go wherever it is offered. Only in the trustee group was the majority place-bound (58 percent, $n = 92$). It is curious to find trustees so committed to the communities whose wishes they must sometimes deny. A community that promotes an individual who has "loyally" refused to go elsewhere may *not* be getting a more responsive individual as a result.

What people think of their jobs and how they evaluate the content of that job makes a difference for their performance. If, for example, a junior high principal believes his job is primarily disciplinary, then he will devote his time and energy to those tasks that another person with another understanding of the position might delegate or at least de-emphasize. The first of these self-defined aspects was whether administrators thought of themselves as being in any sense representatives of the people in their communities. To determine that, we had asked each administrator to describe the major components of his job. Of the administrators 39 percent thought their job dealt with teachers, other administrators, paperwork, and sometimes students—but not with community or even parent relations! Another 55 percent did include at least one reference to the community or parents, but only in the sense of public relations. This group felt that newsletters, social gatherings and other informal, generally informational tasks exhausted the representational dimension of their jobs. Only a small fraction (6 percent) of the administrators acknowledged a major responsibility to make a conscious and binding relationship between the expressed preferences of the community and their own actions. The dominance of the public relations definition among professional educators is not surprising because it has historically characterized school/community relationships. The inadequacy of the public relations approach is responsible for much of the frustration and hostility that many communities feel. We should therefore expect to find a relationship between these representational role self-definitions and the style of representation (or responsiveness) of the administrator. The data indicate that those who verbalize a representational component to their jobs then tend to follow up that verbalization with community-responsive orientations. (The joint occurrence of representational role self-definitions and delegate orientations is .40 gamma.) The evidence suggests that if we can change the way administrators define their jobs, if we can legitimate the representational function, then we may also increase their responsiveness.

After we had asked the interviewees to define their jobs, we next asked them to whom they were responsible. Of the answers 70 percent indicated that the individual felt a responsibility to, and *only* to, the next person up in a bureaucratic hierarchy. Only about a fourth of the administrators indicated that they felt themselves responsible to either part or all of the community. The consequence of bureaucratic versus community lines of responsibility can be seen by comparing the relative proportion of the groups who took trustee or delegate responses. Of those who felt responsible to "bureaucrats only" 72 percent were trustees; but the addition of a perceived responsibility to the community dropped the trustee proportion to 54 percent. Clearly, who the person one thinks one is working for affects one's actions. As long as the bosses are felt to be only within the club of professional educators, community preferences may be overridden with relative impunity.

Much of the media commentary about school administrators in conflict situations such as teachers' strikes, parent boycotts, and student violence, depicts those administrators as fairly helpless creatures of circumstances who lack the legal authority to cope with extreme situations. The administrators were asked if there was anything they would like to do that they could not now legally do, and also whether there were any changes in their legal authority they could suggest. Only about half of the school administrators are unhappy with what the law allows them to do.[a] The most frequently cited source of discontent was the state's authority in matters of discipline (although only 15 percent cited that). Predictably, more trustees were unhappy with what the state allowed them to do (that is, they sought greater autonomy) than the delegates who were generally satisfied or at least indifferent to this aspect of their jobs.

Of course, a state's grant of legal authority is not the only determinant of the autonomy or discretion one will have to perform in a job. To gauge wider aspects, we asked interviewees whether they felt they had "a free hand to do this job?" and also, "Do you have more or less authority as a (principal, super-intendent, etc.) than you used to have? What has changed? What might be done about that?" Only about a third were unhappy with their autonomy, and of that group, only a few felt constrained by those above them in the hierarchy. Apparently, supervision by bureaucratic superiors is not much of a problem for the state's school administrators. Instead, more than half of the malcontents complained that they lacked autonomy in their jobs because of those *below* them in the pecking order, especially teachers' unions, but also including community participants or would-be participants. A small group (14 percent) noted that the era in which building principals had been laws unto themselves ("the sun in the education galaxy" as one put it) had come to an end *and* endorsed that development as a return to a more equable relationship.

---

[a]Because of the variations in state code, this evidence, developed in New York State, may not travel very far.

Respondents were also asked to identify the most important and the most enjoyable components of their jobs. Nine percent said that the most important component of their jobs was dealing with or relating to the community outside the school; even fewer (7 percent) thought that it was the most enjoyable aspect of their work. (Most of those who enjoyed community relations were superintendents.) The largest group put top priority on dealing with teachers and the other adults in the school. Although 15 percent said that educational innovation was at the top of their list, only 4 percent said they enjoyed it the most which indicated the personal costs of introducing change in the schools. It is a difficult and unpleasant business. In any case, the very small number of administrators who give top priority to any externally related aspect of their jobs is disturbing. In 44 of the schools in which we conducted interviews, we judged that the supportiveness of the community for the school as an institution was either declining sharply or had reached a stable and low point. A decline in the community's support for the school would seem to indicate that responsible officials would move aggressively to reverse the trend; yet less than 10 percent of the administrations were willing to give such tasks top priority.

The last of the aspects of an administrator's self-defined institutional relationships is that of expertise. In general, educators delight in avowing that their's is a profession and that it is so because of the distinct knowledge base of its practice. It is undoubtedly true that school administration requires considerable specialized knowledge, and most school administrators will have more of that knowledge than most lay people. School administrators are likely thus to view themselves as expert, and, because that expertise is functional with respect to educational decisions, we can expect to find that as expertise increases so will the propensity to take trustee orientations with respect to the participation of the nonexpert, lay community. The expected relationship is supported by the data. Of those who described their own job performance as being in some fashion expert, fully 72 percent were trustees. (Eleven of the fourteen politicos described themselves as experts, a higher proportion than any other group which lends credence to the picture of them as a self-confident group of trouble-shooters.) The data suggest that belief in personal expertise is a powerful rationale for ignoring the relevance of other people's participation in educational decisions. We shall return to this question in the next chapter when we examine community interactions with administrators.

Institutional Correlates

Are elementary school principals more likely to be trustees than high school principals? Are superintendents more responsive to community preferences if they are employed by elected or appointed boards? Do public school or private school administrators pay more attention to the preferences of their clientele? This section examines changes in representational role orientations as those changes are related to changes in the control and kind of institution being administered.

Some parents who withdraw their children from public schools do so in the expectation that private school administrators will be more responsive to parental preferences. Comparing private with public school respondents, the data indicate that parents sending their children to private schools are slightly more likely to encounter trustee attitudes. Those parents who hope to find in private schools administrators who are more responsive to their preferences may be disappointed.

It is interesting that all fourteen administrators who chose the politico style of representation were public school administrators. The politico orientation appears to be a reaction to, or a defense against stress and conflict, and the fact that almost 10 percent of the public school administrators, but none of the private school administrators, chose this orientation in representing their clientele seems to reflect the turmoil around the public schools.

While we are looking at the control of the institution, we can consider the question of whether or not elected boards are more efficacious in controlling administrators than are appointed boards. We interviewed fifty-one administrators who were responsible to appointed boards, and eighty-two who were responsible to elected boards. (Catholic diocesan and other private school control procedures are not considered here.) The ideology of American politics suggests that those officials who have sought the electorate's approval should be perceived as having greater legitimacy than those who have been "merely" appointed. Elected boards' orders are in this sense more authoritative, so fewer administrators working for elected boards should take trustee attitudes. The data confirm that expectation: while 74 percent of the administrators working for appointed boards are trustees, 61 percent of those working for elected boards are trustees. In addition, over 70 percent of all the delegates are working for elected boards of education.

For many people, the superintendent of their school system is a rather remote figure, especially when contrasted with the almost daily—if informal—interaction that characterizes building principals and many parents. Because superintendents are more removed from face-to-face interaction with parents, are they more likely to override community preferences than are principals? Is there a difference in the way the different administrators represent their communities that can be related to the kind of institution being administered? In exploring the question, we separated responses of principals from those of superintendents, from those other headquarters personnel. When arranged according to the proportion from each group who take trustee orientations, there are fewest trustees among superintendents (60 percent, $n = 10$); the next largest proportion among principals (66 percent, $n = 131$); and the highest proportion of trustees among headquarters administrators other than the superintendents (83 percent, $n = 6$).

A low proportion of trustees among a group indicates a high degree of responsiveness to community preferences. Despite the presumed greater intimacy of community (even neighborhood) contact, principals as a group are not as responsive as superintendents as a group. Instead, the ordering of the three groups suggests that organizational distance from the source of authoritative, legitimate direction—i.e., the school board—may be the key, with superintendents being closest and other headquarters personnel the farthest from the board. There are, of course, other salient differences between superintendents and principals. Principals, for example, are often tenured while superintendents serve at the (often fickle) pleasure of the board of education. The relative insecurity of the superintendents' positions may be forcing their attention to community demands. Abolition of tenure for building principals and the resulting decrease in job security may similarly press other school administrators to be more amenable to community demands and more responsive to their constituents.

Another dimension is the grade level of the individual school. Our sample included 126 principals of whom 68 percent were elementary school principals, 15 percent were junior high or intermediate school principals, and 17 percent were secondary school principals. Elementary principals are slightly more likely to be responsive to community preferences. There may be several explanations for this including the fact that it is probably easier for an elementary school principal to know what the wishes and interests of the parents are. Junior and senior high schools usually serve larger populations where expressed parental interest has declined and where there are many fewer occasions for face-to-face contact than in elementary schools. Thus the trustee style of junior and senior high administrators may be related as much to the difficulty of knowing who or what to represent as it is to their own preferences.

When we compare the frequency with which building principals at the three levels take the politico orientation, both junior high and senior high principals are about three times more likely to be politicos than are elementary principals. If it can be assumed that junior and senior highs are more often the focus of turmoil and community grievances, then the reasons for the politico orientation become clear.

Most people feel that the larger an institution is, the less likely it is that that institution will be responsive to the needs and interests of its clientele. We examined the tendency of public school principals in different-sized institutions to take trustee orientations.[b] We used a several-part scale of size running from an enrollment of less than three hundred to those schools with more than two thousand. Surprisingly enough, there was no tendency for there to be more trustee administrators in the larger schools. There were about as many trustees in the group running schools with enrollments above fifteen hundred as there were

[b]Many private schools in the sample were boarding institutions which are already by design remote from the adult clientele. The relationship should be most clear between the local public school building principal and the surrounding attendance district.

in the group running schools with enrollments between five hundred and one thousand pupils. The only exception to the lack of relationship was for the group of twenty-three administrators in charge of schools with enrollments of five hundred or less. There were noticeably *more* trustees among the administrators of these very small schools than among the rest of the sample (74 percent and about 64 percent, respectively). Thus the data seem to indicate that increasing size does not lead to an increase in the percentage of trustees and that indeed there might even be a reverse effect at the smallest end of the continuum.

We are looking at those orientations that underlie the way administrators incorporate or do not incorporate citizen preferences in their professional decisions. The logistics of processing demands from three thousand rather than five hundred parents is a justifiable source of anxiety for the individual administrator and for the individual parent, both of whom are becoming a smaller fraction of a bigger whole as institutions grow larger and larger. The evidence relates to the administrators' perception of the citizenry and, as we have shown, there is no straight-line tendency for the incorporation of citizen preferences to diminish as the size of the institution increases. Because population, political, and economic pressures are likely to continue to be met by increasing the scale of educational establishments (for example, by building multischool educational parks), it is encouraging that those scale changes do not seem to affect the community representational orientations of the administrators.

The tendency to take politico orientations is related to the size of the institutions. The tendency to be a politico is twice as great in schools with enrollments above a thousand as in those below a thousand. Because the politico style is presumably related to conflict and the amount of conflict is also related to size, it is clear why this is so.

Representing staff needs and interests is the internal counterpart to (and perhaps the competitor to) the administrator's responsibility to represent the external community. Participatory democracy outside the school may be expressed as participatory management inside. Thus we may inquire about the relation between an administrator's internal and external organizational decision style. One way to hypothesize such a relationship is to surmise that, given a fixed amount of administrator energy, the time and effort spent in maintaining an open, democratic, and staff participatory organization will preclude managing external or community relationships in such a fashion. Thus we might expect to find internally open administrators being externally closed (or trustee) and vice versa. To investigate these relations, we began by defining "program decisions" as those macrochoices that had implications for whole groups of people (e.g., all second graders, all nontenured teachers, etc.). Examples of program decisions are the budget formulation processes and curriculum changes.

The budget process is of particular interest, both for what it is and for what it could be. Practicing educators, even including many central office personnel, tend to see the budget as an unintelligible and trivial document that states overall ceilings for things that don't have much meaning to pedagogical activities (especially those in the classroom). But academic economists and social scientists regard school budgets as opportunities for improved resource allocation, the "lifeblood" of an institution, the tangible expression of an institution's values. Whatever the rhetoric of a district's goals may be, the reality can presumably be read from its budget. The inclusion of various groups at the different stages in budget decision-making is potentially quite significant. Of the administrators 44 percent described budget procedures in which the superintendent and school board made preliminary budget decisions with either no involvement, minimal involvement, or after-the-fact involvement by building-level personnel. Another 25 percent described procedures in which community people, building person- nel, as well as the superintendent and the board, were involved in budget deliberations prior to the final decisions. However, most building administrators saw their role in budget matters as superficial and felt that control lay primarily with the boards and superintendents and ultimately with the local general governments that often determine how much money will be made available to the public schools.

Within the school itself, who participates in program decisions? Does an administrator's internal responsiveness reflect his external style of representa- tion? Not surprisingly, all the eight administrators who described themselves as the sole participants in program decisions were trustees. Yet the group that allowed teachers some participation ($n = 100$) was still heavily trustee (70 percent). Two thirds of the principals made the final decisions on curriculum matters unilaterally, only 15 percent (24) included teachers, and only five administrators reported that their community, in conjunction with the profes- sional staff, made the final decisions.

It seemed reasonable to hypothesize that an administrator running a complex school, would be less inclined to be responsive to the community. Does internal complexity drive out external responsiveness? One indication of complexity is the size of the administrative staff, yet it was not related to trusteeness. Another measure of complexity was the number and scope of special or nonstandard programs in the school such as Head Start, Project Follow-Through, etc. There was a very slight tendency for the simpler schools to have more trustees, but, in general, the hypothesis did not hold up.

Institutional characteristics, such as size and programmatic complexity, seem to have little bearing on an administrator's external style. The exception to this generalization is in participation in program decisions where delegates are more likely to feel that community participation is appropriate than are trustees. It will be recalled that the size of an organization was not related to an administrator's community representational style. The evidence presented here reinforces that finding in that the internal complexity of an organization also does not seem to determine, or be related to, representational style. One consequence of this is that those administrators who excuse themselves from public interaction on the grounds that they must attend to the burdens of their large and complicated institutions are taking refuge in an explanation that is not supported by the practices of their colleagues. There is no necessary relation between the two.

Notes

1. When scores are assigned to code trustee and delegate responses, the use of statistical measures of central tendency can push the scores of a respondent with inconsistent attitudes that are nonetheless evenly balanced between trustee and delegate positions into the center of the range. If the center of the numerical range is reserved for the politico position, that procedure assigns inconsistent respondents to the politico orientation when, in fact, politicos are not being inconsistent. To avoid that difficulty, trustee and delegate responses were coded on the same continuum, and politicos were analyzed separately. Politicos are thus categorized according to their behavior and not simply by statistical artifact.

2. R.S. Friedman, B.W. Klein, and J.H. Romani, "Administrative Agencies and the Publics They Serve," *Public Administration Review,* v. 26 (September, 1966), p. 196. Using a dichotomized trustee/delegate distinction that omits the politico orientation, Harmon Zeigler and Kent Jennings have documented the strong trustee orientation of school superintendents. L. Harmon Zeigler and M. Kent Jennings, *Governing American Schools: Political Interaction in Local School Districts* (North Scituate, Mass.: Duxbury Press, 1974), p. 121.

3. Kenneth Prewitt, *The Recruitment of Political Leaders: A Study of Citizen-Politicians* (Indianapolis: Bobbs-Merrill, 1970), p. 196 ff.

4 Administrators and Their Communities

Introduction

School people are at the intersection of many competing pressures. Whether the measure is the nights a principal spends away from home or the civic club appearances the superintendent makes or the single requests made of an administrator, the social nature of the job is easily discernible. But that volume of interaction is not only idle chit chat among neighbors; citizens, in general, and parents, in particular, want definite things from their schools and expect school administrators to deliver them. Many encounters take place under the guise of social events, and, in fact, a large part of any public official's interaction may seem pleasant and purposeless. On the other hand, a great deal of business is conducted at nonbusiness events, as the substitution of Seven-Up for Scotch in the superintendent's glass will often indicate. In terms of role theory, participants in social encounters are attempting to shape each other's behavior. One person will watch another carefully to discover what is expected; that other will send signals to influence the first person's actions. How else but through such subtle signs does a new principal learn what is and isn't acceptable to the neighborhood? How else can a superintendent form independent or validate supplied judgments about a town?

This chapter discusses how school administrators perceive their communities, what they think those communities expect of them, where and under what conditions they think lay participation appropriate, and how they assess citizen participation which is and which is not mediated by elections. It will also discuss the impact of conflict and the drive that many administrators have to deny or avoid it rather than resolve it.

One of the most interesting areas for inquiry is the potential impact the kind of community has on the type of administrative representation. The ten sites for this research were scattered over the entire state. Student enrollment ranged from a high of 32,000 students to lows of about fifteen hundred. Do urban, suburban, and rural school administrators differ with respect to their representational role orientations? Do administrators from the two New York City districts differ from the other urban areas in responsiveness? The data indicate that the type of community does have an effect on the role orientation of school administrators. Of those individuals taking either trustee or delegate orientations, suburban communities have a somewhat larger percentage of trustees (81 percent) than do urban (64 percent) and rural (60 percent) communities. As

51

measured by representational roles, there is a tendency for suburban administrators to be least responsive to their communities, while urban and rural administrators are definitely more responsive, although the majority are still trustees. One suburb, Old Exurbia, had three times the expected number of politicos. The schools of Old Exurbia are an unusually contentious testing ground for race, ethnic, and social class differences.

Oleola is a sprawling manufacturing center for the up state region. Ring City is another of the state's "Big Six" cities (so-named for a sometimes coalition to press for greater state and federal aid). Although already large, Ring City continues to grow rapidly. The two community school districts from within New York City differed not in their heterogeneity, but only in the ethnic and racial groups that contributed to their heterogeneity. School strife in the sixties and the media coverage (as well as the actions of some principals) made New York City school principals notorious for their alleged insensitivity and insularity. But the data document a wide variation in administrative representation within the city (72 percent of the Travis Flats' administrators but only 45 percent of the Hessian Hills' administrators were trustees). There was more similarity among urban districts across the state than among only New York districts. New York City principals are not different from their urban colleagues across the state simply because they are from New York City.

The socioeconomic status of the community has some bearing on administrative representation. Communities were categorized according to a four-part break: (1) those composed predominantly of the nonworking poor; (2) those where the nonworking poor and the working-class poor lived together; (3) middle-class communities, or those that were both middle-class and working-class poor; and, (4) upper-middle class and above. One of the factors complicating the representative's task is the potential for conflict that may arise when there are several sources of signals or cues. We had hypothesized that the wider the range of social classes present in the constituency, the more difficult it would be for an administrator to choose one to represent, and thus the more likely the administrator would be a trustee. It follows that we expected schools serving essentially single-class, homogeneous clientele, to be represented by delegates because the administrators in those situations would have less trouble discerning constituent interests. The data in Table 4-1 destroyed that plausible hypothesis.[a]

Homogeneous attendance areas tended to have distinctly more trustee administrators than heterogeneous attendance areas. The lowest and highest social class areas both have trustee administrators although for very different reasons. In attendance areas composed only of nonworking poor people, many residents are unavailable for civic participation because of the struggle to survive, are alienated from the values of schools dominated by the majority culture, or are cut off from participation by hostility or fear. In addition, school adminis-

[a]Of the politico administrators, 79 percent served broad social class constituencies and thus may be something of an exception to the disconfirmation.

Table 4-1

Percentage of Trustee Principals by Type of Attendance Area and Predominant Social Class(es) of School

Social Class of Majority Group(s) in School	Type of Attendance Area		
	Urban	Suburban	Rural
Nonworking Poor	80% (15)	—	—
Nonworking & Working-class Poor	48% (21)	—[a]	—
Middle Class; Middle with Working-class Poor	64% (58)	82% (17)	54% (13)
Upper Middle & Above	75% (8)	75% (8)	—[a] (2)

Note: $N = 143 + 4 = 147$ (T/D RRO; school principals only)

Three cases were eliminated because no two social classes comprised a majority of the school, and one case was eliminated because no social class(es) could be determined.

[a]Percentages would have little meaning because of small ns.

trators serving such areas often feel that the poor are not capable of participation and thus must be "saved" by the unilateral action of experts. At the other end of the social class spectrum, the attendance areas were also dominated by trustees. In general, those (largely suburban) communities appeared to be allegiant and satisfied with their building level administrators—however they may feel about their superintendents or their taxes. Moreover, it has been suggested that the life style and personal career orientations of the upper-middle class predispose them to accept trustee decision-making.

Of the attendance districts dominated by the nonworking poor, 80 percent have trustee administrators, but the grouping only one rung up the social class ladder has only 48 percent trustee administrators. How can that be explained? The difference seems to be in the addition of working-class parents. Where the school's attendance area is composed of nonworking-class poor people and working-class people, the working-class parents are very likely to feel threatened by their welfare-class neighbors. Because the working-class parents are themselves too poor to escape either to private schools or to the suburbs, they then become actively involved in their own schools. That involvement provides clear representational signals and increases the likelihood of delegate behavior by the administrators.

One of the most persistent and troublesome demands in recent times has been that schools be staffed with only those people who share the ethnic or racial characteristics of the area's dominant group. In our terms, the demand is that school administrators be virtually representative of the community clientele. Virtual representatives are believed to be more sympathetic to the preferences of people with whom they share presumably important characteristics. If we ask, "Is the incumbent more like or more unlike the majority group of enrollment on race, religion, culture, and ethnicity?" then 60 percent of school administrators are not virtually representative of their communities; 40 percent are. Comparing all administrators (principals and superintendents), a slightly smaller proportion of the virtual representatives were trustees than those not virtually representative. [64 percent ($n = 61$) and 69 percent ($n = 85$), respectively]. While the difference is in the predicted direction, the delegate propensity of those who resemble their constituencies is so slight as not to have much impact. That slightness may come as a shock to the many people who have invested a great deal of energy in placing virtual representatives at the top of schooling organizations.

Perhaps the explanation lies in the fact that we have included administrators with relatively amorphous district-wide responsibilities. The effect of virtual representation in the more intimate school/neighborhood context may be sharpened. But considering only principals, 62 percent of those who are virtual representatives of their communities are trustees; 70 percent of those not virtually representative are trustees (n's = 50 and 80, respectively). Again, there is a gain in responsiveness, but not a very large one. What can explain this? First, there is the possibility that a group may be completely satisfied simply to have gotten a virtual representative to head the local school. In the absence of further demands, the administrator's behavior may not be effectively shaped. An additional explanation may lie in the more general propensity of all educators to take trustee orientations. Socialization as a professional may override many of the effects of racial, ethnic, class, or cultural identification that might otherwise have obtained. Another very plausible explanation lies exactly in the identity between the administrator and the community. Because they share characteristics that both believe to be salient, the administrator may believe he already has, in himself, sufficient information about community needs and interests and therefore need not search for any more. Because he is presumed to know the "true" community, he may also feel free to ignore some or all of the groups presuming to speak for it, and to substitute his own ideas of what they need and want for what they say they need and want. In that fashion, a search for a close relationship by recruiting a virtual representative may end up with exactly the opposite results.

The evidence presented here will hardly dissuade anyone who is predisposed to virtual representation from pursuing that search. It is not intended to. Because representation is a sociopsychological relationship and because support for the schools therefore depends heavily on what people *think* is true, all else being equal, the better part of wisdom may be the selection of a virtual representative. However, given the faintness of the imprint of this factor on subsequent representational decisions, communities should not expect that appointment of a virtual representative ends their search for a responsive and productive school system, nor should they arbitrarily limit their candidates to those who happen to be virtually representative of their community.

The next section deals with the descriptive evidence about how administrators think communities should be related to them. Before we turn to that, we should reverse the question and ask how do administrators think they should relate to communities. Three phrases are often used as synonyms for representation: "responsible to," "accountable to," and "responsive to." Administrators were asked to choose which of those words described the most desirable relationship between themselves and the community. Arranged in a roughly increasing order of authoritativeness, the terms should run "responsive," "responsible," and "accountable." The order of desired relationships that begins with "responsive" and ends with "accountable" is the least legally binding. That is also the order that was chosen as most desirable by more administrators (49) than any other. The word "accountable" engendered a lot of antipathy. Half of the administrators felt that, of the three words, "accountability" described the least desirable relationship between themselves and their communities. Although it may seem curious that half the administrators dislike a word that is in such vogue among concerned lay people, at least the figure is much lower state-wide than it is for New York City. In a previous study of NYC elementary school administrators, Mann found that more than 80 percent put "accountable" last on their list of desirable relationships.[1]

Respondents were asked to describe the "procedures or mechanisms" that ensured realization of their desired relationship. If for example, an individual had said that "responsibility" was the most desirable relationship between himself and the community, then we expected to find that he would describe some consciously planned, perhaps formal, procedures or mechanisms designed to realize that state of affairs. However, 70 percent of our respondents could think of *no* such intentional, organizational entity that helped ensure delivery of what they had just said was a goal of their school. Instead, the majority described either information programs (newsletters, etc.); fragmented, *ad hoc* activities (seeing parents who came to the school); or very permissive voluntary groups with little effect of their decision (PTA's, for example). The picture that emerges is not a surprising one. Most school administrators strive for autonomy although they recognize that it is important to be verbally committed to democratic participation. Thus they can maintain their devotion to ideals like "responsibility" and "responsiveness" to the people, but operationalize those ideals with essentially public relations practices that leave control in their own hands. The distinction here is an important one. Representation as a potentially binding interaction between the administrator and the community is much closer to this society's norms for the conduct of public business than is representation as a one-way relationship in which the public is kept informed of what the officials have already decided.

Who or What is "The Community"?

It may be useful in introducing this section to repeat the limits of interview data. Most of what is reported is what administrators told us in response to various questions, statements, and probes. Although there is always a possibility of distortion, it seems minimal. In the first place, school people were genuinely helpful and candid. The research was sponsored by an important state commission that administrators were anxious to have understand the reality of their work. Wherever possible, interview evidence was checked against population statistics, previous research, and other independent sources. The detailed case studies verified the accuracy of what our interviewees had told us, even when the information supplied was not favorable to them. Finally, it should be noted that regardless of its factual validity, what people think influences what they do. If, for example, a principal feels that a neighborhood is personally hostile to him, whether it is or not, he is likely to be anxious and defensive in interacting with it. In that sense, mistaken estimates or wrong notions provide useful information.

The sources of representational cues are the first point to be examined. We boiled the scores of possibilities down to three major categories; the school board, the general community, and both the board and the community. We then analyzed the administrators' responses both for the source of the representational cues that they perceived and for the clarity of those signals. There was a distinct tendency for the delegate orientation to increase as the clarity, community relatedness, and number of representational sources grew. Of those individuals who only grudgingly recognized the board as a source of representational cues, 90 percent were trustees ($n = 20$). At the other end of the spectrum, more than two thirds of those people who clearly recognized both the board and the community as sources of representational cues were delegates ($n = 40$). All school administrators are expected to perform educational functions instead of, or on behalf of, the public. Because they may all be judged by an overall standard of representation, we reanalyzed the interview data in an attempt to determine the reasons for the difference in recognizing representational cues. Obviously there are communities that never present cues, and there are administrators who ignore whatever is presented. The latter explanation (administrator's ignoring cues) accounted for more than twice as many of the cases of lessened representation as did the apathy of communities or boards.

Parents loomed predictably large in the administrator's definitions of their communities, but there are certainly other groups that share an interest in and that bear part of the responsibility for the schools. Only about a third of the administrators recognize that there are other interests beyond those of the parents with a stake in the schools. They named antipoverty agencies, other governmental agencies, business interests, and voluntary associations of various kinds. For two thirds of the administrators, however, the schools exist for the parents and community representational responsibilities have been exhausted when they have been considered.

We asked the administrators if there were areas of educational policy decision-making in which it was appropriate for the community to participate. Only a handful said "no" outright (7 percent); most administrators gave "yes, but" answers. The demurrals generally centered around the putative lack of expertise or interest on the part of would-be participants. About 30 percent enthusiastically endorsed community participation. As expected, there is a strong tendency for the evaluation of appropriateness to vary by representational type.

In what areas was the community granted a role? Each respondent was asked to rank the decision areas of (1) finance and budget, (2) curriculum, (3) teacher personnel, and (4) student discipline in terms of most to least appropriate. We had expected to find that the most esoteric areas would be ranked as least appropriate. Our expected ranking of decision areas ran student discipline (least esoteric and therefore most appropriate), teacher personnel, curriculum, and finance and budget (most esoteric and therefore least appropriate). An additional reason for the expected low ranking of the finance and budget area was the presumption that budgets control programs and that administrators interested in program control would not think it useful to have community participation at that point. The administrators exactly reversed the predicted order. Only 4 percent thought that teacher personnel matters were most appropriate as an area for community participation. They were more unanimous (58 percent) in placing budget and finance at the head of the appropriateness list than in any other choice. Part of the reason may be that "budget and finance" means to most educators that the taxpayers will pick up the bills for the school. Second, in the limited but widely held sense that the fine print of a budget document impersonally distributes dollars for the things the system buys (tons of asphalt, thousands of books, debt service, etc.), then it has very little relation to what goes on in the school (how much of what is taught to whom, and especially to whom *not*). Therefore, in acknowledging budget and finance as the area most appropriate for citizen participation, the administrators probably mean to acknowledge the role of the citizen as payer of educational bills, not as determiner of educational programs. The fact that two thirds of all the trustees chose this area as the most appropriate lends credence to this interpretation because, as we have seen, trustees are not especially solicitous of meaningful community participation.

Administrators tend to define their communities as those people who support them. Selective perception is a common phenomenon, but it can be used to infer that those who do not support the schools—and those who run the schools—are also antieducation. Seventy-three of 165 individuals either denied that there were people in the community who did not support the schools or never included mention of them in any part of the interview. There are indeed some schools that are the object of that kind of unanimous public adulation, but we doubt seriously that that group is as large as 44 percent of all schools. Rather, a good proportion of that figure should be attributed to the drive of educators to maintain the façade of unanimity by denying the presence of nonsupporters. Unfortunately, to the extent that that is true, those administrators are also reducing their own ability to cope with the very people who must be convinced if support is to be built for the schools. Moreover, much of the criticism directed at schools is legitimate and might be usefully incorporated rather than studiously ignored.

By comparing evidence from other parts of the interview, from independent sources, and where possible from the case studies, it was possible to form some judgments about how active the various communities were in pursuit of their interests. There was a distinct drop in the tendency of administrators to be trustees as the public they served moved from apathy toward activity. We can extend this point by looking at the issues around which communities and administrators interact. Apathetic communities with little interaction are heavily staffed with trustees. At the other extreme, where interaction is general and continuous, where the citizens do not wait for an issue to come up before expressing themselves but rather do so constantly and freely, such communities have a much higher proportion of delegate administrators (twice as many as their apathetic counterparts).

In between lie those places in which interaction is issue-specific, that is, in which most school/community interaction is carried on through or stimulated by particular matters of joint concern. We classified this group according to whether or not the issue participation was volatile. Where participation was issue-specific and volatile (twenty-two cases), more than three fourths of the administrators were trustees. Why should issue volatility make a difference for representational orientations? In general, the data will not allow us to determine that trustees are causing the explosive situations associated with their type, or, conversely, that the explosive situations are causing administrators to adopt trustee attitudes. Although we lack the data from this research to test those notions, there is considerable anecdotal evidence in the recent history of school governance to suggest that trustee administrators bear a considerable responsibility for the situations in which they find themselves. Moreover, it is clear that apathy and its opposite—general and continuous participation—are related to the two polar extremes of representation, trusteeness and delegateness, respectively. Parenthetically, it should be noted that the vast majority of politicos are in situations of either issue-specific and volatile, or general and continuous participation.

One function of interest groups is to stimulate, gather, channel, and express opinions. Groups are a kind of antidote to apathy, so the degree and way in which a community is organized should be related to the behavior of its administrators. To test that, we developed definitions of three kinds of communities. Unorganized communities were exactly that—they had no functioning educational interest groups. There were sixteen cases in that category and 87 percent of them were administered by trustees. The second group was called traditional because its only educational interest group was that old standby of public relations—the Parents Association or the Parents and Teachers Association. (Most but not all PTA's are simply an extension of the principal's mimeograph machine.) Ninety-six communities were traditionally organized, and among them the proportion of trustee administrators fell to 69 percent. Highly organized communities were defined as those with two or more continuing interest groups at least part of whose function dealt with the conduct of education (e.g., umbrella coordinating groups from poverty agencies and so on). There were thirty-three of these highly organized communities and 55 percent of their administrators were of the trustee type. Thus, moving past the PTA stage to one in which there are nonschool agencies interested in the school's activities, is highly effective in producing more responsive administrators.

This section has discussed the impact of an increasingly detailed understanding of the community, the impact of opposition, and the impact of organization. In 1958, Wallace Sayre made the following observations about the kind of communities educational administrators preferred:

The community, when it confronts educational questions should be an unstructured audience of citizens. These citizens should not be influenced in their responses to educational questions by their structured associations or organizations: not as members of interest groups of any kind (save perhaps in parents groups) or as members of a political party.[2]

Many administrators prefer to believe that the "people out there" are a kind of a lump with largely similar interests and desires ("everybody wants good schools"). If the community is a mass, then it is much easier to represent. Table 4-2 shows the decline in trusteeness as the community is perceived in increasingly plural terms.

Mass politics is a situation in which the political actor directly engages the constituents served, where there are no intermediate groups, where there are no entities that collect and express the opinions of the public in a continuing fashion. Think for example, of the situation in the United States that would occur if there were no free press, no labor unions, no professional associations, or no voluntary groups like churches, synagogues, etc. Politicians and the public would be in direct and unmediated contact, and the various publics would have lost the relative advantages that accrue to them from the full-time, expert, and sometimes countervailing intercession of interest groups. Of course, because there would be no legitimate alternatives to government programs and because the political actors would dominate the symbols of political allegiance, it would be relatively easy for them to evoke large outpourings of (apparently) popular support. Because the people would be fragmented to the point of atomization, it

Table 4-2
Percentage of Trustees by Administrator's Perception of the Community

Perceived Community	% Trustee
A mass of people, undifferentiated either by amount of activity or attitude to school	91% (22)
All parents inactive (mainly supporters)	82% (33)
Some parents inactive (mainly supporters)	67% (36)
Some parents active (some opponents mentioned)	54% (24)
All parents active (some opponents mentioned)	44% (32)

Note: $N = 147$ (*T/D* RRO)

would also be exceptionally difficult for citizens to gather enough support to affect the course of their government.

The mass politics situation may explain much about the relationships between school administrators and citizens. In the absence of continuing organizations interested in affecting educational policy from outside the educationists' network and given the natural tendency of many public officials to perceive whole, undifferentiated, constituencies—the resulting climate is one in which educators can autonomously control policy decisions far beyond the simply technical sphere. Educators maintain an air of technical competence, and their mastery of how-to-educate is used to justify excluding the participation of the uninitiated. When pressed, they close ranks and assert a claim to definitive answers. (Recall, for instance, the strong relation between high expertise and exclusion of the community from educational decisions.) Yet the scientific journals relevant to education are filled with contradictory evidence, tremendous uncertainty over the relative merits of different programs, and even (perhaps especially) uncertainty over the causes of good teaching and learning. Both cannot be true; either educators have a sufficient mastery of the field to reasonably exclude the uninitiated, or they should admit the points of view of lay people as well. In the absence of convincing demonstrations of reasonably efficacious cause and effect, and in light of the disarray of the most scientifically advanced parts of the education community, the evidence is strongly on the side of those nonprofessional people who seek a legitimate voice in determining educational policy.

Board Relationships

One group of lay people, the board of education, is already inside the circle of education policy decision-makers. In the last chapter, we presented some evidence that suggested that it was more difficult for the administrators to override elected boards than it was to override appointed boards. We attributed the difference to the greater legitimacy that follows selection by the electorate. In this section we will examine that impact in more detail by contrasting the administrators' responses to the boards with their responses to the general community. Boards of education are the official vehicle for citizen participation. Much of the literature about the politics of education revolves around discussions of boards of education as though they were the only contact point for schools and communities. Undoubtedly boards are authoritative actors, they are relatively visible, and, especially where they are elected, they can be studied with techniques of aggregate data analysis that are familiar to political scientists. Most analysis of citizen/school interaction has used data about electoral participation as though it were the only kind of participation, or as though it could be substituted for nonelectoral citizen participation. Yet elections are infrequent events. They ask citizens to summarize a potentially vast array of opinions and attitudes about schools and then to relate that summary to the highly compressed format of a personnel or referendum election. The frustration felt by many voters who must express four years of accumulated discontents about multiple areas of both foreign and domestic policy in a single tug on the lever of a voting machine is a good example of the violence that electoral procedures do to the range of citizen responsibilities. Although electoral participation may be the only access most citizens have to their president, there are plenty of nonelectoral opportunities for participation in school politics.

We can look at this citizen input or demands on two levels. The first has to do with the "little things" of the interaction between communities and schools. Considering only the expressed citizen preferences that are informal, unthreatening, relatively marginal to the operations of the school and thus relatively easy to accommodate, we find that two thirds of all administrators regularly honor and incorporate them. As expected, the propensity to honor even these small demands is strongly related to trusteeness. The gamma measure of joint occurrence between decreasing trusteeness and increasing responsiveness to informal demands is .70 (chi square is .73 with 15 df, significant at the .001 level and tau beta is .47). For that group of trustees who are also responsive to these small demands, there is an interesting variation. High school principals are much more responsive than elementary or junior high principals. Only half of the latter group were trustees, but 70 percent of the high school principals who were responsive to these small demands were also characterized, overall, as trustees. The combination seems a little paradoxical. It may be that the high school principals are responsive in order to trade action on small matters for inaction on larger ones.

The interview schedule also provided opportunities for administrators to make a direct comparison between electoral and nonelectoral citizen participation. Seriate questions asked the respondent,

What if the board were to give you a direct order on an important issue and you thought the order was very bad educational practice? Would you obey it? . . . And if you lost the appeal (or whatever).

And, for nonelectoral citizen participation:

What if you had the same situation, but instead of a direct order from the board, it was a very clear and unanimous expression of the wishes of the people around here, and that went against your ideas of good education. What would you do if you HAD to decide? . . . You choose the issue. Can you imagine such a thing happening?

Of the administrators 60 percent felt free to reject nonelectoral citizen participation even where it was clearly and unanimously expressed, but only 37 percent would reject a direct order from the board. The evidence confirms the wisdom of those who wish to make schools more responsive by providing popularly elected supervisory or policy-making bodies such as New York City's community school boards.

There is a curious discrepancy in the administrators' attitudes toward political bodies and their legitimacy. Although they are willing to be guided by electorally sanctioned citizen participation, they do not approve of the political process as it might potentially affect education. Administrators had been asked questions about local elections and the relation of those elections to educational issues. Only a little more than one quarter of the respondents said that local politics was quite relevant to them, 42 percent thought it was "somewhat relevant," and 22 percent thought it was not relevant at all. Perhaps the traditional walls between "politics," that messy way in which the public will is pursued in public events, and education has not been breeched as widely as one might think. The largest group of administrators, 35 percent, indicated disapproval of any effects spilling over from the larger political arena to the educational arena; 28 percent were indifferent to the possibility of political determination of educational affairs. Only about a fourth of the school officials felt that such interaction was unavoidable and desirable.

In addition to these questions of legitimacy and attitude toward the political process in general, we were curious to know if the amount and kind of interaction individuals had with the board would be related to their representational behavior. About one administrator in three was actively involved with a governing board. Part of the explanation for the small proportion has to do with the strict observance of the chain of command that sometimes insulates building principals from their boards. In spite of the low frequency of interaction, fully 70 percent of the administrators felt that the board was supportive of them. Perceptions of board supportiveness vary by representational type. A higher percentage of politicos (almost 40 percent) believe that they are *not* supported by the board than do trustees or delegates. This belief is probably related to other aspects of the politico's situation such as the prevalence of controversy and conflict in their schools. Because, in addition, many politicos are in high schools, the low level of board support for this group may lend credence to the opinion of some high school principals that they have been made the chief scapegoat for the educational system as a whole. Fewer delegates perceive themselves as not being supported by the board than any other group, which is easily understood because delegates are more sensitive to community participation and more likely to act in accord with it.

Conflict and Opposition

Schools are complex institutions filled with diverse children and, at least ostensibly, serving the needs of a determinedly heterogeneous population. If race differences are not present, class differences are likely to be. Where race and class are similar, ethnicity may not be. The range of students' chronological age and differential learning styles and abilities compound all the rest of the difficulties. Most schools have to serve populations with all of those cleavages, and those differing needs and interests. Because schools are so complex and because society holds such extraordinary expectations for them, we may take it as axiomatic that there will be, at some important level, differing interests and attendant conflict in every educational institution. Considered this way, conflict is nothing more or less than the pursuit by a diverse citizenry of inevitably *and legitimately* differing goals. Considered this way, conflict is good and desirable information which, although it may complicate their jobs, (and burden their lives) administrators can be expected to seek out in order to guide their actions.

How many of the people who run educational institutions recognize conflict? Of the 162 interviews that could be coded on this dimension, 57 percent recognized conflict in response to the question, "Are there important differences between what you think you should be doing as an administrator and what the people around here think you should be doing? . . . None of them ever want you to do something you, as an administrator, don't think is worth doing?" Of the interviewees 43 percent denied that there were such differences. To what extent were those respondents accurately describing the reality of their situation? A little less than half the group that denied the existence of conflict also never described any instances of it during the remainder of the interview. At least their responses were consistent although it is exceptionally difficult to imagine a social institution like a school (and certainly not a school system) that would also be as homogeneous and as tranquil as these administrators would have us believe. The other half of this group first denied its existence and then proceeded to describe substantial fractures between themselves and the community. There were no significant variations between trustees and delegates in the propensity to recognize conflict. However, almost 80 percent of the politicos did so.

We looked at the policy areas that had been the most troublesome in the recent past—curriculum, race relations, staff relations, and student matters. Troubles in all those areas visited the different types of administrators with even-handed frequency except that 76 percent of those reporting the student area as their most controversial policy area were trustees. It may be that as students grow more impatient with their powerlessness, they are less likely to tolerate trustee behavior on the part of their administrators and therefore more likely to provoke controversy. For all decision-making types, the area of race relations was most frequently identified as the most controversial topic.

The part of the general populace that is concerned with schooling matters ordinarily prefers to be able to follow the decisions made by government officials that affect that area. While practically no one wants to be in constant attendance on every schooling decision, there is still a widespread preference for visibility in official decisions. Critics frequently charge that education has become so bureaucratized that it constitutes a closed system in which decisions are made in private councils beyond public scrutiny. We attempted to arrive at a judgment of whether decisions, especially the important programmatic ones regarding budgets, personnel, and curriculum were as open and as accessible to public scrutiny as could be expected. We considered the number of people to whom these decisions were visible and the frequency of that visibility. In general, as the number of individuals to whom decisions were visible increased, the proportion of administrators taking trustee orientations declined. Where the administrator's only scrutiny came from a bureaucratic superior such as a superintendent, 82 percent of those administrators took the trustee orientation. Where all of one's bureaucratic superiors were supplemented by scrutiny of parent groups as well, only 54 percent took trustee orientations. Considering the evidence for building principals alone, an even more striking relationship emerges. The average percent trustee among the three levels of principals (elementary, junior high, and senior high) for the group whose decisions were not visible is 90. The average for the visible group among all three levels is 60 percent (n's = 36 and 95 respectively: T/D RRO n = 131, building principals). Apparently the simple addition of public and especially neighborhood scrutiny to the administrative process, makes a big difference in the tendency to be a trustee.

The last element of conflict we will examine is that dealing with the administrators' allies in a fight. There have been some exceptional controversies lately in which all the possible parties in a dispute took a different side. When such a dispute splits teachers, the community, the board of education, and the central administration one from another, the administrator is likely to be in a real quandary. We were curious to know where, in such a dispute, administrators might go first for assistance? Would they think it most necessary to have community support, board support, or what? Of those who would make a choice, more allied themselves with teachers than with any other group, followed in descending order by the central administration, the community, and the local board. There is a big gap between the number of first-place choices for the central administration (second most frequently chosen) and the community (third most frequently chosen). The gap probably reflects the reluctance of most educators to go outside the educational fraternity for support and assistance. The last place position of the local board seems curious because its directives are perceived as being legitimate and its assistance might therefore be presumed to be welcome. The infrequency of its choice probably reflects the fact that it is also the employer of educators and thus a potential source of conflict as well. Predictably, the group that would turn first to other professionals for assistance was heavily trustee; those who would turn first to the community and/or the board, tended to be delegates.

Notes

1. Dale Mann, "Representational Role Orientations of New York City Elementary School Principals" (New York, Columbia University, unpublished Ph.D. dissertation, 1971).
2. Wallace Sayre, "Additional Observations on the Study of Administration," *Teachers College Record*, v. 60 (November, 1958), p. 75.

5

The Impact of Involvement

A premise of this book is that schools and communities exist in political interaction. The previous chapters have concentrated on how administrators regard their community representational responsibilities. But the view from the administration out is only one half of the school/community circle. In this second part, we will be looking at the other half, at the involvement of communities in school decision-making. These two halves of the same whole—the leader's representation and the followers' participation—are what the struggle over the democratic control of schools is made up of. These chapters develop an argument about shared control. The basic position is that the goals that both lay and professional people have for schools can be achieved by sharing the control of those schools. In this chapter the evidence relating increased involvement to increased goal achievement is reviewed. In essence, the chapter presents the "why's" of community involvement. The next chapter discusses the nature of that involvement, delineates its operational features, and presents the research-based knowledge about those features. The final chapter presents those features as an operations manual and applies them to the situation of a school principal. Together these materials show how community involvement may become shared control.

One of the most highly touted, hotly contested, and poorly defined techniques for school improvement in our recent past has been that of community involvement. Increasing community involvement in educational decisions was supposed to lead directly to a large number of sometimes contradictory goals. For some, involvement was to be used for the material gain of citizens,[1] or it was supposed to provide "educational therapy" and to encourage "behavioral change."[2] Others suggested that increasing participation was supposed, to "relieve psychic suffering"[3] and to develop "community cohesion."[4] Radical critics suggested that the purpose of increasing client involvement was to shift responsibility for the failure of schools to the poor ("blaming the victim") who might then be abandoned even more completely. Even moderate critics recognized that increased involvement was often used to co-opt or placate dissidents and defuse legitimate complaints.

Except as a grand abstraction, there never was much agreement about community involvement. Most school people were as threatened by it as social planners were mesmerized by it. Still, there are goals or purposes for involvement that both citizens and educators might share. In political situations, the discovery (or creation) of common interests can sometimes facilitate progress.

67

This chapter reviews the evidence on the impact that community involvement in education decisions has had in four areas where lay communities and school people may be assumed to have very similar goals. (The chapter concentrates on evidence from urban situations for some very simple reasons. That is where schools are most in trouble; that is where the most dramatic increases have come from; and, that is where most of the research and evaluations have been done.)

It is important to keep in mind that the major focus here is on the involvement of people in decision-making, not the involvement of people in parenting. The demonstrated association between high levels of parent involvement and high levels of student achievement was often used to justify increased general involvement by parents and others in school decision-making. But the two situations are not comparable—not all community members are parents, the school's enrollment is more than an individual child, the school is not the home, policy decisions are not (only) personal decisions, and decisional participation is therefore not the same as parental participation. Although parent-training strategies will be reviewed insofar as they contribute to decision-making, the focus is on the consequences of having involved people in decisions, not on having involved people in parenting.

There are four goals that may be shared between communities and administrators, each one of which has been supposed to be reached by increasing community involvement. The first goal, that of improving the *responsiveness* of schools to their community clientele, is intended to increase the congruence between what schools do and what their clientele want them to do or need for them to do. The second goal is that of increasing the affective and material *support* that communities give to schools. The third goal, *educational achievement*, is widely regarded as the most important. Achievement levels are a source of profound dissatisfaction, and a hope for community involvement has been that it would increase such levels. The fourth goal, *democratic principle*, expresses the norm in this society that the people affected by a public institution should participate in its governance.

The empirical content of studies relating community involvement to goal achievement varies wildly from nil through thoroughly valid and reliable. Unfortunately, there is not as much of the latter as anyone might wish. Where good, nonschool-based studies disclose important facets of phenomena that are reasonably linked to schooling, we have not hesitated to make use of them. Where, as often happens, the only "evidence" available is anecdotal, we have considered the source along with the contributions that (even) conjecture may make to an important topic. The procedure strains the limits of inference but can be justified because the guidance it yields may be better than unrefined speculation for people who cannot afford the luxury of inaction.

Goal I: Institutional Responsiveness

It is easy to see why the residents of a community should want schools to be responsive to them, but less easy to see why school people should endorse the same goal. There is a sense in which it is "right" for public schools to be responsive to the communities they serve. Practically all school people will espouse that symbolic goal, but the reality of its achievement is more problematic. With limited resources to fulfill an enormous number of needs, school people are inevitably the subject of uncomfortable pressures. When the disparities in the knowledge base and legal responsibility between the two groups are considered, exclusion of lay participation in quasi-technical decisions like education may be further justified. The bureaucratic walls around schools were erected in part for that purpose. Why then should school people actually want to be responsive to practically insatiable, potentially less-informed, and legally nonaccountable communities? Why should administrators want "their" schools to be responsive to communities? The big carrot in eliciting responsiveness from administrators is the support of the clientele. Support is no longer freely given. It is exchanged for something.

Responsiveness is the price schools pay for community support. The responsiveness-support quid pro quo is the first reason that educators should share this goal. The second has to do with improvement. The importance of responsiveness is inversely proportional to the quality of schooling. Where the community is satisfied, responsiveness may be less important than where the community is dissatisfied. Improving schools has been an extremely arduous business in part because of insufficient knowledge about the causes of good teaching and learning, in part because of the complexity of the educational task and the paucity of material resources, and in part because of such features as bureaucratic inertia, vested interests, and so on. Thus it is difficult for schools to respond to community demands—especially when those demands come from new groups, when the changes involved are substantial, or when professional educators do not agree with what is being demanded. In those cases, the impetus for improvement must often be supplied from outside the school. Averch et al., found that "Research suggests that the larger the school system, the less likely it is to display innovation, responsiveness, and adaptation, and the more likely it is to depend upon exogenous shocks to the system."[5] Because the outside community can be an important assist to school improvement and because such improvements may lead to increased support, educators inclined to reform may be very interested in responding to their communities.

But that presupposes something to respond to. The community must present its demands and interests. The content of what is learned, the process through which it is taught, the identities of the people who do the teaching, and other similar factors are often of considerable concern to neighborhoods. As the neighborhood presence grows in terms of numbers, time, and scope of involvement, the likelihood increases that its demands will be presented and their resolution pursued in ways that ensure greater congruity between school and community. That process works in both directions. The more that professionals and lay people interact, the more opportunities that professionals have to persuade lay people of the wisdom of professionally recommended policy. In the first instance, the school changes in response to the citizens; in the second, the citizens' own goals come to coincide with those of the institution.

The evidence that most clearly relates increases in community involvement to increases in the responsiveness of social welfare institutions (including schools) is the work of Robert Yin *et al.* In their study of citizen participation in the governance of local programs, Yin *et al.*, reported that about half of the citizen involvement mechanisms that had only "advisory" or limited authority over their programs succeeded in getting agency implementation of new ideas. Yet 69 percent of those citizen boards with "governing" authority got their agencies to accept new ideas.[6]

The most easily visible proxy for responsiveness is innovation.[a] Marilyn Gittell and T. Edward Hollander studied the propensity to innovate in six large cities. They argued that because of the changing socioeconomic characteristics, the ability of those cities' school systems to adapt themselves to new demands was their single most important characteristic. They studied the effect of (1) administrative organization, (2) citizen participation, and (3) the allocation of financial resources on the propensity to innovate. "The most direct and clear cut cause and effect relationship with innovation appears to be public participation."[7] Marian Sherman Stearns and Susan Peterson cite, "Evidence from Follow Through case studies conducted between 1968 and 1970 [which] suggested a connection between the level of parent participation in a local project and the level of institutional change within the project and the community."[8]

The previous chapters presented the evidence from this study of administrative representation that suggests that administrators are most responsive where community participation was most organized. A related finding appears in James Vanecko's analysis of community action programs in one hundred cities. Where the programs stressed the provision of services to clientele, there was very little change in the service-providing institutions themselves. But in programs that emphasized community organization and citizen mobilization, the institutions themselves changed and became more responsive. Vanecko found that the simple presence of a school-related community organization was often sufficient to provoke change in the schools. Compared to other kinds of social-welfare organizations, Vanecko found that: "Schools are less susceptible to the threat of militant activity and the pressures of citizens. They are most likely to change simply because the neighborhood is organized."[9]

It is not surprising that participation through community organization should be associated with institutional responsiveness; people get involved exactly because they want to make a difference in what schools do. The premium

[a]Schools are also being responsive where communities do not want to change, and schools accommodate that desire. But there is considerable evidence about discontent, especially in the big cities, with school performance, so the cases of a status quo school reflecting a status quo community are probably much less frequent than administrators would have people believe.

organization yields in political influence should apply in school affairs just as certainly as it does in other sectors. Because lay people bring new perceptions, new biases, and new attitudes, some response from the school is a logical outcome. Gittell notes the eagerness that newly elected community school board members brought to their responsibilities in New York. "There is no question but that boards and their professional staffs in the districts sought new methods which would produce immediate results."[10]

Goal II: Support for Schooling

There is a lot of rhetoric about the plight of urban schools and the culpability of administrators for that condition. Those indictments have helped to call attention to needed reforms, they have mobilized communities, and they have sensitized administrators. But no single group bears total responsibility for what hasn't been done in urban education. If professionals are believed to have bad intentions and the failures of urban education are their fault, then it is only an easy step to believing that the schools run by those administrators do not deserve the support of the community. Momentum originally designed to mobilize people's concern for the schools can damage the very institution it was intended to help. Two questions arise: Is increasing support for the schools a goal that can be shared by communities and administrators; and can support be built by increasing community involvement?

Supporting the schools as an institution does not mean endorsing every feature or consequence of the status quo. Nor does it mean that support cannot be conditional on important changes. What support means as a goal for community involvement is that the local school is an object generally worthy of assistance, cooperation, and reinforcement. Schools can survive on acquiescence, but they need support to succeed. Thus both communities and administrators share an interest in seeing schools become stronger, more effective places for teaching and learning.

Can support be generated through involvement? Ronald Havelock made an extensive survey of the literature related to educational innovation including the work of Kurt Lewin and his associates. Havelock has summarized the effects that lead those who have been involved in a group to become more supportive of the group's decisions.

Group atmosphere has certain important effects in and of itself. Anderson and McGuire demonstrate the lowered resistance that results from peer support. The greater the peer support, the lower the resistance and therefore, the greater the susceptibility to influence from sources acceptable to the group.... Thus, participation with others in decision-making groups usually leads to a commitment to the group's actions.[11]

Havelock also discusses Edith Bennett Pelz's validation of Lewin's early studies on the efficacy of group participation as a way of influencing individual behavior. Havelock notes that the two factors most closely related to an individual's acceptance of a new behavior were "(1) the perceived consensus among their peers and (2) the fact that they had made a decision."[12]

For the individual, the act of involvement requires the expenditure of some minimum amount of resources—time, concentration, intellectual and emotional expression. Investing personal resources is likely to increase one's commitment to the group being participated in, regardless of the outcome of any particular decision, simply because most people are loath to invest resources without receiving some benefits in return. If they do make the effort to participate and nothing happens, then their effort was wasted. Thus people tend to reinterpret unfavorable decisions as favorable or at least neutral rather than acknowledge the unpleasant outcomes of their own involvement. As involvement increases, so does support for the institution that was, after all, "good enough" to have made use of the involved person.

But how can that initial participation be stimulated? Political participation is related to an individual's sense of efficacy. A person who places a high value on himself is more likely to believe that an institution will be responsive to his input and is thus more likely to make such input. When the institution does respond, or even seems to respond, the person's estimate of both his own worth and of the institution's is reinforced, making further input even more likely. The cycle of self-efficacy contributing to political efficacy contributing to self-efficacy and so on is probably more common, more powerful, and more socially significant in the direction of negative reinforcement than it is in the positive direction. Lester Milbrath has said of those people who habitually do not take part in public affairs, "Failure to participate contributed to ... [a] sense of political impotence and [the] lack of a sense of efficacy increases the probability that they will not participate."[13] The most likely question for an administrator is, how can the downward spiral of self-efficacy be reversed? How can people be provided with a participatory experience sufficient to increase their sense of political self-efficacy and hence their potential identification with and support for their institutions? (Those "how-to-do-it" questions are addressed in the last chapter.)

However it begins, once the involvement is under way, other people identify the involved person with the school. They call on that person to explain or justify the school's actions, and that identification increases the felt commitment. Where poor school/community relations are a product of a lack of knowledge and familiarity, broadening the base of community participation in institutional decisions may decrease hostility and increase support. A participant will become more familiar with the setting. Simply by virtue of the act of participation, the individual has become more accessible and perhaps more amenable to influence than people who do not participate. As we have said, involvement in the school exposes the community person to a group of professionals and other community members, all of whom are much more likely to support the school than are people who are uninvolved. Thus, at a personal psychological level, the involvement of individuals may aggregate to community support because acts of participation are likely to change the person's relation with the school.[14]

Perhaps the clearest example of these effects in education has been the experience of community-based paraprofessionals many of whom have moderated their criticism of the schools precisely for these reasons. From the school's point of view, there has been co-option. Crucially, the amount of support available to the schools has increased. Richard Andrews and Ernest Noack in their paper on "The Satisfaction of Parents with Their Community Schools" cite the work of Hess and Shipman and of Rankin as confirming that, "The participation of parents in various facets of the school's operation was found to improve the parent's attitude. . . ."[15]

Gittell's evaluation of the Ocean Hill-Brownsville experience indicated that the community's support for its schools increased during the first years of the community control experiment. In two surveys taken a year apart, support for the teachers more than doubled from 38 percent responding positively to 77 percent;[16] support for building principals jumped from 40 percent to 75 percent; support for the community superintendent doubled from 29 percent to 58 percent; and, support for the community school board itself increased from 31 percent to 57 percent. Even that "heavy," New York City's central Board of Education shared in these more supportive attitudes, going from 24 percent approval to a 50 percent rating in a year.

When asked to evaluate the schools in the district in comparison to the way they were before the creation of the Ocean Hill-Brownsville district, 72 per cent rated the schools better or about the same while only 17 per cent thought that they were worse and 10 per cent were not sure.[17]

She concluded,

that more parents were in the schools more frequently and felt more positively towards the locally selected professional staff and the local board. Informal visits to the schools were greater and knowledge of what was going on appeared to be more widespread. Certainly, parents felt school personnel were more responsive to them. Participant observations and interviews with staff suggested greater parent attendance and interest at meetings and more use of the schools as community facilities.[18]

Gittell's finding lends credence to an earlier speculation by Robert Lyke:

It is likely that community control of the schools will very quickly change the character of political interaction in ghetto communities. Citizens will no longer trace all problems in the schools to a repressive white society, hostility and tensions are likely to diminish as reforms are made, and future debate over education policy will be less likely to be as ideological as it currently is.[19]

The aggregate or community version of the participation hypothesis holds that, as involvement increases, so does supportiveness. In a moment we will turn to the evidence about relations between involvement and support for the financial aspects of schooling. Before reviewing the evidence, however, we need to consider an exception to the general relationship between increased involvement and increased support. Two studies have found that as involvement increases, so does the tendency to be critical of the schools. Working with a national sample of two thousand parents, Kent Jennings found that those parents who were PTA members had fewer grievances against the school than did parents who, in addition to being PTA members, also belonged to other education-related groups.[20] For members of any group, once a grievance had been expressed and pursued, there was a tendency to have another. The second study is that of Richard Cloward and James Jones. They found that the more a person was exposed to the schools, the more likely it was that that person would define education as either the first or second greatest problem in the community.

These results would tend to suggest that school administrators must be prepared to deal with more negative attitudes toward the school if greater efforts are made to involve people in school activities. Such involvement ... is functional for attitudes toward the importance of education generally, but as attitudes toward education improve the school as an institution is more likely to come under attack. Skillfully managed, however, these negative attitudes can become a source of pressure for better educational facilities and programs.[21]

That complaints increase as involvement increases will have the shrill ring of truth for many school principals. However, an important distinction needs to be made in both cases. Neither Jennings' "grievances" nor Cloward and Jones' "negative appraisals" are necessarily related to support. A person may believe that cancer is an enormously important problem and may be very critical about research to discover its cure, yet still support the attempt. That an individual thinks of the local schools as the community's most significant problem may mean that the person thinks efforts at educational improvement should have the highest priority. The task, as Cloward and Jones rightly point out, is to turn criticism to constructive purposes.

One way in which the prospects for constructive criticism can be increased is by providing a mechanism for authentic community involvement. Donald Haider notes that, "representational devices tend to be important to a citizen's sense of efficacy and overall support for a political system. It is at the heart of the democratic process and should not be minimized."[22] Luttbeg and Griffin set out to see whether a lack of accurate representation by education officials of citizens' preferences would affect the amount of support those citizens had for the system. They had hypothesized that "the low salience of politics for the average man means that the lack of representation in no way affects the level of public support for the political system."[23] But instead they found that as misrepresentation or nonrepresentation increased, support decreased. Although the amount of the association was slight (about 10 percent of the variance in public support was explained by misrepresentation), it was still significant.

Dollar support for the schools is critical. The extensive school/community communications studies conducted by Richard Carter and others at Stanford University,

began with the hypothesis (and implicit hope) that public understanding leads to support for public education. We found some evidence for this hypothesis. But we found it for the degree of understanding among informed observers in school districts, not among the citizens as a whole. From what we have seen of citizen participation, there is little to suggest that we would find support related to understanding among citizens generally.[24]

Carter's findings indicate that understanding is indeed related to support, but understanding itself is also related to and increased by participation in school affairs. Thus involvement and understanding may be used to increase each other, and the result in turn conduces to support, in this case willingness to financially support the schools. George Gallup traced the same relation in the opposite direction in his 1969 national survey of public attitudes toward the schools:

1. While the American people seem reasonably well informed about school activities, they are ill-informed about education itself.

2. Since they have little or no basis for judging the quality of education in their local schools, pressures are obviously absent for improving the quality.

Thus, in the absence of more sophistication and information, they can hardly be expected to be stronger supporters of more money.[25]

The so-called turnout hypothesis suggests that school bond issues pass more easily when voting participation is in the light than in the intermediate range. In *Voters and Their Schools*, Richard Carter and John Suttoff report that for more than a thousand school districts over more than a decade, bond election experience indicated that

when the percentage of voters is less than 30 percent, many more elections succeed than fail; when a moderate turnout of 30 to 60 percent of the voters occurs, more elections fail than succeed; and when the turnout is over 60 percent, the chances of success and failure are equal.[26]

Most school people have concentrated on the diminished chances of success in the portion of voter turnout from 30 to 60 percent. The relationship exists because of the differences in attitudes that characterize successive participatory strata of the electorate. In general, the stratum of frequent voters contains a higher proportion favorable to government action (e.g., more money for schools) than does the stratum of infrequent voters. A light voter turnout will be made up disproportionately of those who favor schooling expenditures (parents, school people, and their friends and neighbors). But as voter turnout increases, it begins to tap a stratum of voters that has a higher proportion of "anti" attitudes. Evidence is not unanimous on this relation,[27] but the conclusion frequently drawn is that success can be enhanced if voting can be depressed.

There are two difficulties with that conclusion. In the first place, it is ethically objectionable for educators to make the public schools' (short-term) success rely on restricting the public's franchise. The second objection is a practical one. It is difficult to control voter turnout. When issues are important and opinions are strongly held, turnout may be heavy. In the most important issues, that is exactly the case, so it is preferable for educators to work on the attitudes that characterize *all* strata of the electorate prior to the need for mobilizing support. A reservoir of informed voters is a more reliable resource in times of crisis than people who are intermittently called upon for only marginal participation.[b]

After one of the few longitudinal studies of school/community interaction, Robert Agger and Marshall Goldstein concluded that there was an ominous gap between professional educators and the less mobilized stratum of citizens. They found an

increasing tendency for the alienated to organize and be organized by what the dominant overstructure might term "demagogues." The increasingly effective leaders of the opposition are demagogues but not in the pejorative sense. They are men and women who represent the less articulate but substantial numbers of people whose potentially sympathetic support has increasingly been wasted by an elite which partly does not comprehend the existence of an alien cultural perspective, partly does not care, partly does not know how to cope with it, and partly fears both personal and professional self-searching and the kinds of professionally prohibited political involvement which might then have to follow.[29]

What Agger and Goldstein are talking about is the manipulative use of involvement, the practice of asking for community input only at the point of crisis, in only one direction (support for the status quo), and then only for something that has already been unilaterally determined.

---

[b]Finance is not the only critical area in which the public's supportiveness of the school's programs seems to turn around levels of public understanding. The U.S. Civil Rights Commission in an extensive national survey dealing with school desegregation found "a close relation between understanding the facts and more favorable response toward desegregation. The more people know, the less willing they are to restrict the Constitutional rights of Black children."[28]

Goal III: Educational Achievement

Students' educational achievement comes close to being the reason for the school's existence. Student achievement in all its forms is at the same time a widely accepted and widely disliked metric for the school's performance. The importance of student achievement and its central place as a criterion for school performance suggest that professional and lay people share an acute interest in it.

Historically, proponents of community involvement have argued that educational achievement could be increased through community participation. Carol Lopate, Erwin Flaxman, Effie Bynum, and Edmund Gordon's statement is a good introduction to this area. Their 1969 review of the literature indicated that, "When parents are involved in the decision-making process of education, their children are likely to do better in school."[30] At what was about the high-water mark for rhetorical support of the direct linkage between community involvement and achievement, Maurice Berube wrote:

There is every reason to believe that community control of city schools will enhance educational quality. *Equality of Educational Opportunity* discovered that the secret to learning lay with student attitudes. Attitudes toward self, of power to determine one's own future, influence academic achievement far more than factors of class size, teacher qualifications or condition of school plant. "Of all the variables measured in the survey, the attitudes of student interest in school, self concept, and sense of environmental control show the greatest relation to achievement," Coleman concluded. Furthermore a pupil's attitude— "the extent to which an individual feels that he has some control over his destiny"—was not only the most important of the various elements studied, but it "appears to have a stronger relationship to achievement than do all the 'school' factors together."[31]

Another very prominent defender of community involvement, Marilyn Gittell, evaluated those aspects of New York's Intermediate School 201 and Two Bridges experiments in local control. In defending the beneficial impact of community involvement, she wrote:

To a certain extent, the results of these educational experiments were reflected in the standardized testing. The hard data on I.S. 201 and Two Bridges shows that the school district was able to at least keep some children on reading level and in some cases in some schools there was marked improvement. Both I.S. 201 and Two Bridges reflected a stable standardized test achievement at a time when the city *declined* in reading achievement primarily because of the teacher strike.[32]

The national study of the effects of parent participation in Head Start programs conducted by Charles Mowry found that,

There is a strong relationship between high participation by parents and better performance on intellective and task-oriented measures. The children of parents with extensive participation in both roles [as decision makers and as learners] produced better scores on verbal intelligence, academic achievement, self concept behavioral rating in classroom and at home, and change rating in both learning and activities.[33]

As Mowry recognizes, despite their encouraging direction, there are several problems with these findings, including the probability that parents of children who were already high achievers prior to their Head Start exposure, self-selected those children (and themselves as decision-makers) into program participation.

There are other difficulties of interpreting the evidence that links the decisional involvement of parents to the educational achievement of students. The first and most important distinction that should be made concerns the difference between causation and association. Milbrey Wallin McLaughlin, for example, found that although "parental involvement of any kind is conspicuously absent in [Title 1] programs which fail to meet their objectives, all that can be said with justification about this finding is that successful programs and parental participation covary together."[34] Because more parents with middle-class attributes participate in more school activities than do lower-class parents and because middle-class children perform at higher levels on standardized tests does not mean that the parents' participation in the school's activities causes the students' achievement. Increasing the involvement of lower-class communities in education decisions will not by itself make up for the tremendous range of educational advantages that are not available to them or their children. Changing decision-making patterns will not by itself dramatically alter the school's performance. Diane Ravitch has noted:

It still remains true in New York City as elsewhere, that schools with middle-class children—whether white or black—record higher achievement scores than schools with lower-class children, no matter who controls the schools. And it is equally true that the problems of poverty—hunger, family instability, sickness, unemployment, and despair—cannot be solved by the schools alone. No amount of administrative experimentation seems to be able to change these facts.[35]

Averch's survey of the question of educational achievement and its causes found that:

The current status of research in this area can be described by the following propositions:

Proposition 1: Research has not identified a variant of the existing system that is consistently related to students' educational outcomes. . . .

Proposition 3: Research tentatively suggests that improvement in student outcomes, cognitive and non-cognitive, may require sweeping changes in the organization, structure, and conduct of educational experience.[36]

We have now had several years' experience with levels of community involvement somewhat higher than those that had previously characterized urban schooling. Although there have been some gains, a breakthrough in student achievement has not been made. It is difficult and depressing to document something that has not happened. Robert Hess, Marianne Bloch, Joan Costello, Ruby Knowles, and Dorothy Largay have provided a useful summary.

A compelling line of argument . . . contended that early experience affects subsequent intellectual and educational growth and achievement, and that children who grow up in homes disadvantaged by racial discrimination and poverty have a deficit of the experiences presumably essential for academic achievement in the public schools. . . . Therefore compensatory programs should involve parents and assist them in providing a more adequate educational environment for their young children. In view of our present knowledge about early experience in ghetto and low income homes, this view obviously is simplistic and in some aspects false.[37]

With the clarity honed by hindsight, it is easy to recognize that citizen involvement with school decision-making is not the same as parental involvement with children and that the benefits of association between the last two sets of factors can not be translated into causally increased benefits from the first two sets of factors. To make matters worse, community involvement tumbled into the implementation gap along with virtually every other programmatic reform of the sixties. Programs that began with grand hopes got watered down; their implementation was imperfect, very partial, hesitant, poorly supported, and fickle. To justify their claims on resources and to overcome resistance to change, proponents of political reforms like community involvement overstated their original case. The uneven results from those partial reforms have been interpreted as demonstrating the foolhardy nature of having tried to do anything different in the first place. This cycle will be familiar to political scientists and to historians. The community involvement movement was not the first to wrap its political goals (control, responsiveness, etc.) in educational clothes (student achievement). The irony is that school people who have been doing exactly that for years should be so adept at criticizing community involvement on their own grounds.

Again, with hindsight, it is easy to say that we should have known better than to expect very dramatic, quick, or widespread results from the sorts of changes in community involvement that have usually been instituted. The new involvement practices have been in place too short a time for their effects to be manifest. The problems are too severe to yield to a mere management reform; serious attempts at improving achievement in urban schools appear now to require quantum jumps in material and political resources. When effects do emerge, they may be faint and they will certainly be very difficult to attribute to involvement. They may not be adequately registered by standardized tests. And finally, it seems certain that we will not get important changes in achievement associated with involvement until we have moved that involvement to a level of significance such as shared control.

There are several implications that need to be drawn from this experience. The first is that community involvement in education remains an important strategy for the improvement of urban education; it should not be discarded simply because it turns out to be as complicated and subtle as other education change strategies. The gains may be modest and slow to arrive. The second implication is that the resources devoted to community involvement (time, energy, support, etc.) need to be increased significantly if significant gains are to be realized. Recall Averch's conclusion that improvement in student outcomes may require, not the sort of incremental change so far attempted, but "sweeping changes in the organization, structure, and conduct of educational experience."[38]

To this point, we have reviewed some of the original expectations about the linkage between community involvement and educational achievement; we have described the subsequent disappointment; and we have outlined some of the more plausible explanations for that melancholy reality. The other benefits associated with community involvement may, by themselves, provide a nearly sufficient rationale for its maintenance or even increase, but the central role of student achievement is so important that it should not be abandoned prematurely. The following section identifies four paths through which involvement may affect achievement. It cites the existing evidence that supports these paths and speculates about needed additional research. (Figure 5-1.)

Path 1: Parent Self-efficacy. Parents, as citizens, participate in educational decisions, become more knowledgeable and confident, and then encourage their children to higher levels of achievement.

Path 2: Institutional/Child Congruence. Parents and other citizens participate in educational decisions and in so doing, affect the school which becomes more responsive to the children who then perform better.

Path 3: Community Support. Parents and other citizens participate in educational decisions, become themselves more interested in the school, turn to the community to get more support for the school, which is then better able to help children to higher achievement levels.

Path 4: Student Self-efficacy. In this relatively direct pattern, the child notices the parent's involvement in the school and is stimulated by that example to perform better.

These patterns are graphically represented in Figure 5-1 and then discussed in more detail.

81

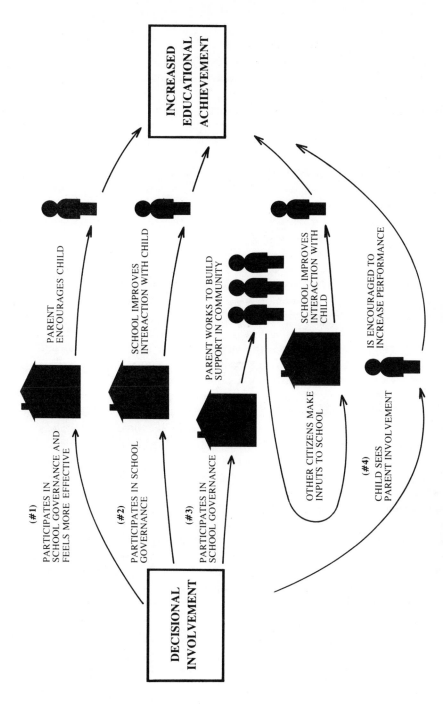

Figure 5-1. Paths of Increased Educational Achievement through Decisional Involvement

Path 1: Parent Self-efficacy

Of the four, this is the most thoroughly (but still insufficiently) documented path. It begins with the parents' involvement in decision-making which increases the parents' knowledge and self-confidence. Those increases are then translated into increased and improved attention to the child who then does better in school. What evidence is there on the effect of involvement on the parents and second, on the generalization of the parents' involvement to the child's achievement?

McLaughlin's review of Title I evaluations indicated that "It is . . . typically reported that, as a result of increased parent participation, parents know more about the 'special' program in which their child is enrolled."[39] Gittell's evaluation of community school boards in New York "indicated that the knowledge, perceptions and attitudes of board members were developed in the new citizen boards. All the board members showed increased knowledge as a result of their participation and became more articulate about their views." She continues: "The net effect of [the] developing sense of community . . . was to reduce the amount of alienation of parents towards the schools and to make them more aware of educational policy."[40] Yin, *et al.*, looked at the extent to which leadership skills had been developed as a result of citizen service on social-welfare governing boards. Not only did significant numbers of people develop such skills as a result of their service, but also more leadership skills were developed where the responsibility of the board was the greatest.[41]

The sense of political efficacy measures the confidence a person feels that government will be responsive to his or her input. People who feel that their actions will be responded to are more likely than those who do not to take part in government activities. The act of participating itself encourages people to feel more efficacious. There is a circular relationship here between efficacy and participation, and it works to decelerate involvement as well as to accelerate it. Hess's extensive review of the parental involvement literature reinforces the point in an educational setting. "There are indications that many Black mothers, and probably those of other ethnic minority groups, feel a sense of powerlessness regarding their ability to help their children to achieve in school."[42]

But can decisional participation help? Hess believes that although such participation is hardly a sufficient cause, membership in community organizations and the consequent increased feeling of control can contribute to educational achievement.[43] He continues:

Participation may have some impact on the development of competence and self-esteem in the parents involved (Miller, 1968; Scheinfeld, 1969; Hadger, 1970). It can be noted that these programs actively engage and involve parents in teaching their own children while emphasizing respect for their potential worth as individuals and confidence in this potential for continuous development.[44]

Mowry's study of parental participation in Head Start found that,

Parents who were high in participation, especially those high in decision-making, were also high in feeling of ability to control their environment. . . . Parents who were high in participation also viewed themselves as more successful, more skillful, and better able to influence their environment.[45]

McLaughlin makes a similar point. "Parent training programs and a number of parent participation programs have accomplished what many Manpower Development Training Act programs have failed to do. They have given parents a sense of competence and confidence."[46]

That participation and the sense of personal efficacy reinforce each other is well established in educational governance and in other settings.[47] The sense of political efficacy is important in its own right, but it also deserves to be cultivated for its contribution to other values. In the achievement context, the sense of efficacy is important because of its bearing on the parents' interactions with the child. There is a spillover from political to parental efficacy. McLaughlin cites a reanalysis of the Coleman data undertaken by Marshall Smith at the Center for Educational Policy Research which indicates that for

a representative sample of sixth grade students in the urban north . . . even when a large number of individual background characteristics such as SES and school-wide measures were controlled, the relation between [parental] PTA attendance and three measures of academic achievement were significant at the .05 level for black students.[48]

In her own excellent review, McLaughlin distinguished between programs of parent participation and parent training. Moving beyond participation to

parent training of even a modest sort . . . can be said to positively and significantly effect the cognitive development of children—both the target youngsters and the younger siblings. Of the two parent models, then, parent training appears to combine most successfully all the virtues of economy and attainment of cognitive and affective objectives for both parents and children.[49]

Stearns and Peterson make a similar point.

The evidence indicates that involving parents as trainees and tutors can indeed improve children's performance—at least with young preschool children. [Several carefully controlled investigations] . . . have noted positive effects of such participation both on parents' attitudes about themselves and on children's IQ scores.[50]

And Wilbur Brookover, et al., found that low-achieving junior high school students whose parents had become involved in the school and made more aware of the developmental process of their children showed heightened self-concept and made significant academic progress.[51]

Adelaide Jablonsky asserts that compensatory programs in "schools which have open doors to parents and community members have greater success in educating children. . . . The children seem to be the direct beneficiaries of the change in perception on the part of their parents."[52] Joe L. Rempson states that

school-parent programs can help to increase the school achievement of the disadvantaged child. Both Schiff . . . and Duncan . . . discovered that children of low SES parents who participated in programs of planned contacts made significantly greater achievement gains in reading and in new mathematics, respectively, than comparably matched children of no or few contact parents.[53]

The evidence indicating that children of parents who are actively involved in their education perform better than do other children hardly needs emphasis. The point here is that successful involvement in school decision-making can provide parents with the confidence and the knowledge to support a more active role at the more immediate family level.

Path 2: Institutional/Child Congruence

Responsiveness is the key to the second of the paths through which community participation may be linked to educational achievement. We had earlier hypothesized that in this path, parents and other citizens would be found to be participating in educational decisions and that participation would affect the schools which might then become more responsive to the children who would in turn perform better. The studies reviewed in the earlier section dealing with the responsiveness goal clearly indicate that its achievement increases as community participation increases. Here we are concerned with evidence about the next step, i.e., its possible linkage to student achievement.

The strongest evidence is the so-called Pygmalion effect. Parents who express confidence in their children's ability to their teachers have an effect on the teacher's subsequent view of those children. Rosenthal and Jacobson reported that children who profited from positive changes in teachers' expectations of their ability *all* had parents who had demonstrated some interest in their child's development and who were distinctly visible to the teachers.[54] Similarly, Rankin compared high- and low-achieving inner-city children and found that the parents of the higher-achieving group were more able to initiate contacts and pursue school-related matters with school officials.[55]

Although PTA's are weak forms of participation in governance, Coleman found that there was a significant relationship between the amount of community participation in the PTA and the achievement of students in 684 urban elementary schools. Where PTA attendance was reported as being high, children's performance was two to four months ahead of those schools that had no PTA. Christopher Jencks reanalyzed the Coleman data to discover whether race and social class might explain the relationship between PTA attendance and achievement.

> PTA attendance was ... significantly related to achievement. Race and class explained about 15 percent of the variance in schools' PTA attendance. But even after this was taken into account, schools whose principals reported that almost all parents attended PTA meetings scored between two and four months above schools whose principals reported not having a PTA. Schools with more moderate PTA attendance were strung out between. PTA attendance seems to be a proxy for district-wide parental interest in education ... the relationship did hold for reading or math scores.[56]

Another of the analyses done of Head Start, the Kirschner report, concluded that significant institutional changes were identified more often at those sites where parent involvement was classified as high than at those sites with low involvement of parents. The difference was significant, and the researchers concluded that a relationship did seem to exist between the degree of parent involvement and the extent of Head Start impact on institutional change.[57] Mowry's study of parental participation in Head Start investigated several types of institutional change including greater emphasis on the educational needs of poor people. "The number of reported changes was significantly greater in centers where parents were highly involved in decision-making and learning activities."[58]

The importance of such responsiveness can hardly be underestimated. As NYC's Bundy Commission said: "If peers and family regard the school as an alien, unresponsive, or ineffective institution in their midst, the child will enter the school in a mood of distrust, apprehension or hostility."[59] The clear intention is to require the school to facilitate the child's achievement by becoming more responsive to parental desires. McLaughlin's review of the lay participation aspects of Title I evaluations also documented the frequent finding of "a change in teachers' attitudes about and understanding of low income children and their families."[60] The linkage between participation and responsiveness is clear, but even though it is reasonable to presume that responsiveness may be being translated into achievement, it has yet to be empirically demonstrated.

Path 3: Community Support

In the first two patterns, educational achievement was affected through the actions of participants in the schools. In this pattern the focus of the participants' action is on other citizens. Participating in the school's affairs arms people with information and motivation that can be directed to other citizens. We have already reviewed the considerable stock of research that related increases in participation to increases in support by primary participants. Documentation on the persistence of that effect as it ripples outward is more scanty. There, the greater supportiveness of primary participants should encourage them to recruit others in the community, and the resulting increased reservoir of positive attitudes should help the schools to facilitate the child's achievement. The path is long but there are some indications that at least part of it is being traversed. For example, with respect to parent training, a number of sources document the "vertical" and "horizontal" diffusion of benefits from such training. Not only does the trained parent perform better with the siblings of the child ("vertical" diffusion), but those skills also get communicated to other people in the community ("horizontal" diffusion).[61] If those "horizontal" or second-generation participants feel more efficacious, have more knowledge about the schools, and so on, then it is also reasonable to assume that they will be more supportive of the school as an institution. Similarly, McLaughlin's review of Title I evaluations found that participants in program decisions led to increases in parent morale about the school.[62]

Path 4: Student Self-efficacy

In some ways, this is the simplest and most direct of the paths. It suggests that the children observe their parents taking part in school decision-making and are therefore encouraged to think more highly of their own participation in school. The U.S. Office of Education has made a succinct case for this pattern. "There is a subsidiary asset of parental involvement. As children see their own parents more involved in school affairs, they will be encouraged to take a more active interest in school."[63] The logic underlying this path is apparent: If you believe that there is no way to succeed, you are unlikely to try. A sense of self-efficacy is as necessary a precondition for success with students as it is with their parents. The question is, can it be built through parental and community participation?

The experience of the Flint Michigan School and Home Program supports the possibility. The evaluation of the parent-training aspects of that program indicate that the child's awareness of their parents' participation stimulated the children to greater activity. The children in the group whose parents had the training experience showed gains on the Gates Revised Reading test that were double those of the control group of children.[64]

The best-known study relevant to this question is the Coleman Report. Coleman measured three attitudes of students toward themselves:

(1) Student's interest in school (2) self-concept specifically with regard to learning and success in school, and (3) sense of control of the environment. [This analysis demonstrated that] of all the variables measured (including family background and school variables) these attitudes showed the strongest relation to achievement at all three grade levels. [Grades 6, 9, and 12.][65]

Coleman's data indicate how important it is that students believe in themselves and in their ability to achieve. Parents can affect the child's attitudes toward school and toward their prospect for success in the school. The key attitude may be what Coleman called "The sense of control of the environment," the school's administrators, teachers, decision procedures, governance roles, etc. Students who perceive that their parents are effective in that environment are more likely to believe that they too can successfully negotiate it. In addition, they are more likely to perceive their school environment as one that is supportive of them.

Mario Fantini has suggested an analogy between community involvement in urban schools and the control of Catholic schools. Andrew Greeley and Peter Rossi speculated that students in Catholic schools performed well academically at least in part because of the sense of security those schools generated. Similarly, Fantini says,

Under community-directed schools, the educational environment is far less likely to be hostile or intimidating to the minority child. He will thus have a sense of being able to function in the school environment and, in turn, a greater sense of internal control—the prime prerequisite to effective learning, according to a growing body of educational evidence as well as psychological insight.[66]

In some research that would support Fantini's speculation, Joan Abrams has documented the extent to which school principals' ideology of pupil control covaries with their attitude toward decentralization. Those who support decentralization are much more likely to employ more humanistic, child-centered, and pedagogically effective methods with children.[67]

The findings linking the general concept "sense of fate control" to educational achievement have been criticized by Judith Kleinfeld on three grounds.[68] Kleinfeld points out that "fate control" in the context of community control has overtones of racial self-determination and aspects of racial and ethnic pride and self-esteem. Coleman's measure of fate control did not refer to the community's self-determination but rather to whether or not the student felt his or her own academic achievement was controlled by others or by self. Kleinfeld then attacks the validity of Coleman's fate control idea by demonstrating its ambiguity and by suggesting that the items on which it was based are susceptible to additional measurement errors. Kleinfeld's own research (with 166 black eleventh- and twelfth-grade students in Washington, D.C., public schools) shows that those students who believe their fates to be externally controlled do not achieve less in school than those who feel themselves to be in more personal control. Kleinfeld's factor analysis of the Coleman data indicates that student attitudes toward academic achievement and not student attitudes toward fate control are related to their measured achievement levels. Even if Kleinfeld is correct, the question remains whether increases in control by the community (or more specifically, decisional involvement by parents) can contribute to students' sense of their own fate control and through that to their estimate of their own academic ability. Kleinfeld is (sometimes) pessimistic. " . . . [I] t is hard to see how redistributing power from external forces to the black community would affect black students' estimates of their academic ability."[69] However, just two pages before that statement, Kleinfeld notes, "Community control of the schools might well increase black students self-esteem and racial pride, and this increased sense of self-worth may increase achievements. . . ."[70] A more encouraging conclusion would revolve around such factors as the availability of role models, and an identification (and cooperation) with officials presumed to be less discriminatory and more sympathetic.

In another look at fate control, Marcia Guttentag administered the Coleman instrument to black fifth graders in New York's Intermediate School 201 where community involvement has been intense, visible, and prolonged. Coleman had found that poor children and those who attended ghetto schools had a low estimate of the prospects of their own success. Moreover, they believed (perhaps realistically) that people were against them and that good luck would play a major role in determining their success or failure. Guttentag indicates that,

Perhaps the most striking finding in this fifth grade group is the percentages of yes (19%) and no (79%) to the first question: "Everytime I try to get ahead something or somebody stops me." Typically, ghetto children overwhelmingly answer "yes" to this question. These I.S. 201 fifth graders had answered overwhelmingly "no." Particularly the boys feel that they are not being stopped in their attempt to get ahead. Answers to this attitude item are directly related to later academic achievement. This data is markedly different from the Coleman finding. . . . It seems reasonable to suppose that the new atmosphere induced by community control of schools was related to this dramatic difference in attitude. It should also be noted that this was one item which explained much of the variance in later achievement test scores for black children in the Coleman report. This difference in attitude is therefore likely to be related to later changes in achievement.[71]

Early proponents had hoped that involvement would simply, directly, and dramatically increase achievement levels. While there is reason to believe that pupil achievement can be affected by parental (and other) involvement, the relationship is more subtle and the paths linking the two seem more tortuous than was originally suspected. Evidence about the second route, "Institutional/ child congruence," is fairly well developed but stops short of closing with achievement. The third path, community support, still lacks a conclusively demonstrated link between the participation of the individual and subsequent proselytizing of the school's cause among the individual's peers. Although the proposition that involvement leads to support among those so involved is very well documented, it has yet to be demonstrated that the school's supporters do what we may reasonably expect them to do—i.e., recruit other supporters.

There is a similar problem with the student self-efficacy pattern. Self-efficacy of some kind is associated with achievement, and it seems reasonable to believe that parental self-efficacy (generated, or at least enhanced, through decisional involvement) can percolate to the children of the involved parents, yet evidence documenting that is not yet conclusive.

Thus the state of our research-based knowledge concerning the individual patterns through which decisional involvement may lead to increased achievement must be described as promising but incomplete.

Although the beneficial impact of involvement on achievement has yet to be conclusively demonstrated for any of the paths, there is some evidence supporting each of them. In the real world, as well as in the world of research, the community's involvement travels all four of the paths. To the extent that there is an effect, it is a cumulative one.

Goal IV: Democratic Principle

One of the root norms of a democratic society is that those people whose lives are affected by a public institution should, in some fashion, participate in the control of that institution. Schools affect important aspects of the social and material well-being that their students enjoy. Schools are directly relevant to the ambitions that parents have for their children, and they are major public agencies in terms of taxes spent and social missions performed. At the neighborhood level these effects suggest that there should be neighborhood participation in school decision-making. In fact, this basic democratic principle is so strong that even if involvement could not be expected to affect (a) educational achievement, (b) the congruence between the child and the institution, and (c) support for schooling, it would still be justified on this democratic principle alone. Melvin Mogulof, whose wide practical and academic experience with citizen participation in social-welfare matters makes him an exceptionally well-qualified observer, has pointed to democratic principle as an intrinsic and sufficient justification for community involvement:

It is not that citizen participation helps us to get any place faster; although it may in fact do all the good things that have been claimed for it (e.g., decrease alienation, create a program constituency, calm would-be rioters, etc.). Rather we base the case for a broadly conceived Federal citizen participation policy on the argument that participation represents an unfulfilled goal in and of itself. It fits us well as a society. It is what the American experiment is all about. And perhaps in the process of giving aggrieved groups influence over their resources and communal decisions *because it is right* we will increase the life chances for all of us.[72]

The problem is that decisions about many parts of the schooling enterprise are facilitated by expert knowledge. That knowledge is not very widely spread through the population. Those who possess it have used it to control schooling for outcomes they believed in. But where major parts of the community disagree with the values and actions of the experts, it is necessary for the community to assert, on its own behalf, its own interests. The problem of lay involvement in areas that are at least in part technical is a persistent one.[73]

Almost fifty years ago, John Dewey wrote:

No government by experts in which the masses do not have the chance tò inform the experts as to their needs can be anything but an oligarchy managed in the interest of the few. And the enlightenment must proceed in ways which force the administrative specialists to take account of the needs. The world has suffered more from leaders and authorities than from the masses. The essential need, in other words, is the improvement of the methods and conditions of debate, discussion and persuasion. That is the problem of the public.[74]

Notes

1. Sherry R. Arnstein, "Eight Rungs on the Ladder of Citizen Participation," in Edgar S. Cahn and Barry A. Passett (eds.) *Citizen Participation: Effecting Community Change* (New York: Praeger, 1971), p. 96.

2. Edmund M. Burke, "Citizen Participation Strategies," *Journal of American Institute of Planners* (September, 1968), p. 288 ff.

3. James V. Cunningham, "Citizen Participation in Public Affairs," *Public Administration Review*, v. 32 (October, 1972, special issue), p. 597.

4. Douglas Yates, "Neighborhood Government," *Policy Sciences*, v. 3, n. 2 (July, 1972), p. 213.

5. Harvey A. Averch, Stephen J. Carrol, Theodore S. Donaldson, Herbert J. Kiesling, and John Pincus, *How Effective is Schooling? A Critical Review and Synthesis of Research Findings* (Santa Monica, Calif.: The Rand Corporation, March, 1972, R-956-PCSF/RC), p. X.

6. Robert K. Yin, William A. Lucas, Peter I. Szanton, and James A. Spindler, "Citizen Participation in DHEW Programs" (Washington, D.C.: The Rand Corporation, R-1196-HEW, Xerox, January, 1973), p. vii. The final report (April, 1973) is available under the title referred to above. Citations in this chapter refer to the January, 1973, document.

7. Marilyn Gittell and T. Edward Hollander, *Six Urban School Districts: A Comparative Study of Institutional Response* (New York: Praeger, 1968), p. 51.

8. Marian Sherman Stearns and Susan Peterson with Anne H. Rosenfeld and Meredith L. Robinson, "Parent Involvement in Compensatory Education Programs: Definitions and Findings" (Menlo Park, Calif., Educational Policy Research Center: Stanford Research Institute, mimeographed, March 16, 1973), p. 38.

9. James J. Vanecko, "Community Mobilization and Institutional Change: The Influence of the Community Action Program in Large Cities," *Social Science Quarterly* (December, 1969), pp. 615-616 and 628-629.

10. Marilyn Gittell, Maurice R. Berube, Frances Gottfreid, Marcia Guttentag,

and Adele Spier, *Demonstration for Social Change: An Experiment in Local Control* (New York: Institute for Community Studies, Queens College of The City University of New York, 1971), p. 129.

11. Ronald G. Havelock, *Planning for Innovation through Dissemination and Utilization of Knowledge* (Ann Arbor, Mich.: Institute for Social Research CRUSK, 1971), pp. 5-2 and 5-3.

12. Ibid., p. 5-2. Pelz's research is available in "Discussion, Decision Commitment and Consensus in 'Group Decision,'" *Human Relations 1955*, v. 8, pp. 251-274. The Levin study cited by Havelock is "Group Decision and Social Change," in G.E. Swanson, *et al.*, *Readings in Social Psychology* (New York: Holt, Rinehart, Winston, 1952), pp. 459-473. Sidney Verba also reviews this literature and relates it specifically to political action in his *Small Groups and Political Behavior: A Study of Leadership* (Princeton, N.J.: Princeton University Press, 1961), especially Chapters IX and X, which deal with the participation hypothesis.

13. Lester W. Milbrath, *Political Participation: How and Why People Get Involved in Politics* (Chicago: Rand McNally, 1965), p. 58.

14. For an excellent summary, see Frederick C. Mosher, *Governmental Reorganizations: Cases and Commentary* (Indianapolis: Bobbs-Merrill Company, Inc., 1967), p. 518. In addition to the sources cited immediately above, much of the basic literature from the human relations school is collected in *Readings in Social Psychology*, ed. by E.E. Maccoby, T.M. Newcomb, and E.E. Hartley, 3rd ed. (New York: Holt, Rinehart, Winston, 1958). For a treatment of the participation hypothesis in a general political context, see Lester W. Milbrath, *Political Participation: How and Why People Get Involved in Politics* (Chicago: Rand McNally, 1965). The participation hypotheses in an educational context are dealt with in Fred D. Carver and Thomas T. Sergiovanni (eds.) *Organizations and Human Behavior: Focus on Schools* (New York: McGraw Hill, 1969).

15. Richard L. Andrews and Ernest G.S. Noack, "The Satisfaction of Parents with their Community Schools as a Measure of Effectiveness of the Decentralization of a School System," American Education Research Association, Annual Meetings (New York, February, 1971), p. 3. The studies cited are: Robert D. Hess and Virginia C. Shipman, "Maternal Attitudes Toward the School and the Role of Pupils: Some Social Comparisons." Paper prepared for the Fifth Work Conference on Curriculum and Teaching in Depressed Urban Areas, New York, Teachers College, Columbia University, 1966 (mimeographed); Paul T. Rankin, Jr., "The Relationship Between Parent Behavior and Achievement of Inner City School Children." Paper presented at the 1967 Annual Meeting of the American Educational Research Association, New York, February, 1967.

16. Gittell, *Demonstration for Social Change*, p. 59.

17. Ibid., pp. 51, 54.

18. Ibid., p. 133.

19. Robert F. Lyke, "Political Issues in School Decentralization," in Michael

W. Kirst (ed.) *The Politics of Education at the Local, State and Federal Levels* (Berkeley, Calif.: McCutchan, 1970), p. 127. Copyright 1970 by McCutchan Publishing Corporation. Reprinted with permission of publisher.

20. M. Kent Jennings, "Parental Grievances and School Politics" (ERIC ED 010 0900, June, 1966). A revised version is available under the same title in *Public Opinion Quarterly*, v. 32, n. 3 (Fall, 1968), pp. 363-378.

21. Richard A. Cloward and James A. Jones, "Social Class: Educational Attitudes and Participation" in A. Harry Passow (ed.) *Education in Depressed Areas* (New York: Teachers College Press, 1963), pp. 213. Reprinted with permission.

22. Donald Haider, "The Political Economy of Decentralization," *American Behavioral Scientist*, v. 15, n. 1 (September/October, 1971), p. 121.

23. Norman R. Luttbeg and Richard W. Griffin, "Public Relations to Misrepresentation: The Case of Educational Politics," Florida State University, no date (mimeographed).

24. Richard F. Carter and W.R. Odell, *The Structure and Process of School Community Relations, Vol. V: A Summary* (Stanford: California Institute for Communications Research, Stanford University, 1966: ERIC ED 017 058), pp. 53-54. Other studies in this series include: Richard F. Carter, Bradley S. Greenberg, and Alvin Haimson, *Vol. I: Informal Communications about Schools*; Richard Carter, Steven Chaffee, *Vol. II: Between Citizens and Schools*; Richard Carter, W. Lee Ruggels, and Richard Olson, *Vol. III: Structure of School Community Relations*; and Richard Carter, and W. Lee Ruggels, *Vol. IV: The Process of School-Community Relations.*

25. George Gallup, "How the Nation Views the Public Schools" (Princeton, N.J.: Gallup International, 1969), p. 23. See also Dale Mann, "Public Understanding and Education Decision-Making," *Educational Administration Quarterly*, v. 10, n. 2 (Spring, 1974), pp. 1-18.

26. Richard F. Carter and John Sutthoff, *Voters and Their Schools* (Stanford, Calif.: Institute for Communications Research, Stanford University, 1960), pp. 108 ff. See also Warner Bloomberg and Morris Sunshine, *Suburban Power Structures and Public Education* (Syracuse: Syracuse University Press, 1963); Marshall Goldstein and Robert Cahill, "Mass Media and Community Politics" in Robert S. Cahill and Stephen P. Hencley (eds.), *The Politics of Education in the Local Community* (Danville, Ill.: The Interstate Printers and Publishers, Inc., 1964), pp. 171-173; and, *Who Will Rule the Schools: A Cultural Class Crisis*, Robert E. Agger and Marshall N. Goldstein. © 1971 by Wadsworth Publishing Company, Inc., Belmont, California 94002. Reprinted by permission of the publisher, Duxbury Press.

27. See the sources cited by James D. Wilson, "Research for School Board Members: School-Community Relations," No. 7-D, "Community Support for Education: Elections Involving School Issues" (ERIC ED 034 083, 1969).

28. U.S. Commission on Civil Rights, "Public Knowledge and Busing Opposi-

tion: An Interpretation of a New National Survey" (Washington, D.C.: March 11, 1973, mimeographed).

29. Agger and Goldstein, *Who Will Rule the Schools*, p. 190. © 1971 by Wadsworth Publishing Company, Inc. Reprinted by permission of the publisher, Duxbury Press.

30. Carol Lopate, Erwin Flaxman, Effie Bynum, and Edmund Gordon, "Some Effects of Parent and Community Participation on Public Education," (New York: ERIC Information Retrieval Center on the Disadvantaged, Teachers College, February 1969), pp. vi-vii. ERIC ED 027 359.

31. Maurice Berube, "Educational Achievement and Community Control," *Community Issues*, v. 1, n. 1 (November, 1968), p. 3. Italics in original.

32. Gittell, *et al., Demonstration for Social Change*, p. 112.

33. Charles E. Mowry, "Non-Technical Report: Investigation of the Effects of Parent Participation in Head Start" (Denver: Midco Educational Associates Inc., prepared for OCD, HEW-OS-72-45, November, 1972), p. 46. Reprinted with permission.

34. Milbrey Wallin McLaughlin, "Parent Involvement in Compensatory Education Programs" (Cambridge: Center for Educational Policy Research, Harvard University, 1971), p. 37.

35. Diane Ravitch, "Community Control Revisited," *Commentary* v. 53, n. 2 (February, 1972), p. 74. "Reprinted by permission from *Commentary*: © The American Jewish Committee, 1972."

36. Averch, *et al., How Effective is Schooling?*, p. X.

37. Robert Hess, *et al.*, "Parent Involvement in Early Childhood Education," in *Day Care: Resources for Decisions*, ed. by Edith Grotberg (Washington, D.C.: Office of Economic Opportunity, reprinted by the Day Care and Child Development Council of America, Inc., no date), pp. 265-266. The authors also distinguish among the various roles for parent involvement. See Ibid., pp. 276-278.

38. Averch, *How Effective is Schooling?*, p. X.

39. McLaughlin, "Parent Involvement in Compensatory Education Programs," p. 19.

40. Gittell, *et al., Demonstration for Social Change*, p. 32 and p. 12. For a similar finding, see Louis A. Zurcher, "The Poverty Board: Some Consequences of 'Maximum Feasible Participation,' " *Journal of Social Issues*, v. 26, n. 3, pp. 85-107.

41. Yin, *et al.*, "Citizen Participation in DHEW Programs," p. 34.

42. Robert Hess, *et al.*, "Parent Involvement in Early Education," in Grotberg, (ed.) *Day Care: Resources for Decision*, p. 269.

43. Ibid., p. 269.

44. Ibid., p. 279.

45. Mowry, "Investigation of the Effects of Parent Participation in Head Start," p. 45. Reprinted with permission.

46. McLaughlin, "Parent Involvement in Compensatory Education Programs," p. 68.

47. For a useful summary, see Carole Pateman, *Participation and Democratic Theory* (London: Cambridge University Press, 1970), especially Chapter III, "The Sense of Political Efficacy and Participation in the Workplace," pp. 45-66.

48. McLaughlin, "Parent Involvement in Compensatory Education Programs," pp. 11-12.

49. McLaughlin, ibid., p. 64.

50. Stearns and Peterson, "Parent Involvement in Compensatory Education Programs," p. 22.

51. Wilbur B. Brookover, *et al., Self-Concept of Ability and School Achievement (II)* (East Lansing: Bureau of Educational Research Services, Michigan State University, 1965) cited by Carole Lopate, Erwin Flaxman, Effie M. Bynum, and Edmund Gordon, "Decentralization and Community Participation in Public Education" *Review of Educational Research*, v. 40, n. 1 (February, 1970), p. 142.

52. Adelaide Jablonsky, "Some Trends in Education of the Disadvantaged," quoted by Carole Lopate, *et al.*, "Decentralization and Community Participation in Public Education," p. 142.

53. Joe L. Rempson, "School-Parent Programs in Depressed Urban Neighborhoods," in Robert A. Dentler, Bernard Mackler, and Mary Ellen Warshauer, *The Urban Rs: Race Relations as the Problem in Urban Education* (New York: Praeger, 1967), p. 145. Rempson cites six studies that associate increased achievement with increased parent participation.

54. Robert Rosenthal and Leonore Jacobson, *Pygmalion in the Classroom* (New York: Holt, Rinehart, Winston, 1968) cited by Lopate *et al.*, "Decentralization and Community Participation in Public Education," p. 142.

55. Paul T. Rankin, Jr., "The Relationship Between Parent Behavior and Achievement of Inner-City Elementary School Children" (American Educational Research Association, February, 1967), cited by Lopate, *et al.*, ibid., p. 142.

56. Christopher Jencks, "The Coleman Report and the Conventional Wisdom," in Frederick Mosteller and Daniel Moynihan (eds.), *On Equality of Educational Opportunity* (New York: Vintage, © 1972), pp. 89-90. Reprinted with permission of publisher.

57. Cited by Stearns and Peterson, "Parent Involvement in Compensatory Education Programs," p. 39.

58. Mowry, "Investigation of the Effects of Parent Participation in Head Start," p. 35.

59. Mayor's Advisory Panel on Decentralization of the New York City Schools, McGeorge Bundy, chairman, *Reconnection for Learning: A Community School System for New York City* (New York: Mayor's Advisory Panel, November, 1967), p. 12.

60. McLaughlin, "Parent Involvement in Compensatory Education Pro-

grams," p. 19. McLaughlin cites the following sources dealing with the impact of consistency and mutuality of values between the school and the home. Bloom, *Compensatory Education and Cultural Deprivation* (New York: Holt, Rinehart, Winston, 1965); Martin Deutsch, "The Disadvantaged Child and the Learning Process, in Passow (ed.), *Education in Depressed Areas*, ibid., "Social Intervention and the Malleability of the Child," in M. Deutsch (ed.), *The Disadvantaged Child* (New York: Basic Books, 1967); and S.L. Wolf, "The Identification and Measurement of Environmental Process Variables Related to Intelligence," (Chicago: University of Chicago, unpublished dissertation, 1964). See also the sources cited for "Goal II, Institutional Responsiveness."

61. See McLaughlin, ibid., pp. 52-53.

62. Ibid., p. 19.

63. U.S. Office of Education, "Parental Involvement in Title I ESEA, Why? What? How?" (Washington, D.C., DHEW Publication No. OE 72-109, 1972), p. 1.

64. Cited by McLaughlin, "Parent Involvement in Compensatory Education Programs," pp. 57-58.

65. James S. Coleman, *Equality of Educational Opportunity* (Washington, D.C.: U.S. Office of Education, USGPO, 1966), p. 319.

66. Mario Fantini, Marilyn Gittell, and Richard Magat, *Community Control and the Urban School* (New York: Praeger, © 1970) (reprinted by permission), pp. 192-193. Paul Lauter and Florence Howe express a similar conclusion and extend it to suburban schools. See "The School Mess," *The New York Review of Books* (February 1, 1968), pp. 16-21; also available in Marilyn Gittell and Alan G. Hevesi (eds.), *The Politics of Urban Education* (New York: Praeger, 1969), p. 260.

67. Joan Dianne Abrams, "Relationships Among Responses of Elementary School Principals in the New York City Public School System to School Decentralization, Their Perceptions Concerning Teacher Professionalism and Their Public Control Orientation" (New York: New York University, unpublished Ph.D. dissertation, 1971), p. 1.

68. Judith Kleinfeld, " 'Sense of Fate Control' and Community Control of Schools," *Education and Urban Society*, v. III, n. 3 (May, 1971), pp. 277-300.

69. Kleinfeld, ibid., pp. 282-283.

70. Kleinfeld, ibid., p. 281.

71. Marcia Guttenberg in Gittell, *et al.*, *Demonstration for Social Change*, pp. 118-119.

72. Melvin B. Mogulof, "Citizen Participation: A Review and Commentary on Federal Policies and Practices" (Washington, D.C.: The Urban Institute, 1970), p. 80. (mimeographed) Cited by John H. Strange, "The Impact of Citizen Participation on Public Administration," *Public Administration Review*, v. 32 (September, 1972, special issue), p. 469. Italics in original.

73. For a review of the relevant literature, see Dale Mann, "Public Under-

standing and Education Decision-Making," *Educational Administration Quarterly*, v. 10, n. 2 (Spring, 1974), pp. 1-18.

74. John Dewey, *The Public and Its Problems* (Chicago: Sage Books, The Swallow Press, Inc., 1927, 1954), p. 208. Cited by Harry L. Summerfield, *The Neighborhood-Based Politics of Education* (Columbus, Ohio: Merrill, 1971), p. 2.

6

Involvement and Shared Control

Previous chapters have made several points about the modern context of school/community interaction. Many federal programs and many pressing problems (especially race) require that administrators and communities work together more closely than ever before. The early chapters presented the data gathered in a series of studies of the representational behavior of school administrators in a variety of situations. We talked about the trustee style of representation as the most common pattern and discussed a number of consequences that follow from that pattern. The burden of that argument is that administrators are being forced into greater responsiveness to their communities, even at the expense of their own professionally indicated solutions.

Conflict and tension may push some administrators in that direction, but we have argued that there are positive reasons for increasing responsiveness as well. The previous chapter reviewed the available evidence that links increased responsiveness to increases in the achievement of four goals central to schooling. Thus the turbulence of school/community interaction may combine with its promise to both push and pull administrators in the same direction.

This chapter and the next one discuss a particular model of involvement that is called shared control. This concluding part of the book moves from analysis to application, from diagnosis to prescription. One test of an applied social science is its ability to inform practice, yet there are no illusions in this part that it will persuade anyone to share control who is not already inclined in that direction. We hope to suggest some promising practices that could contribute to the quality of school/community interaction even where they are not adopted *in toto*. While we are advocating a general orientation, we are not mandating a particular or single solution.

The last chapter is a handbook for shared control that has been designed for use by school principals. It is a kind of nuts-and-bolts, how-to-do-it statement that stresses operational features of shared control. It is also a practice-oriented summary of the dimensions of school/community relations that have occupied so much of the rest of this book. In keeping with its practical intent, it does not include the documentation necessary to support its recommendations. That is the purpose of this chapter.[1]

What is shared control? It comprises three characteristics: (1) the regular opportunity for community participation in a comprehensive range of policy matters; (2) the inclusion of all relevant points of view; and, (3) the probability that the community's participation will have an effect on school policy. Each of these characteristics is defined in the next chapter. Here we should distinguish shared control from the much more common types of interaction between schools and community. There has been a great deal of emphasis on advisory groups, on involvement that leaves decisions and the final determination up to the professionals. Control is not shared when advisory groups may be heeded or not at the discretion of the educator. Most school administrators will recognize this public relations model of community involvement.

Involvement as Public Relations

In involving communities, principals are responding to several needs: to keep the community informed, to build support among friends and allies, and to minimize interference with the professional's autonomy. As one source puts it: "The sound administrator wants as much parent activity as he can muster because he can thereafter channel it appropriately, knowing how to protect his staff, how to use the parents in the community, how to use the interplay to strengthen the school, and how to keep the reins of responsibility untangled."[2] The public relations approach stresses (1) one-way communications, (2) a concentration on support for existing arrangements, (3) a definition of the citizen as dependent consumer, and (4) a definition of the educator as autonomous professional.

Most administrators interpret their main responsibility in school/community relations as keeping the public informed, which they do generally through PTA bulletins, school newsletters, occasional fliers, and in a few cases annual reports to their school boards. The emphasis is aptly expressed in the textbooks of educational administration which counsel administrators "how to tell the school story," "selling the school mission," "letting the people know."[3]

In general, when textbooks discuss the need for "closer" school/community relations, they refer to a closer understanding by the community of the schools, not vice versa. Lay advisory groups serve mostly as conduits for the principal's views, not for soliciting the community's opinions. The literature details how to use the media for various purposes, but with one recent exception,[4] there is very little attention to systematic procedures for tapping community opinion. When asked how they find out what their communities might want or expect, the stock answer of administrators is to refer to an "open-door policy" which means that anyone who is willing to come to the administrator can get a hearing.

Within the framework of the public relations model, communications has a very particular purpose: to motivate greater support for the schools. One author describes this as follows: "Public relations are necessary (1) to secure continued and stronger support, (2) to render an accounting, (3) to advance the educational program, and (4) to promote the concept of community partnership in educational affairs."[5] The most extensive study of school/community communication ever undertaken set for its task "... to discover those factors which influence school-community relations, and, by implication, support of public education."[6] Precisely to the extent that schools deserve it, they should be supported, but no one has a duty to be uncritical. If the schools need to change and to be changed, then running school/community interaction through the public relations screen is not always useful. Mario Fantini points out that:

The chief motivation of most professionals in the current prevalent concept of community relations is to make *their* system work more smoothly. From the parents' point of view their concept has a basic flaw: when a school system is dysfunctional, the community is acting against its own interests and those of its children in maintaining the system, in failing to criticize it. In short, the existing concept of parent and community participation in education is basically misdirected toward supporting the school's status quo.[7]

The efforts of the public relations model resemble marketing and relegate the citizen to the role of a dependent and passive consumer of education services. In the marketplace, the consumer must be "sold" or motivated about the virtues of the product. Competition among various suppliers provides a slight degree of protection to consumers in the marketplace, but not in education. There, selection is not preceded by comparison, one brand may not be replaced by another, there is only support or nonsupport. Moreover, while the market consumer is playing a somewhat voluntary role, in education that role is portrayed as a duty. Administrative practices reinforce the dependence and passivity of the consumer. One author recommends: "An advisory committee must be oriented from the beginning to recognize that its advice does not constitute interference with the workings of the legal organization: on the contrary it insures a greater amount of *invulnerability* in the functioning of the entire school organization."[8]

As consumers, citizens are assumed to all have the same interest. Viewing citizens as consumers and school/community involvement as public relations leads to an intolerance for the legitimately differing interests and opinions that characterize any urban community. The attitude is closely linked to what Robert Salisbury has criticized as the "myth of the unitary community," that the best community will be "consensual, integrated, [and] organic" and that, therefore, there is no need to endure the kind of conflict over educational issues that affects other, crass "political" areas.[9] As Salisbury remarks, this attitude decreases the chances that the special needs of particular groups of children will be met appropriately. For example, Leslie Kindred sets out some rules to be used by administrators in controlling citizens committees: "(2) The committee should work only as a whole on the assigned task. . . . (3) Any dissension should not be made public and dissenting members should withdraw and then act as individuals."[10] Another author counsels that "The advisory group may pervert its true function by exerting pressure upon the board of education or upon the community. . . . Objectivity and disinterestedness are essential to the effective functioning of the advisory committee."[11] The attitudes are reminiscent of Henry Ford's dictum that the public could have any color automobile as long as it was black.

In the public relations-as-manipulation model, the professional occupies a central, defining, and autonomous position. That role is clear in the foregoing quotations where professionals are safeguarding their own autonomy by limiting that of the consumers. The community relations portions of many job descriptions reveal the same thing.[12] They stress cooperation (by the people with the school), not participation; information, not involvement. The principal "keeps them informed" but does not report to, and is certainly not accountable to, the community. The community is a discretionary resource to be used approximately like any other material. From a legal-institutional point of view, it is neither a source of authority nor of direction. The prevailing orientation is well expressed by Myron Leiberman: "Local control by laymen should be limited to peripheral and ceremonial functions of education."[13] The manipulative version of the public relations model concentrates on one-way communications, selectively stresses support, assigns citizens a passive and dependent consumer role, and preserves the autonomy of professionals. Citizen involvement, regardless of the intent with which it is offered, is acceptable only if it is supportive and even then it is carefully restricted to trivial and tangential concerns. Sherry Arnstein writes:

In the name of citizen participation, people are placed on rubber-stamp advisory committees or advisory boards for the express purpose of 'educating' them or engineering their support. Instead of genuine citizen participation, the bottom rung of the ladder [of involvement] signifies the distortion of participation into a public relations vehicle by power-holders.[14]

Obviously, all public relations efforts do not deserve a blanket indictment. Similarly, the 43,000 units of the Parent Teachers Associations are not all someone else's puppets. Many existing school community involvement mechanisms are good vehicles for interaction among citizens and administrators. But most are not, and public relations, when it is practiced only for manipulative purposes, has some serious consequences. In the first place, it often preempts more legitimate involvement. The U.S. Office of Education's guidelines for parent involvement in Title I point out that "A 'paper' or 'figurehead' council will accomplish nothing; in fact, it may increase the public's distrust of the school system."[15] Involvement mechanisms which are solely oriented to public relations also tend to dilute serious participation or to preclude the formation of other more effective organizations. School communities have a finite number of parents and other interested people. Splitting their numbers among two or more groups may deprive parents of the influence they might otherwise have.[16]

Perhaps the most serious of the consequences attached to the manipulative version of the public relations model is its debilitating effect on the public. When citizen interaction is viewed as manipulation, the educator's conception of the citizen's role is one of simple, uncritical supportiveness. That is communicated to the public. The response expected from the public is a minimal one that stresses an affective orientation more than independent judgment or constructive criticism. Administrators often justify inculcating that attitude by pointing to how little (they believe) the public knows about schools. However, the rule that learning is a function of incentives applies just as surely in communities as it does in classrooms. Where involvement has little likelihood of effecting significant change, there is little incentive to become informed or involved. Where only the most trivial involvement is possible (the opportunity to vote for an unsatisfactory status quo, for example) why become better informed? The professional's expectation of the limited role of the public becomes a self-fulfilling prophecy. Low expectations that were originally justified by low levels of information produce inauthentic opportunities for involvement, and they in turn are met with indifference and unimproved levels of information on the part of the public. Robert Agger and Marshall Goldstein collected evidence that indicated that, although poor people wanted to participate in decisions, they did not vote as frequently as others. Agger and Goldstein believe that the explanation lies in the significance of the opportunity offered.

We can see that the paradox . . . lies not in the fact that the less educated wish to decide but fail to vote. Rather, they wish to decide but are offered only the most limited, last-stage means of participation through the vote. By the time they are called upon, the definitions of the issues have been made by others without their being consulted, and thus the range of choice presented to them is narrowed. Typically, the alternatives are limited to approval of the program as defined by others, disapproval of the program with little hope that a major new definition will be presented for their evaluation, or wrecking the program entirely by consistently voting against the budget.[17]

This downward spiral will be familiar from the discussion of political self-efficacy in previous chapters. Here we wish only to point out that it results in grievances that are legitimate but unexpressed. That prior stifling of interest articulation deprives officials of the signals they need to improve public systems.

Finally, when something more than mere opinion is required, fewer citizens are equipped for serious participation than might otherwise be the case. After decades of having left schooling to educators, it should come as no surprise that people have as little relevant experience as they do. Civic abilities have atrophied and are not available in the times of crisis when they are most needed. The stormy history of community control in New York City should be viewed as a process through which an enormous conurbation is learning to govern its schools. The only question is not, will people take part, but how well will they take part. Or, as Betty Levin has said, "Whatever meaningful participation by ghetto parents may mean, it clearly does not mean membership in the PTA. What we need are new strategies of parental involvement, and new definitions and measures of parent participation."[18] And Edgar and Jean Cahn say of citizen participation that "it does not mean the illusion of involvement, the opportunity to speak without being heard, the receipt of token benefits or the enjoyment of stop-gap, once-every-summer palliative measures."[19]

There is a basic difference between community involvement as public relations and as shared control. *Community involvement is successful when it is significant.* The benefits to be derived are related to the opportunities offered; important opportunities will be rewarded by goal achievement. It should come as no surprise that what you get depends on what you invest. Still, most mechanisms for community involvement fall short of effectiveness on precisely these grounds: They are not opportunities for significant involvement. The U.S. Office of Education, in its recommendations to local Title I programs, notes the relationship: "While all parental involvement efforts are important, informal arrangements, largely because they have no advisory or decision-making powers built in, often have uncertain impact. It was with this understanding that Title I required parent councils, a structured organized means of involving parents in all facets—from the planning to the evaluation of programs that affect their children."[20]

Community involvement is a purposeful act, it is intended to be effective. The best and most direct evidence documenting the positive relation between the amount or significance of involvement and the successful achievement of organizational goals is the Yin study cited earlier. That research related the amount of authority (or involvement) that citizen governing boards had to the responsiveness of programs to community interests. For each of the cases in their sample of programs incorporating citizen participation, the following question was asked: "Has the organization been successful in obtaining implementation of ideas or approaches the participants favor that would not otherwise have been put into effect?" As the communities' authoritative involvement increased, so did their ability to make a difference in the governance of their institutions.[21]

In another national study confirming the significance/efficacy relationship, Brandeis University examined twenty community action agencies to determine the conditions that led to successful community representation in the governance of such programs. The findings reinforce the general relationship between the significance of the involvement and the chances of its success.

The significance of target area participation through membership on the CAA board is reduced by restrictions on the ability of the entire CAA board to make important decisions. Federal ear-marking of funds for particular programs, and reductions in local initiative funds have reduced the range of program choices with which the board can deal. . . . The significance of participation is also limited by a restricted definition by the CAA board of its responsibilities.[22]

The study's general conclusion was that "the significance of target area membership on the CAA [community action agency] is increased if the CAA board itself controls a wide range of substantive decision-making."[23]

Yin, *et al.*, made a systematic examination of the literature about decentralization in education to discover whether the amount of involvement could be related to various outcomes. They differentiated weak forms of decentralization (e.g., public relations approaches) from stronger, more political forms and found that the latter were related to increases in client control. Twenty-one of the thirty-four studies they examined reported improvement in service as an outcome of decentralization.[24] This fairly straightforward proposition about community involvement that its effectiveness rests on its significance—is crucial to moving beyond manipulative public relations models of involvement. The implication is clear: Something more must be done.

If public relations does not work, what does? The evidence indicates that when community involvement reaches the level of shared control, then the probability of its success is much greater. Shared control is a relatively simple idea, even if operationalizing it is not. It means that the decisions that stick about what happens in the school, are made *with* the participation of the community. Shared control has three characteristics: (1) the regular opportunity for community participation in the determination of a range of policy matters; (2) the inclusion of all relevant points of view; and (3) the probability that the community's participation will at some meaningful level have an effect on policy. Control sharing means a partnership in decision-making between communities and administrators. Wilson Riles, the California State Commissioner of Education, distinguished such a control-sharing arrangement from both weaker and stronger forms of community involvement.

1. As *participation* is conceived here, with its possible combination of advisory and policy making functions, there is no guarantee that community parents and residents would really have an effective role in the governance of programs in their local schools. . . .

2. With *partnership* described here as a division of authority, there is a sharing of the decision-making power—either in an informal arrangement (e.g., a set of understandings worked out with the local school board and administration) or a formal agreement (e.g., a legal contract stipulating the precise division of authority and responsibility). . . .

3. With *control* conceived here as full authority in fiscal, programmatic, and hiring matters, the community board or authority legally replaces the central school board. Within the limits of state laws and municipal regulations, including any other agencies with which it must deal (e.g., the teachers' union), the community can operate its school or sub-system making such changes as it deems necessary and can afford.[25]

Defining shared control as a regular opportunity for all points of view to be heard and to some extent heeded on significant educational matters immediately provokes a number of questions. First, of course, is what is the meaning of "to some extent"? Who is "the community"? How are they to be organized to share control? On which matters should they be involved? How much should they be involved? These reasonable questions are also subtle, complex, and interrelated. The following sections deal with those topics.

When to Share Control and
What to Expect

Administrators contemplating control sharing are ordinarily apprehensive. Before they get into such an arrangement, they want to know what they can expect. Their understandable anxieties are caused, among other things, by the specter of conflict. Why, they ask, should they do anything that may increase tension, surface disagreements, or otherwise turn up the heat in their own kitchens? Why indeed?

Is conflict a good thing or a bad thing? That depends on the answers to several questions: Conflict between whom? About what? How is it pursued? What are the outcomes? When teachers and boards disagree and teachers strike or take "job actions," that may or may not be acceptable. When administrators seek new pension benefits and struggle with different groups and factions in the state legislature, the struggle may or may not be justified. When national coalitions fight for full funding of federal legislation, that too may be all right. In each case, one's attitudes toward the acceptability of the disagreements being pursued to the level of conflict will depend on the issue at stake (is it important to you? do you agree with what is being demanded?); the methods being used (are they fair and appropriate to what is being sought?), and who the different protagonists are. (It's usually the conflicts involving other people, or those where we may be the loser, that we object to.)

The first reaction of most administrators to the prospects for conflict is a negative one: "It's bad," "The children can only suffer," etc. Like everyone else, most administrators would prefer that their community relations be harmoniously free of conflict. But real harmony is extremely rare. At the beginning of this book we described the circumstances that combine to make the school the center of competing forces. We outlined how the range (and inconsistency) of society's expectations for schools could never be satisfied by the finite stock of resources available to the schools. That mismatch inevitably creates winners and losers for significant stakes and in itself is a nearly sufficient explanation for the ubiquity of conflict.

But there are several additional forces that make conflict and conflict management a central administrative skill. George La Noue and Bruce Smith point out: "Unlike institutions in other policy areas, most citizens have had some sustained involvement with schools. Although that may not give them any insights into the technical problems of either budget or pedagogy, it does provide an important reservoir of intuitive evaluations and value judgments."[26] When those sometimes "intuitive" judgments are multiplied by what Aristotle referred to as "parental overfondness" and then applied to the multibillion dollar business of schooling, the result is seldom true harmony.

The local school is a visible institution with which practically everyone has had some experience; it affects central values about cultural and political identity and economic mobility; there is great uncertainty about how schooling can be improved, yet everyone is positive that it needs to be. What the Brandeis University study said of citizen participation in general is particularly true for education: "Disagreements, controversy, and conflict over the implementation of target area participation can be expected regardless of the nature of the program or the nature of the community setting."[27] The point here is not that every urban school is surrounded by a constantly critical community. Some are, but more are not. If administrators can't have harmony, then why not settle for apathy which leaves their control undiluted? Urban parents have a reputation for being notoriously difficult to involve in school affairs. Joe Rempson summarized the reasons commonly offered for the gulf between urban schools and parents.

It is held that parents do not care, that they resent the school, that they think that the teacher, whom they perceive as belonging to a higher social class, looks down on them; that they do know how to help their children; that they do not think they can influence their children's school life; that they have had unpleasant experiences with the school; that they have no concern for long-range problems and therefore do not see the need to go to school unless their children are in trouble; and that they are pessimistic and uncertain about the future.

On the other hand, the schools are held responsible for the gulf because teachers fear parents; because teachers live outside the school neighborhood; because school authorities are not interested in the welfare of the pupil, some even being antagonistic toward parents and children; because teachers use educational jargon; because the reading level required by communications from the school is too high; because the school does not know what should be done; because the formalized activities of the school discourage parents; because the school has not developed sound machinery to provide for improved relations and because inadequate staffing precludes having the time for parental contacts.[28]

Rempson also points out that most of the characteristics that make urban parents difficult to involve in the school are linked to lower-class status. Involvement is difficult to stimulate and unpredictable. It is quite understandable that administrators do not want to recognize, risk, or cope with the problems of greater involvement. In discussing the earlier data about administrators, we found that about a third described their communities as passive or apathetic. Most then interpreted that as being due to the supportive posture they believed characterized their communities. But leaping from perceived silence to received support is a long jump. Luttbeg and Griffin compared evaluations of the job that principals and the public thought schools and teachers were doing. Among principals, 90 percent felt that the teachers were doing either a "good" or a "very good" job, and 98 percent felt the same way about the local schools. But the percentage of the public holding the same high evaluation of the school was only 49 percent for both objects.[29] Thus lay people are not nearly as favorably disposed to the schools as are administrators. Principals who choose to believe that people are quiet because they are satisfied may be misleading themselves.

Moreover, apathy does not last forever. The Carter *et al.*, study of school community communications found that "Achieving support through quiescence is largely fortuitous—at least it is for now. There is no control on the emergence of conflict, only attempted control of it when it becomes threatening."[30] The suggestion is that administrators in such communities may be living on borrowed time. Robert Crain, Elihu Katz, and Donald Rosenthal made a nationwide study that determined, among other things, the conditions under which ordinary conflict became destructive or rancorous. The apathy of the community was one of those factors that contributed to such uncontrollable conflict.[31] Why should that be? Truly apathetic communities are unlikely to be interested in anything about the school until the needs, problems, controversies, or whatever have become too acute for any but major changes. But, with little or no civic experience, their last-minute participation is more likely to be severely critical, demanding, and dogmatic at precisely the point when those qualities are least useful. Leigh Stelzer says that "A body of literature on school as well as generalized conflict suggests that the anomic outbursts that plague school politics are the results of closed decision procedures (Coleman, 1957; Iannaccone, 1967)."[32] Neighborhoods that are temporarily quiet may tip easily into disruptive conflict that other, more fractious neighborhoods, with different histories and mechanisms, might handle more effectively. The choice facing the principal in an apathetic community is like that facing a boilerroom engineer. The steady hiss of an escape valve may be irritating, but it is better than the occasional roar of an explosion. Apathy may not be entirely eliminated by a successful mechanism of community involvement, but it and its effects should certainly be ameliorated.

Still, not many administrators are willing to risk conflict for the benefits it may entail. Education is a discipline that draws heavily on the knowledge base of several sciences; the practice of education is a profession requiring extensive preparation. As we have documented, the more seriously an educator takes the scientific and professional aspects of education, the less likely it is that the participation from an inevitably less-informed public will be seen as legitimate. In *Education and Public Understanding*, Gordon McCloskey writes about what is a common approach among professionals:

Any consideration of school community relationships rightly involves consideration of a basic question frequently phrased as follows: "Is school policy to be based on scientific definitions of the educational needs of children and youth, or on the whims of public opinion? Are educators going to sacrifice educational principles to the pressures exerted by uninformed groups?"[33]

Put that way, the answer is obviously "no," educators should not sacrifice principles to whims. But are whims the exclusive province of the public and principles the whole property of professionals? Harold Howe has pointed out some of the abuses that get cloaked in expertise. "Educators sometimes tend to regard themselves as annointed by a holy oil that confers a unique wisdom upon them, and they literally regard laymen as their flock; sheep to be herded toward a destination they have picked out."[34]

What happens when it is necessary to return to the public for financial support, for sanctions, for help with controversy? In those times, educators have paid a high price for their nonpublic politics. When public business is conducted with only intermittent involvement, the emphasis can seldom be on issues (which have been defined as "technical" and not appropriate for the public) and instead focus on personalities. That leaves the school administrator, who has sought to avoid conflict, instead personally spotlighted by it. Crain notes,

avoiding controversial matters does not, of course, make them go away; indeed, the political executive's neutrality should lead, in the long run, to greater controversy, since he is not using his influence to prevent issues from being brought up. Thus "personality" politics, weak political leaders, and high levels of controversy all seem to be products of nonpartisanship.[35]

David Minar suggested that the isolation of education from other municipal functions also meant that conflict and opposition could be easily mobilized against the lonely target of the educator rather than dispersed among numerous others.

The consequence of this situation is not only that demands are focused on specifics ... but also that the authority system usually is not accustomed to being opposed and therefore lacks resilience. Conflict is likely to be a disorganizing shock. Whereas, in most democratic governments, structured conflict is recognized as the way the game is played, in school government it often seems to be regarded as a rude and foreign intrusion."[36]

Harmon Zeigler, a political scientist whose research interests for the last several years have been directed to the area of school system responsiveness, writes:

School systems are not equipped to deal with conflict, and therefore, respond to escalated demands defensively. Defensive reactions anger those who made the original demands, and thus conflict—normal in any well functioning system—becomes a *cause celebre*. The constant *brouhaha* about schools should not mask the relatively routine nature of most educational decisions. City councils and legislatures deal with equally intense conflicts in the normal course of doing business. In contrast, school systems do not contain personnel emotionally or intellectually capable of handling conflict.[37]

Luvern Cunningham reached a similar conclusion:

Inability to deal with discontent has caused school people to withdraw, to isolate themselves from their constituencies (even their students), and to communicate an intensely defensive posture. The tragic part of this phenomenon is that no one really wills that it be this way. Such institutional withdrawal and protectionist behavior is simply the natural response of an organism that has failed to locate an adequate coping capacity.[38]

There is a long line of received wisdom that equates effective management with running a quiet ship. Good administrators are supposed to keep people happy and contented. They are not supposed to go looking for trouble. Few people wish to be known as trouble-makers. They are not supposed to overreact (many problems, left untended, simply disappear). Good administrative practice requires that support appear to be widespread and that dissent be minimized. Good administrative practice requires that compliance be perceived as voluntary and the product of persuasion, not compulsory and the product of power. Good administrators are also supposed to be decisive, choosing forthrightly in complex situations, making constant progress on difficult tasks. Yet, as Robert Aleshire points out,

Participation puts the spotlight on the fact that . . . we really don't know very much about social problems or their solution. We are still very much in an experimental stage. We don't like to make our uncertainty a matter of public record, burned into the minds of men through endless hours of debate and conflict. The quiet frustration of an administrator or an elected official making a decision masks the uncertainty more than the open process of participation.[39]

Good administrators are supposed to recognize the personal risks of conflict (it can cost them their jobs). All of these things contribute to a powerful sense among administrators that conflict is to be avoided. No one likes it; few people can stand the strain of jobs that are ridden with it. It is an easy step, then, to equate "outsiders," the unknown and unpredictable "community" with trouble. Why risk decreasing whatever support may exist by widening participation? Why stir people up?

Increased involvement can lead to increases in the amount of disagreements that get expressed, but it should also be recognized that conflict comes in different amounts and that it has different outcomes. Many school communities are so quiescent that they could easily tolerate substantial increases in the level of expressed disagreement, especially since that disagreement vents legitimate concerns of the school's clientele. David Austin's research indicates that conflict can stabilize the gains from social programs. "The political and social movements among black citizens that were strengthened through adversary patterns of participation were able to maintain those gains and move forward on an independent basis."[40]

Gittel says,

Some conflicts may well be healthy and in themselves, may activate new elements in the community. If the goal is greater participation and citizen interest, conflict may be a necessary component. Such clashes should not be viewed as necessarily negative in their impact. They must be evaluated in terms of the goals set or the model of political relations considered most productive to developing responsive policies.[41]

Administrators are not helpless to intervene in the outcomes of conflict. The same skills of mediation, compromise, reconciliation, judgment and so on that determine their success or failure in other management areas are equally important in school/community relations. The mechanisms of community involvement are part of the administrator's responsibility. Where they are properly constructed, they can make an important contribution. Iannaccone and Lutz report that:

The analysis of the operation of the semi-formal mediating organizations that clustered around the formal decision making organizations of the Jefferson School District indicated that the parents and teachers of Jefferson had developed mechanisms through which they simultaneously resolved their differences and attempted to influence school policies. The machinery had a healthy effect on the school district because [they] . . . "fought out" their differences in joint committees.[42]

Bloomberg and Kincaid draw similar encouraging conclusions about the results of widespread participation.

Extensive efforts to optimize the understanding and operational skills of activist parents and to educate and train a majority of teachers and administrators to react positively to the new situation could minimize the disruptive consequences of such movements and projects and maximize their contributions to changes that enhance the educational opportunities and experiences of ghetto children.[43]

Part of the responsibility of administrators is to make it possible for citizens to participate. Emmette Redford, writing in *Democracy in the Administrative State* says, "We cannot accept the idea that the citizen must depend upon self-help to learn what the government is doing and how it affects him. In a democratic society each agency must bear responsibility for informing people of the benefits and liabilities of its program and . . . for making its processes known to society."[44]

Creating and maintaining systematic procedures for involvement is one responsibility, but it is not the only one. If involvement is not to be the occasion of dysfunctional conflict, it must be accompanied by responsiveness on the part of the institution. Again, this points to the importance of escalating involvement to a level of considerable significance in order that its benefits be realized. Yin *et al.*, found that the weaker of the community boards that they studied simply raised people's expectations which then went unfulfilled which in turn increased alienation.[45] Gamson's study of rancorous conflict makes a similar point:

Participation does not automatically remove strain . . . As long as the underlying sources of stress are not dealt with, such participation simply increases structural conduciveness and thus makes other expressions more likely. Of course, if the action also helps to remove the strain, for example by aiding the passage of remedial legislation, then the *net* effect may be to reduce the possibility of other less orderly expressions.[46]

Thus, institutions that meet the needs of their clientele can foster involvement and avoid the worst kinds of conflict.

Involvement can lead to conflict, but that may be useful, and it may also be contained or managed. Involvement creates expectations for responsiveness that may tax the school, but which, if met, can help it gain support. Still there is no denying the personal and programmatic risks associated with significant levels of community involvement. The situation is very likely to test the responsible administrators' commitment to democratic procedure.

Wide-spread participation may lead to something resembling chaos, but it is chaotic because there are many different people involved with many different goals. Under such circumstances, clear-cut policies are difficult to achieve. But such are the circumstances of democracy.[47]

Who Should be Involved?

Everyone agrees that groups should be "representative of the community," but realizing that goal requires careful attention. The various bases for representation and the various methods of selecting representatives are considered in this section.

Many groups are, in effect, self-selected through the emergence of particular issues or crises. They spring up around some controversy and just as rapidly go out of business when the issue is resolved or subsides. The sporadic nature of that sort of involvement has several consequences. For one, because it is regrettably easier to mobilize people to be against something, intermittent groups are more likely to take anti- than pro-school positions. Second, the narrow mobilizing base of special-purpose groups will attract only those people sympathetic to their position and thus such groups are more likely to take extreme positions. Third, the short career of such groups keeps their participants from developing the knowledge and sophistication that might contribute more usefully. Thus, on the whole, special-purpose groups give community involvement a bad reputation. (Many of the same characteristics deprive them of much influence on the schools.) Despite their drawbacks, it is sometimes possible to use special-purpose groups as a base on which to build. They have, after all, already mobilized some people. They can make a contribution as long as care is taken to augment them with others more inclusive of the full range of topical interests and attitudes. The same point applies when Parent-Teacher Associations, Parent Associations, and Home-School Leagues serve as the basis for a shared-control group.

The need for broad representation and for an independent and legitimate point of view must be considered. Research indicates that the groups with the best prospects for success are those in which members have had some prior experience with each other in a group setting.[48] The presence of prior organizational ties increases the cohesion of the new groups and facilitates its involvement with the institution. In addition, when conflict arises, the extent to which members have worked together prior to the conflict is positively associated with successful resolution. These are important benefits from building the shared-control group on an existing base, but the necessity of modifying that base so that it serves its new purpose should be kept in mind.

The principal's activity at the point of group formation is another of the junctures at which care and discretion are essential. On the one hand, the principal has a responsibility for and an interest in the group's success. The temptation is obviously to use the professional's organizing resources and other advantages to set up a shared-control group quickly and efficiently. But several factors argue against that approach. The ability of the group to strengthen the school will depend on how people in the neighborhood perceive it. If it is seen as simply an extension of the school's established powers, it may not do much to reduce mistrust and alienation. But if neighborhood people play a central role from the beginning, then the group will be seen as a much more legitimate vehicle of involvement. The most important thing is that the group have the legitimacy, identification, and information that comes from early indigenous leadership.[49] Thus the professional's job is essentially one of technical assistance, providing some guidance and help without displacing community people.

The kind of group that will emerge, the quality of its activities, and the value of its contribution to the school depend on its membership. Selection determines those aspects by determining the personnel. The selection process is also the key ingredient in keeping the group responsive to the community. Selection can occur by appointment, by election, and by a combination of the two.

Regardless of who does the appointing, its use is not recommended. Appointment leads to mistrust and does not contribute to an effective group.[50] Group members who are appointed have a difficult time establishing their independence from those who appointed them. Stelzer's research on school board members, for example, indicates that appointed board members are more likely than elected ones to have prior ties to educators and educational associations and that those members are less receptive to community opinion than their colleagues without such associations.[51] And, despite the best intentions, appointing a group of people who will display the proper range *and* balance of important characteristics (age, sex, parental standing, race, ethnicity, occupation, and so on, through a long list) is very nearly impossible. If it is attempted solely though the appointment route, it is a thankless task and an inevitable target for criticism.

Most observers agree that elections are preferable. One of their major benefits is that they can increase the responsiveness of the institution. The path runs something as follows. The office holders would like to stay in office, and the candidates who would like to get into office compete to win the support of the public. This competition between the "ins" and the "outs" goes on in terms of which one can better satisfy the interests of the public. This simple description of electoral dynamics has three important parts: (1) incumbents who would like to stay on, (2) candidates who oppose them, and (3) an electorate that judges the competition in terms of what the candidates have done or will do for it. But the aspects of ambition, competition, and consciousness are not nearly as vividly present in public life in general as they are thought to be.[52] Jennings and Zeigler, for example, after their examination of school board politics, conclude "... The force of competition, the threat of defeat, and the desire to remain in office are of little moment for many school boards in keeping them responsive to their publics."[53] In a constituency as small as a neighborhood, there may be even less interest in serving on a shared-control group. The problem is a real one, but there seems to be no alternative but to face it.

There is some evidence, again at the level of school boards, to indicate that elected boards do a better job at representation than do appointed boards. Stelzer found that, in general, the more competition there was for places on the board, the more receptive board members were to citizens. "Members with high receptivity increases by 9 percentage points, from 12 to 21%, when all three competitive aspects are present in the respondent's first election. The aspects of competition were (1) opposition candidate for board seat (2) active contention between candidates (3) differences of ideas among candidates."[54] Similarly, Peterson found that competition among candidates in poverty program boards was associated with "universalistic" rather than "particularistic" representation; that is, where there was no competition, board members tended to pay most attention to satisfying the needs of individuals, not groups. Where competition was a factor, representatives concerned themselves with more broadly based interests.[55] The evidence developed earlier in this book demonstrated that there was a marked decrease in the willingness to override community opinion from those administrators who worked for appointed boards to those who worked for elected boards. Of those working in districts with appointed boards, 74 percent took a "trustee" representational role orientation while 61 percent of those working for elected boards did so. From their own national surveys, Jennings and Zeigler conclude:

Electoral characteristics of the school districts do leave an imprint on the responsiveness of school boards because these characteristics provide differential settings within which the strong elements of sociopolitical complexity (and mass support) operate. It seems probable therefore, that tinkering with the legal framework and fostering more competition for office would—sooner or later—affect the response linkage between constituents and school boards.[56]

How should the election be organized? Its features are very important, for, as Ralph Kramer notes in his comparative study of community action programs:

An election might appear to be intrinsically more democratic and more likely to insure a representative [target area organization] than any other process, but its success depended on the conditions under which it was conducted, the criteria established for candidates and voters, and the extent to which the neighborhood was organized for voting, as well as the number of persons casting ballots.[57]

The first matter for consideration is who should be eligible to vote? It is clear that only those people who reside within the attendance district should be allowed to vote in the school election. Teachers, administrators, paraprofessionals, and other school employees who live in the area should be allowed to vote in the election even though it is not recommended that they hold office in the control-sharing group (see p. 138). An underlying question is should residents other than parents be allowed to vote? Some people argue that parental interest in the school is too important to risk it being overridden by nonparent interest.[58] If other than public school parents can vote, it may be that the control-sharing group can be captured by a faction destructive of the purposes of public education, by a group vehemently opposed to the cost of public education, or by a militant (partisan) political group. On the other side, proponents of a wider franchise argue that interest in the school is more broadly shared than simply the parent group, and it is desirable on ethical and pedagogical grounds to allow those interests an opportunity to participate. If we are to follow the norm of a democratic society, then those people who are affected by an issue should have an opportunity to participate in deciding it. Nonparents are affected by what happens in the school. They help pay for education just as do parents. And as we learn more about the noninstitutional, nonschool, truly community-based ways in which children learn, it is clear that nonparents also have a role to play in the education of children. (It is natural and inevitable that far more parents than nonparents will take an interest in the local school election and turn out to vote.[59]) Therefore, anyone who shows proof of residence should be allowed to vote. No other restrictions on the franchise (except, of course, age) are advisable.[60]

An often controversial question revolves around whether school employees should be allowed to hold office. In general, they are already well represented in the policy-making process through their unions and associations and through the access and role that is built into their status in the school. Moreover, as employees of the public, their participation on a control-sharing group constitutes a conflict of interest. Therefore, both paraprofessional and professional employees of the local school should be excluded from holding office even when they reside within the school's attendance area.[61]

Other recommended election procedures are straightforward adaptations of fair election practices to the neighborhood situation. The single exception may be the areal or other basis for election. There it is recommended that all candidates run-at-large, that is, that they not run either for a specific position ("second grade representative,") or from a particular part of the neighborhood. The important consideration here is the physical size of most urban attendance areas. Because of population density and neighborhood life styles, such areas are already quite compact, often comprised of not more than a few square blocks. This is especially the case with elementary schools. Yin, *et al.,* found

... that success is negatively related to the size of the target population. Of the citizen participation organizations involving activities serving less than 20,000 citizens, 68 percent were successful in implementing their ideas, compared to less than one-half of those involving over 20,000 citizens. The greater success for all criteria was for target populations between, 5,000 and 20,000 citizens.[62]

Andrews and Noack found that parents in a decentralized community school district were significantly more satisfied with their schools than parents in a centralized district.[63] Similarly, Kramer's comparative study indicated that smaller election units resulted in better representation of low-income residents.[64]

Larger attendance districts—those that encompass more than a single neighborhood—present complications. It may be desirable to break up such areas into smaller election subdistricts and select representatives from the smaller areas. If that seems useful, its probable impact on the composition of the group needs to be weighed *very* carefully. The evils of gerrymandering are well known. The effect of drawing lines around any given area should not unfairly diminish ethnic or racial or other representation. This is a very complicated subject that cannot be assessed without attention to the geographic- and issue-orientation distributions of specific electorates. One plan, for example, may concentrate a school's opponents in one area where they have but a single representative; another plan may distribute opponents so evenly that they are never able to elect a representative. The guidelines here have to do with the critical importance of maximizing the representing of whatever characteristics are salient to school policy, fairly and impartially on the shared-control group.

Elections are the preferred method of selecting group members because they begin the process of involvement early and on a broad basis. They contribute to adequate representation between group members and their constituents, and they are perceived as fairer and more legitimate in their results. However, special circumstances may require another procedure. One of these might be a neighborhood that has a firmly established base of voluntary associations. If those groups have a history of interest and interaction with the school, it may be desirable (and sometimes unavoidable) to allow them to delegate representatives to the local school's control-sharing group. One potential problem with this procedure is establishing just which groups should be allowed this sort of representation. Two other circumstances may justify the use of this selection procedure. If election itself seems unlikely to deliver a shared-control group that is broadly inclusive of the neighborhood's legitimate points of view, then this alternative may be considered. If it is considered, the principal needs to be acutely aware that allowing some organizations to send representatives will be perceived as special and perhaps unfair treatment. Who is to decide what "broadly inclusive" means? On whose authority is the selection process "supplemented?" The procedure may well debase the selection process itself, and that is a very serious consequence. Still, the delegate assembly approach has worked fairly well on a city-wide basis in the community-action area. The crucial difference between that experience and the neighborhood experience is very likely to be the relative dominance of established organizations. If the strategy is employed, it should be done with great care to minimize the possibility of abuse and to minimize the damage done to more broadly-based selection procedures. It seems reasonable to conclude that a shared-control group should be only partially constituted through this procedure, and then only with the cooperation and assistance of as many of the appropriate neighborhood people as possible.

What They Should Do

A shared-control group exists to realize the goals of the school and the community. That means involvement that may make a difference in what happens in the school. It is involvement that can determine, influence, or change what the school does. The existence of a group to express community interests is not enough. The possibility has to exist that those expressions can impact school policy. It should be obvious that what is intended here is not a one-to-one correspondence between community expression and school policy. Some of what the community wants may, on some occasions, be reflected in school policy and sometimes not. Whether it is or not depends on a number of contextual factors that have already been discussed.

But the essential point remains. On some level, involvement must make a difference. Kenneth Clark's study of a dozen big city community-action programs indicated that among the features that distinguished successful from unsuccessful programs was the involvement or representation of the program's clientele on the policy-making level.[65]

Whether such an impact is justified depends *inter alia* on the substance of the decision. There are four major areas of school policy: curriculum, budget, personnel, and student affairs. Jeffrey Raffel's study of black parents in Boston found that they were interested in participating in more policy areas than was any other group.[66] In earlier chapters we indicated that administrators feel that lay participation is most appropriate in budget and finance matters and least appropriate in teacher personnel decisions. Yin *et al.*, report that "When the citizen participation organization (CPO) has substantial influence over the services budget, 79 percent of the time it was successful in implementing citizen views into policy."[67] However, while the overall proposition linking significant involvement to goal achievement is well established, the component attributes of that involvement are less clearly demonstrated.

Control can be shared in rather precise amounts and those amounts can vary according to local circumstances and the policy areas implicated. Both "how much" and "in what" can be modified to achieve a balance that school people and neighborhood people can agree on. Legitimate questions may still be raised about what sorts of decisions should be shared with respect to particular matters. The diagnosis of the reading problems of a group of children, the location and evaluation of various reading curricula, the selection and adoption of one curriculum and the assessment of its results pose very specific dilemmas for school people and citizens. What should be done in any particular decision will depend to a large degree on such factors as the knowledgeability of the participants, the history of their interaction, and their relative influence over one another. None of those things can be determined except by reference to specific situations that obviously cannot be described here except in terms of general, overall components.

Uncertainty about situational aspects is one of the things that makes administrators reluctant participants in shared-control arrangements. The fierce rhetoric that characterized the early part of the 1960s is certainly another contributing factor. School people were often pictured as incompetent villains, and community people often arrogated to themselves sufficient decision-making power and authority. Reality is more complicated than rhetoric. Out of that strife has come a much more realistic mutual appraisal of the strengths and weaknesses of both sides. An important part of that reappraisal is the recognition that very, very few communities want to run schools themselves. They do not wish to replace professional educators, only to participate with them in important policy decisions. Philip Meranto, for example, in *School Politics in the Metropolis*, writes:

Although the degree of envisioned local control is often ambiguous, the proponents feel that community control can only be successful if there is "significant" community involvement in key policy decisions, particularly in the areas of personnel, curriculum, budget, and overall evaluation. This does not mean that parents and other community participants seek to run the school themselves. It does mean that they want to be involved in key policy decisions and want to insure that the professionals working in the schools are responsive to the needs of the community and its children.[68]

And Fantini, *et al.*, have observed, "Most parents want nothing more than the assurance that their children's schools are being run by men and women who truly believe in the capacity of all children to learn. Ironically, the more accountable the school is to the community, the lower the degree of community control is likely to be."[69] The relationship here is an interesting one because it suggests that as long as the school is accountable, professional autonomy may be largely unhindered. A good deal of the justification of a shared-control group is to deliver accountability from the school to the community. If the group increases that accountability, then (in what will seem paradoxical to many) it may also increase, not decrease, the personal autonomy of the administrator.

Nonetheless, the temptation to use community involvement for manipulative purposes remains a strong one. The definition of manipulation is always difficult—the old saw says, "I teach but *you* manipulate!" Where professionals have a responsibility for encouraging and stimulating people to do things they might not do unassisted, it will always be difficult to know where leadership stops and manipulation begins. Referring to people's "best interests" does not help because those interests are so varied, and practically no action is ever undertaken except in the sincere belief that it is serving "The Public Interest." However, when a different version of people's interests is substituted for the version that people themselves had originally expressed, then manipulation is taking place. As we have discussed at length, the test case comes when the neighborhood persists in wanting to do something the principal feels is wrong. The principal's first resort is persuasion and exhortation. The principal may also wish to marshall his or her own supporters. If that fails, the principal may assert legal authority, or, perhaps, if the issue is important enough, consider resigning. There is an alternative. If the consequences are not too severe and if the estimated results—although lamentable—are still acceptable, the principal may wish to accede to something he or she cannot endorse. The freedom to fail is, after all, one of the risks all responsible decision-makers (including communities) run. Two long-time observers of the community involvement scene, S.M. Miller and Martin Rein, say, "Efficiency and participation do not necessarily converge. It may not always be possible to bring together without conflict ideals of efficiency, humanity, and democracy. But we cannot surrender to efficiency as the highest social value."[70]

A frequent criticism of education is that it has become so bureaucratized, especially in the big cities, that it is a closed-decision system in which public decisions are made in private beyond reach of public scrutiny. Practically every feature of the shared-control mechanism described in the next chapter can be interpreted as an assault on the closed nature of that decision system. The introduction of new groups into school policy formation will certainly contribute to more communications between schools and the public. We may also recall that the number and kind of people to whom administrative decisions are visible and the frequency of that visibility are related to administrator's responsiveness to the community. Where only bureaucratic superiors can oversee program decisions, the tendency to override community interests is strong. When oversight by a neighborhood group is added to the supervision of the chain of command, that tendency diminishes sharply.

How the Group Should be Organized

The responsibilities of a shared-control group dictate that it have a structure appropriate to the community- and school-related tasks it performs. It must take its decisions in a democratic fashion, and it must be organized to utilize the best available advice. Organizational features of the group include its decision procedures, constituent relations, aspects of its meetings, and provisions for self-change.

Procedures for group decisions are discussed in the next chapter. A distinction between "consensus" and "consent" is introduced there. Briefly, where groups are cohesive or where they share goals, most decisions can be expected to emerge by mutual agreement. Such consensual decisions are desirable but not always accessible. Because the group should respect the right of minorities to disagree, it should not attempt to force dissidents to participate in a consensus. In such cases, it is appropriate that those who do not agree simply consent to the group's decision. Where consensus is not present, the prior establishment of fair procedures for arriving at a decision is very important. The next chapter also refers to the standard reference for group decision-making, *Robert's Rules of Order.* In a neighborhood where most participants are known to each other and where the group is created and operates under amicable circumstances, adopting parliamentary procedures may seem unnecessarily formal. In one sense that is true: If decisions can be reached fairly and with little effort, more formal structure is not necessary. However, if the shared-control group is to engage significant policy matters, some disagreement can be anticipated. Formal procedures channel conflict, ensure fairness to all interests, and preserve the integrity of the group. Prior familiarity with formal decision procedures in nonstressful circumstances can help groups through disagreements that might otherwise be much more acrimonious.

The sort of relation that individual group members should have with their constituents is always a thorny business. Practically everyone is agreed that any group that intends to pursue a neighborhood's interests or that will be acting on behalf of a neighborhood should have represented in its membership the salient descriptive characteristics of the neighborhood. This does not mean that Puerto Ricans cannot represent the interests of Chicanos, or that blacks from the American South cannot act on behalf of those from the West Indies. On the other hand, where a large and vocal part of the school's clientele consists of mothers who are employed outside their homes, a shared-control group will be hampered in its operation without some representation of their interests. A neighborhood group that is not accurately representative of its community constituency will have a difficult time acting on their behalf. If the group is not a representative one, professionals feel it is less legitimate and are less likely to cooperate with it.[71] Despite the desirability of having a fairly close match between the descriptive characteristics of the group and the neighborhood, there is not much the principal can do about an imbalance if it results from an election. Where elections are used to select group members, about all the principal can do is to be alert to the possibility of an imbalance or gap in representation and perhaps encourage people to run for office to avoid those situations.

Another aspect of constituent relations is the extent to which a group acts to satisfy individual interests rather than group interests. (Earlier, we pointed out that competition for positions on the group reduces the tendency of groups to serve only individual interests.) What are the conditions that inhibit the tendency of a group to "do favors for certain people"? In their study of a national sample of school boards, Jennings and Zeigler found that the more complexity present in the community being represented (measured by metropolitanism, urbanism, and size), the less likely the group was to represent individual as opposed to group interests. Thus, to the extent that the shared-control group indeed represents or is chosen to reflect the entire range of interests in a community, to that extent it will be less likely to enact individual's wishes and interests at the expense of those groups.[72]

How to Help

The next chapter is organized around the specific things school principals may do to help shared-control groups succeed. This concluding section of this chapter considers some additional things that principals may do for the group. It deals in sequence with requisite features for democratic participation.[73]

The first requisite is, of course, the opportunity to share control. That is not as tautological as it may seem because schools ordinarily offer many involvement opportunities that do not reach the level of authenticity or intensity of shared control. Saul Alinsky stressed,

the necessary physical links to start the communication and the democratic bargaining. Without that it becomes literally impossible. You cannot have the democratic process and you cannot have the democratic involvement of people in the community as long as they do not have representation. If they are not organized, they don't have the circumstances from which they can derive legitimate representation. . . . Principals who have ideas about community involvement in the operation of the school must, of necessity, have a method of securing legitimate representation from the community.[74]

The existence of a mechanism of shared control is a necessary but not a sufficient condition for successful involvement. One of the most important of the additional resources is material support for neighborhood people. In many circumstances, the participation of urban residents is precluded because of family responsibilities or because of the necessity to work at two or more jobs or because of the simple inability to pay the small amounts entailed in carfare between home and meeting place. Modest per meeting or lump sum stipends may be used to make up for those lacks. Stipends can also contribute to the neighborhood group's motivation and attention to details of its work. Title I of ESEA specifically provides for stipends to parent representatives.[75] Several researchers agree about the usefulness of this provision. Lyke, for example, recommends that city-wide school board members be paid for their time as are many state and federal representatives.[76] Gittell says, "The traditional civic concept of unpaid board membership developed by a middle-class community and for a limited concept of the role of a school board is not practical in a system of community control."[77]

The information on which to base involvement is a vital support component. It is so important that the U.S. Office of Education has mandated that each parent representative on a Title I ESEA advisory council must, as a minimum, receive free of charge,

1. Title I legislation

2. Federal regulations, guidelines, criteria pertaining to Title I

3. State Title I regulations and guidelines

4. The LEA's current Title I application and past applications and evaluations

5. Any other information the council members may need to perform their duties effectively.[78]

The Office of Education's regulations also referred to an "affirmative information program" for parents that included recommendations about exemplary programs, a description of the process for planning and developing grant applications, and full information about the starting and ending dates of all programs.[79] Malcolm Provus expanded on the sorts of information to be provided. Public and educators alike may come to expect that all programs will be described in terms of:

Who is to be changed by the program? In what way and by what time? How are the changes to be brought about? Who must be involved? What process will be used? What is the sequence of the steps in each process and what are the immediate effects of these steps? What staff training is needed? What administrative functions are essential? What kind of institutional cooperation is needed? What facilities, material, and equipment are needed and will these be used? What dollar and nondollar costs are involved? How much money comes from Federal, state, and local resources?[80]

Along with more information, members of the shared-control group are also likely to profit by training in its application to school-level decision-making. Again, the Title I guidelines stress the need for "long-term, on-going training of Parent Advisory council members."[81] The study of DHEW programs by Yin, *et al.*, documented that when additional training was provided to group members, the participants developed new skills and were successful in getting their views translated into policy.[82]

The provision of formal training experiences can reinforce the learning that will already be taking place simply by virtue of membership in the group. Fantini, *et al.*, point out the benefits to be had by this "learning-by-doing" approach:

The question should involve not what parents know now about the technicalities of education, but what they can come to know. Participation affords direct knowledge and facilitates understanding and insights far more effectively than attempts to learn and understand from a distance. Experience is the great teacher.[83]

The availability of staff help is also extremely important. Zeigler concluded that "elected bodies must be provided with *full time* staffs, capable of matching the administration fact for fact, jargonistic phrase for jargonistic phrase. Otherwise, the inevitable erosion will occur."[84] The study of citizen participation in DHEW programs reached a similar and emphatic conclusion. "The most important organizational characteristic for a CPO is that it has a staff under its own control . . . the simple presence of staff was associated with a 75 percent success rate."[85] But despite this clear indication of the relation between staff assistance to community boards and program success, Gittell reports that, by 1972, not more than five of New York City's thirty-two decentralized boards had executive assistants at the district level.[86]

The final characteristic to be considered is probably equally important. The professionals within the schools, especially the teachers, must be receptive to and supportive of community involvement. The next chapter will discuss some of the things that can be done to foster those attitudes.

Notes

1. This chapter is an extensively revised version of Dale Mann, "Shared Control in Urban Neighborhood Schools: An Interpretive Essay and Bibliography" (NIE, ERIC ED083355, September, 1973).

2. Abraham Bernstein, *The Education of Urban Populations* (New York: Random House, 1967), p. 283.

3. For a similar conclusion, see Frederick M. Wirt and Michael W. Kirst, *The Political Web of American Schools* (Boston: Little, Brown, 1972), p. 61.

4. James A. Conway, Robert E. Jennings, and Mike M. Milstein, *Understanding Communities* (Englewood Cliffs, N.J.: Prentice-Hall, 1974).

5. Clifford Lee Brownell, Leo Gans, and Tufie Z. Maroon, *Public Relations in Education* (New York: McGraw-Hill, 1955), p. 70.

6. Richard F. Carter and John Sutthoff, *Voters and Their Schools* (Stanford University: Institute for Communication Research, 1960), p. 1.

7. Mario Fantini, Marilyn Gittell, and Richard Magat, *Community Control and the Urban School* (New York: Praeger, © 1970), pp. 91-92. Italics in original. Reprinted by permission.

8. Arthur B. Moehlman and James A. van Zwoll, *School Public Relations* (New York: Appleton-Century-Crofts, 1957), p. 441. (Emphasis added.)

9. See Robert H. Salisbury, "Schools and Politics in the Big City," *Harvard Educational Review*, v. 37, n. 3 (Summer, 1967), p. 413.

10. Leslie W. Kindred and Associates, *How to tell the School Story* (Englewood Cliffs, N.J.: Prentice-Hall, 1960), p. 390.

11. Moehlman and van Zwoll, *School Public Relations*, p. 441.

12. For example:

1. Inform the public about the schools.
2. Establish confidence in the schools.
3. Rally support for proper maintenance of the educational program.
4. Develop an awareness for the importance of education in a democracy.
5. Improve the partnership concept by uniting parents and teachers in meeting the educational needs of children.
6. Integrate the home, schools, and community in improving the educational opportunities for all children.
7. Evaluate the offerings of the schools and the needs of the children of the community.
8. Correct misunderstandings as to the aims and objectives of the school.

from Stephen Knezevich, *Administration of Public Education* (New York: Harper and Brothers, 1962), p. 502. The community related responsibilities of New York City School principals are defined as follows:

4.1 To encourage the use of school services and facilities by responsible, interested people and agencies of the community.

4.2 To utilize community resources in implementing, enriching, and improving the school program, and to train teachers in doing so.

4.3 To provide democratic and competent direction in assisting the people of the community to cooperate with the school in its efforts to attain worthwhile goals and improve the educational program and in keeping them informed of the work of the school.

4.4 To encourage and sponsor a Parents' Association and a School Council.

4.5 To cooperate with other agencies in protecting the health, moral well-being, and safety of children.

4.6 To recognize valuable resource persons in the community and to interest them in giving of their special talents to the school.

Source: Board of Examiners, "Preliminary Notice: Next Examination for License as Principal of a Day Elementary School" (Brooklyn: Board of Education of the City of New York, 1970), pp. 3-4.

13. Myron Leiberman, *The Future of Public Education* (Chicago: Phoenix, 1960), p. 281.

14. Sherry R. Arnstein, "Eight Rungs on the Ladder of Citizen Participa-

tion," in *Citizen Participation: Effecting Community Change*, ed. Edgar S. Cahn and Barry A. Passett (New York: Praeger, 1971), p. 74.

15. U.S. Office of Education, "Parental Involvement in Title I ESEA: Why? What? How?" (Washington, D.C.: DHEW Publication No. OE 72-109, 1972), p. 5. See also Joseph L. Falkson and Marc A. Grainer, "Neighborhood School Politics and Constituency Organizations," *School Review*, v. 81, n. 1 (November, 1972), p. 57.

16. Cf. Fantini, Gittell, and Magat, *Community Control and the Urban School*, p. 74.

17. Robert E. Agger and Marshall N. Goldstein, *Who Will Rule the Schools: A Cultural Class Crisis* (Belmont, Calif.: Wadsworth, 1971), p. 146. © 1971 by Wadsworth Publishing Company, Inc., Belmont, California 94002. Reprinted by permission of the publisher, Duxbury Press. See also William A. Gamson, "Stable Unrepresentation in American Society," *American Behavioral Scientist*, v. 12 (November-December, 1968), pp. 15-21; reprinted in *Group Politics: A New Emphasis*, ed. by Edward S. Malecki and H.R. Mahood (New York: Scribner's, 1972), pp. 60-81.

18. Quoted in Alan Altshuler, *Community Control: The Black Demand for Participation in Large American Cities* (New York: Pegasus, 1970), p. 54n.

19. Edgar S. Cahn and Jean Camper Cahn, "Maximum Feasible Participation: A General Overview," in *Citizen Participation: Effecting Community Change*, ed. Edgar S. Cahn and Barry A. Passett (New York: Praeger, 1971), p. 39.

20. U.S. Office of Education, "Parental Involvement in Title I ESEA," p. 5. See also Altshuler, *Community Control*, p. 126; and Marilyn Gittell, *et al.*, *School Boards and School Policy: An Evaluation of Decentralization in New York City* (New York: Praeger, 1973), pp. 38-39.

21. Robert K. Yin, William A. Lucas, Peter I. Szanton, and James A. Spindler, "Citizen Participation in DHEW Programs," (Washington, D.C.: The Rand Corporation, R-1196-HEW, Xerox, January, 1973), p. vii. The final report (April, 1973) is available under the title referred to above. Citations in this chapter refer to the January, 1973 document unless otherwise specified.

22. Brandeis University, "Community Representation in 20 Cities," in *Citizen Participation*, ed. Cahn and Passett, p. 210.

23. Ibid., p. 212.

24. Yin, *et al.*, "Citizen Participation in DHEW Programs" (April, 1973), pp. 164-165.

25. *The Urban Education Task Force Report*, Wilson C. Riles, Chairman (New York: Praeger, © 1970), pp. 269-272, (reprinted by permission). Quoted in John Hughes and Anne O. Hughes, *Equal Education: A New National Strategy* (Bloomington: Indiana University Press, 1972), p. 118. (Emphasis added.) See also Peter K. Eisinger, "Control Sharing in the City," *American Behavioral Scientist,* v. 15, n. 1 (September/October, 1971), pp. 38-39.

26. George LaNoue and Bruce L.R. Smith, *The Politics of School Decentralization* (Lexington, Mass.: Lexington Books, 1973), p. 238.

124

27. Brandeis University, "Community Representation in 20 Cities," in *Citizen Participation*, ed. Cahn and Passett, p. 203.

28. Joe. L. Rempson, "School-Parent Programs in Depressed Urban Neighborhoods," in Robert A. Dentler, Bernard Mackler, and Mary Ellen Warshauer, *The Urban Rs: Race Relations as the Problem in Urban Education* (New York: Praeger, © 1967), pp. 134-135. Reprinted by permission. Rempson's twenty-five sources supporting the reasons listed have been omitted here. See also Jeffrey A. Raffel, "Responsiveness in Urban Schools: A Study of School System Adaptation to Parental Preferences in an Urban Environment," unpublished Ph.D. dissertation, Massachusetts Institute of Technology, 1972, p. 99.

29. Norman Luttbeg and Richard W. Griffin, "Public Reactions to Misrepresentation: The Case of Educational Politics," Florida State University, occasional paper, undated (mimeographed), p. 14.

30. Carter, *et al.*, "The Structure and Process of School Community Relations, Volume V, A Summary," pp. 105-106.

31. Robert L. Crain, Elihu Katz, and Donald Rosenthal, *The Politics of Community Conflict: The Flouridation Decision* (New York: Bobbs-Merrill, 1969), p. 223.

32. Leigh Stelzer, "School Board Receptivity," *Education and Urban Society*, v. V, n. 1 (November, 1972), p. 84.

33. Gordon McCloskey, *Education and Public Understanding*, 2d ed. (New York: Harper and Row, 1967), p. 27.

34. Harold Howe, "Should Educators or Boards Control our Public Schools," *Nation's Schools*, 78 (December, 1966). Cited in Michael D. McCaffrey, "Politics in the Schools," *Educational Administration Quarterly*, v. 7, n. 3 (Autumn, 1971), p. 54.

35. Crain, *et al., The Politics of Community Conflict*, p. 200.

36. David Minar, "Community Politics and School Boards," in *The American School Board Journal* (March, 1967), p. 35.

37. Harmon Zeigler, "Creating Responsive Schools," *Urban Review*, v. 6, n. 4 (1973), p. 41. Italics in original.

38. Luvern Cunningham, *Governing Schools: New Approaches to Old Issues* (Columbus, Ohio: Merrill, 1971), p. 177.

39. Robert A. Aleshire, "Power to the People: An Assessment of the Community Action and Model Cities Experience," *Public Administration Review*, v. 32 (September, 1972, special issue), p. 438.

40. David Austin, "Resident Participation: Political Mobilization or Organizational Cooptation?" *Public Administration Review* (September, 1972, special issue), p. 419. See also Gittell, *School Boards and School Policy*, p. 21.

41. Marilyn Gittell, "Urban School Reform in the 70's" in *Confrontation at Ocean-Hill Brownsville*, ed. Maurice R. Berube and Marilyn Gittell (New York: Praeger, 1969), p. 332.

42. Laurence Iannaccone and Frank Lutz, *Politics, Power and Policy: The Governing of Local School Districts* (Columbus, Ohio: Merrill, 1970), p. 19.

43. Warner J. Bloomberg and John Kincaid, "Parent Participation: Practical Policy or Another Panacea," *The Urban Review*, v. 2, n. 7 (June, 1968), p. 11.

44. Emmett S. Redford, *Democracy in the Administrative State* (New York: Oxford, 1969), p. 139.

45. Yin, *et al.*, "Citizen Participation in DHEW Programs," p. 47.

46. William A. Gamson, "Rancorous Conflict in Community Politics," in Willis D. Hawley and Frederick M. Wirt, *The Search for Community Power* (Englewood Cliffs, N.J.: Prentice-Hall, 1968), pp. 251-252.

47. Sidney Verba, "Democratic Participation," in B.M. Gross, ed., *Social Intelligence for America's Future: Explorations in Societal Problems* (Boston: Allyn and Bacon, 1969), p. 75.

48. Wendell Bell and Maryanne Force, "Urban Neighborhood Types and Participation in Formal Associations," *American Sociological Review* (February, 1956); Robert Hollister, "Citizen Participation in Health Planning," *Planning for Health Services and Facilities and Its Relation to City and Regional Planning Activities* (Cambridge, Mass.: Joint Center for Urban Studies of MIT and Harvard University, June, 1968).

49. Neil Gilbert, *Clients or Constituents* (San Francisco: Jossey-Bass, 1970).

50. Sherry R. Arnstein, "Eight Rungs on the Ladder of Citizen Participation," in *Citizen Participation: Effecting Community Change*, ed. Edgar S. Cahn and Barry A. Passett (New York: Praeger Publishers, 1971), pp. 69-92; Sumati N. Dubey, "Community Action Programs and Citizen Participation: Issues and Confusions," *Social Work*, v. 15 (January, 1970), pp. 77-84. See also Melvin Mogulof, "Coalition to Adversary: Citizen Participation in Three Federal Programs," *Journal of the American Institute of Planners* (July, 1969), pp. 225-232.

51. Stelzer, "School Board Receptivity," p. 82.

52. See, for example, the analysis of their faint impact on city councils as reported in Kenneth Prewitt and Heinz Eulau, "Political Matrix and Political Representation: Prolegomenon to a New Departure from an Old Problem," *American Political Science Review*, v. LXIII, n. 2 (June, 1969), pp. 412-427; Kenneth Prewitt, "Political Ambitions, Volunteerism, and Electoral Accountability," *American Political Science Review*, v. LXIV, n. 1 (March, 1970), pp. 5-17. For a recent discussion of the extent to which issue consciousness governs the electorate's judgment, see Gerald M. Pomper, *et al.*, "Issue Voting," *American Political Science Review*, v. LXVI, n. 2 (June, 1972), pp. 415-428.

53. Reprinted from "Response Styles and Politics: The Case of School Boards," *Midwest Journal of Political Science*, v. XV, n. 2 (May, 1971), by M. Kent Jennings and Harmon Zeigler, p. 311, by permission of the Wayne State University Press. Copyright 1971 by Wayne State University Press.

54. Stelzer, "School Board Receptivity," p. 80.

55. Paul E. Peterson, "Participation of the Poor," *American Political Science Review*, v. LXIV, n. 2 (June, 1970), pp. 491-507.

56. Reprinted from "Response Styles and Politics: The Case of School Boards," *Midwest Journal of Political Science*, v. XV, n. 2 (May, 1971), by M. Kent Jennings and Harmon Zeigler, p. 318, by permission of the Wayne State University Press. Copyright 1971 by Wayne State University Press.

57. Ralph M. Kramer, *Participation of the Poor: Comparative Case Studies in the War on Poverty* (Englewood Cliffs, N.J.: Prentice-Hall, 1969), pp. 195-196.

58. Gittell, *School Boards*, p. 164.

59. Louis Massotti comments on the natural dominance of parent interests in "Patterns of White and NonWhite School Referenda Participation in Cleveland 1960-64," in *Educating an Urban Population*, ed. Marilyn Gittell (Beverly Hills: Sage, 1967), pp. 240-256.

60. Fantini, *Community Control*, p. 170. See also Ellen Lurie, *How to Change the Schools* (New York: Vintage, 1970), p. 249.

61. For similar positions, see Fantini, *et al., Community Control*, p. 170; and Gittell, "The Balance of Power," in Levin, *Community Control*, p. 125.

62. Yin, *et al.*, "Citizen Participation in DHEW Programs," pp. 50-51.

63. Andrews and Noack, "The Satisfaction of Parents with their Community Schools," p. 5.

64. Kramer, *Participation of the Poor*, pp. 195-196. For additional discussions of the scale of the governance unit, see, Altshuler, *Community Control*, p. 130 ff; Fein, *The Ecology of the Public Schools*, pp. 89-93; Kotler, *Neighborhood Government*, p. 2; and Schmandt, "Municipal Decentralization: An Overview," pp. 571-588.

65. Kenneth Clark, *A Relevant War Against Poverty: A Study of Community Action Programs and Observable Social Change* (New York: Metropolitan Applied Research Center, Inc., 1968), p. 212. See also Harold Savitch' discussion of nominal versus effective access in "Powerlessness in an Urban Ghetto: The Case of Political Biases and Differential Access in New York City," *Polity*, v. V, n. 1 (Fall, 1972), p. 50; Gittell, *Demonstration for Social Change*, p. 7; and Lyke, "Representation," in *Community Control*, p. 159.

66. Raffel, "Responsiveness in Urban Schools," p. 153.

67. Yin, *et al.*, "Citizen Participation in DHEW Programs," p. 53.

68. Phillip Meranto, *School Politics in the Metropolis* (Columbus, Ohio: Merrill, 1970), pp. 76-77.

69. Fantini, *et al., Community Control*, Preface, p. xviii.

70. S.M. Miller and Martin Rein, "Participation, Poverty and Administration," in *Public AdministratioReview*, v. 29, n. 1 (January/February, 1969), pp. 15 and 25.

71. See, for example, Gilbert's discussion of the attitudes of community organizers in *Clients or Constituents: Community Action in the War on Poverty*, pp. 137-138.

72. Reprinted from "Response Styles and Politics: The Case of School Boards," *Midwest Journal of Political Science*, v. XV, n. 2 (May, 1971), by M.

Kent Jennings and Harmon Zeigler, p. 301, by permission of the Wayne State University Press. Copyright 1971 by Wayne State University Press.

73. See Verba, "Democratic Participation," pp. 53-78. For a similar list of resources necessary to support popular participation, see Michael Lipsky, *Protest in City Politics: Rent Strikes, Housing, and the Power of the Poor* (Chicago: Rand McNally, 1970), pp. 167-168.

74. Saul Alinsky, "Organizing Low-Income Neighborhoods for Political Action," in *Urban School Administration*, ed. McKelvey and Swanson, p. 43. See also Hess, "Parent Involvement," in *Day Care: Resources for Decisions*, p. 280; Kirst, *The Politics of Education*, p. 124; Russell L. Isbister and G. Robert Koopman, "Citizen Participation in School Affairs," in *Vital Issues in American Education*, ed. Crow, p. 86.

75. Office of Education, "Parental Involvement," p. 11.

76. Lyke, "Representation," in *Community Control*, ed. Levin, p. 167.

77. Gittell, "The Balance of Power," in *Community Control*, ed. Levin, p. 133.

78. "Parental Involvement in Title I ESEA," p. 8.

79. USOE, "Memorandum to Chief State School Officers/Advisory Statement on Development of Policy on Parental Involvement in Title I, ESEA Projects" (Washington, D.C.: USOE/DHEW, October 30, 1970), pp. 2-3.

80. Malcolm Provus, "In Search of Community," *Phi Delta Kappan*, v. 54, n. 10 (June, 1973), p. 661.

81. Office of Education, "Parental Involvement," p. 10.

82. Yin, *et al.*, "Citizen Participation in DHEW Programs," p. 56.

83. Fantini, *et al., Community Control*, p. 97. See also Cunningham, *Governing Schools*, p. 171; and Rempson, "School-Parent Programs," in *The Urban Rs*, ed. Dentler, Mackler and Warshauer, p. 140.

84. Zeigler, "Creating Responsive Schools," p. 43.

85. Yin, *et al.*, "Citizen Participation in DHEW Programs," p. 55. See also Rempson.

86. Gittell, *School Boards and School Policy*, p. 64.

7

A Principal's Handbook for Shared Control in Urban Community Schools

This handbook should help building principals to create, support, and utilize neighborhood involvement in school decision-making. Here "involvement" means participation in, and sharing of, decisions about the education of children. A number of guides are already available for the creation of advisory or public relations-oriented involvement. But despite the increasingly frequent official mandates from state and federal agencies and public pressures from communities, school principals who wish to share some amount of control with communities have not had much operational help with that process. This manual is designed to fill that need.

Shared control (which is explained in more detail later) is the first premise of this work. The second premise is a commitment to local options. Every principal must respond to a very specific combination of neighborhood goals, needs, and resources. That local situation will determine much about how neighborhood involvement is realized. The handbook is a synthesis of the best and most recent research and evaluation in its field; it is intended to be a comprehensive listing of the practices that empirical data and field experiences indicate have led to successful shared control.

Nonetheless, the building principal still faces a great many choices about how to combine the practices described here to fit the particular needs of his or her particular neighborhood. The handbook will be most useful to those principals who want, or who cannot avoid, shared control. But there are undoubtedly some principals who do not believe in that. They will not be persuaded by any handbook supported by any accumulation of evidence. If they change their practices, it will be because they have been forcefully convinced to do so by the communities they serve. At that point, if they retain their jobs, these principals may discover a use for the techniques and procedures outlined here.

Some of the factors that determine success at the neighborhood level recur at other organizational levels as well (e.g., goals, structure, process, support, etc.). Community district superintendents or headquarters specialists in community relations may wish to check their own practices against those recommended here. They may also make use of this guide in in-service training courses and in community-involvement workshops. The same general point applies to citizens. Both lay citizens and professional educators should be equally interested in what makes for successful involvement. These options and recommendations are written specifically for school principals, but because they identify the key points in a shared process, they should be useful to communities as well.

129

Finally, it should be pointed out that the handbook concentrates on community involvement in the urban setting. How people relate to their social institutions varies by such factors as urban/suburban/rural setting, class, region of the country, and so on. For many reasons the task of effective community involvement is more difficult in the neighborhoods of the big cities than it is anywhere else. But just as every neighborhood is to some extent a unique constellation of strengths and needs, there are also regularities among neighborhoods. The principles and practices outlined here should be of interest to anyone who wants to improve relations between public schools and the communities they serve.

Few things are more difficult to arrange than the authoritative interaction of lay people and professionals in an area of largely technical decision-making that is of extreme importance to both of them. When, as it must be, that interaction is complicated by differences in race, ethnicity, and political purpose, the difficulties of what is essentially an exercise in constitution building are apparent. The task is at least as complicated and perhaps as important as the design of a school's curriculum, yet it seldom gets the same careful attention.

This handbook has six sections, each of which deals with a major component of neighborhood involvement. The sections reflect operational necessity in that they are grouped by areas for action and are arranged in the order a principal needs to consider as he or she develops community involvement. The appendixes at the end of the chapter provide suggested by-laws and prototype budgets for the support of neighborhood groups at various resource levels.

Why Share Control?

The importance and complexity of school governance suggest caution in changing it. Current decision-making arrangements place a great deal of the available control at the discretion of the principal. That control should only be shared if there is reason to believe that significant increases in goal achievement will result. This section defines control-sharing and relates it to the achievement of the most important and most commonly accepted goals of public schooling.

Shared control has three characteristics: (1) the regular opportunity for community participation in a comprehensive range of policy matters, (2) the inclusion of all relevant points of view, and (3) the probability that the community's participation will have an effect on school policy. One term in each of the three parts needs clarification. "Policy" refers to important or significant matters that affect the children of the school. "Relevant" points of view include the interests of all the school's parents; it also includes nonparent community members such as businessmen, religious groups, social-welfare agencies, etc. "Probability" refers to the fact that because we are talking about shared, not total, control, we can expect to find the community's will prevailing some of the time on some issues. Probability refers to compromise and cooperation, and that applies to both communities and administrators within the control-sharing arrangement. It is extremely important to recognize at the outset that control is not an either/or situation. It can be shared in almost infinite (but poorly understood) gradations. For principals this is significant because it means that the control situation can be shaped precisely to the needs of both the community and the school's professional staff. Control can be shared both with respect to "how much" and "of what," and those determinations can be based on the local reality.

Being a school principal takes years of training, a great deal of judgment, and lots of energy. Most school principals feel that they have little enough power to deal with the tasks they face; why should they diminish what they have by sharing it with others? The most persuasive reason to do so would be evidence that sharing resulted in increased achievement of the school's goals. Increases in community participation have been associated with increased goal achievement in four areas: (1) educational achievement of pupils, (2) institutional responsiveness, (3) support for schooling, and (4) democratic principle.

Recent research has made the case for an association between high (or increased) student achievement and high (or increased) parent involvement. The kind of involvement that is most clearly related to student achievement is the child-centered involvement of parents with the family-based activities of their own children. But parents who build civic skills by participating in educational policy determination for an entire school should also be more inclined to work purposefully with their own children. Beyond that, there may be a transfer of the sense of personal efficacy the parent experiences upon participating in school decision-making to the child who may then also feel more personally efficacious, more in control, and thus more motivated to learn. The parent's sense of increased control may generalize to the child's sense of increased control. In *Equality of Educational Opportunity*, James S. Coleman found that the pupil attitude factor which measured the extent to which a pupil felt control over his own destiny, "appears to have a stronger relationship to achievement than do all the 'school' factors together. . . ." In addition, the parent's interest in the school may set an example for the child to emulate, and the fact that the school is responsive to the parent may help persuade the child that the school is a relevant and empathetic institution. All of these effects are strongest where the involvement itself is the most intense and significant. Parents who participate the most are most likely to reap these benefits.

One major way in which the neighborhood school responds to its clientele is by increasing the educational achievement of students. However, the content of what is learned, the process through which it is taught, the identities of the people who do the teaching, and other similar factors, are often of vivid interest to the school's constituents. As the neighborhood presence grows in numbers, time, knowledgeability, and scope of involvement, the likelihood increases that it will present demands and follow up on them in ways that ensure greater congruity between school and community. The evidence shows that administrators and especially teachers recognize concerned and actively involved parents and pay increased attention to their children and to the needs expressed by their parents. That process works both ways. The more that professionals and lay people interact, the more opportunities professionals have to persuade lay people of the wisdom of professionally recommended policy. In the first instance, the school changes in response to the citizens; in the second, the citizens' own goals come to coincide with those of the institution. Responsiveness is thus a two-way street, and the leadership role, like the participation in decisions, is shared between lay and professional people. In both cases, the perceived distance between the two is lessened.

To exist, urban schools need the acquiescence of their neighborhoods. To succeed, urban schools need the support of those neighborhoods. Getting more support for the schools, both financial and affective, has been one of the traditional purposes for involving communities. Support for the schools goes up if what the school does is close to what the neighborhood wants it to do. When neighborhood participation makes the school more responsive to neighborhood desires, then the agreement between the two also leads to increased support for the school.

This relationship is reinforced at the individual level. People tend to approve of what they have had a hand in determining. When a person invests time and energy in something, there is a tendency to value that thing and to become more closely identified with it on a personal and social basis. Being around professionals, paraprofessionals, and other people who are committed to the school increases the amount of favorable information a participant will receive about the school. Thus at the personal level, increasing involvement should increase the support that most participants feel for the school and its staff.

The last of the reasons for control being shared has to do with the norm of a democratic society that those people whose lives are affected by an institution should, in some fashion, participate in its control. Schools affect important aspects of the social and material well-being that their students will enjoy. Schools are directly relevant to the ambitions that parents have for their children; they are major public agencies in terms of taxes spent and social missions performed. At the neighborhood level these effects suggest that there should be neighborhood participation in school decision-making. Participation affects educational achievement, institutional responsiveness, and support for schooling, but even if it did not, it would still be justified on this principle alone.

Achievement of these four very important goals can be increased through community involvement. The benefits to the school and community are related to how many people participate how much in important decisions. The evidence clearly indicates that *community involvement is successful when it is significant.* In this field, where little is risked, nothing is gained. A second point is that the four goal areas are cumulative. Where a school involves people because it wishes to increase achievement, that involvement will also contribute to responsiveness, support, and the democratic principle. Involvement is justified on the *total* goals achieved, not simply on any single goal.

When to Share Control and
What to Expect

The most obvious answer to the question, "when to share control," is that control should be shared whenever the need is felt to raise goal achievement. Involvement is a purposeful strategy that is directly relevant to what administrators want the schools to do. The second answer to the "when" question relates to the need for help from the community. The creation of a temporary "citizens committee" is a common tactic in districts that raise their own money through elections. The fact that such committees are often seen by the voters as undemocratic ruses should tell urban administrators something about the timing of involvement. If participation is expected to provide a reservoir of support, then it must be built well before it is needed. The two most profound problems of urban education are race relations and money. Neither can be solved without the cooperation and involvement of urban communities. Urban school conflicts often turn around deeply felt racial and ethnic beliefs; the more experienced and knowledgeable the group is, the more likely it is to be of assistance. That suggests that in order to have such a resource, even those principals who believe their neighborhoods to be quiet, passive, and allegiant should seriously consider increasing involvement. In other words, involvement should begin when increased goal achievement is sought; it should start well before it is needed. It should be sought in quiet as well as in volatile communities.

Historically, increases in involvement have come episodically in response to crisis and conflict. That has made a lot of administrators apprehensive. Inviting lay people into school decision-making will seem like asking for trouble. On a general level, the goals of community involvement may seem uniformly desirable, but on a practical level, there is likely to be disagreement about them. Some may feel that their local school does not deserve support because they are dissatisfied with the building or the curriculum or the personnel. Groups in the neighborhood will almost certainly disagree about which specific aspects of their school should be how responsive to which people, how soon. Where interests differ and resources are limited, disagreement about priorities is practically inevitable. But such conflicts exist whether or not a mechanism for involvement exists. The presence of a well-designed mechanism for community involvement provides a channel for conflict and enhances the prospect it will be successfully resolved.

There is another frequently overlooked point that is perhaps even more important. A great deal of the disagreement inherent in neighborhoods reflects differences of interst and of perception that are quite legitimate. Conflict arises simply from the pursuit of many *different* people's self-interests. It is to be expected when important public values are at stake. It is probably fair to say that most schools are surrounded by neighborhoods that appear to be quiescent about school policy issues. When public decisions are made, they are often surrounded by what seems to be consensus. Everyone appears to agree on a course of action. Consensus is an important thing. Where it is possible to make decisions unanimously, the benefits of harmony and good will are desirable. But, there are many instances in which some people will be unwilling to agree with a particular course; they will want to continue to pursue their own interests because they feel they are right. In those instances the most that can be hoped for is that people will *consent* to the decision although they will be unwilling to join a consensus about it. (It is relevant to note that American government rests not on consensus, but on the consent of the governed.) Thus, when some people's interests are not reflected in a decision, they allow it to be carried out but reserve the right to continue to press for their belief. The difference between these two patterns can be crucial for school administrators who are used to superficially harmonious community "participation." Consensus is a useful way to proceed, but if it is unobtainable, principals should not expect people to give up the differences that prompted the disagreement.

Conflict is not a sign of failure. The absence of unanimity does not mean something is wrong. Where interests differ and resources are limited, citizens should understand their differences, agree to a resolution of them, but *not* abandon the pursuit of their own interests. The informed consent of the neighborhood is as honorable a goal as consensus and, quite often, more realistic. There are different kinds of conflict. Some conflict accurately registers what people want the school to do. It signals the school about the different interests it must try to serve and provides valuable and constructive guidance. Then there is destructive or rancorous conflict in which people pursue their differences to the point that they are no longer willing to work together to solve common problems. That willingness to work together is the definition of "community," and it can be destroyed by uncontrolled conflict. There has been much less rancorous conflict in schools than the media's attention to newsworthy events might indicate. There are very few places where communities wish to replace professionals in operating the schools. Nonetheless, principals are right to be concerned about the possibility of uncontrolled conflict. Where it has destroyed communities (and careers and the teaching/learning environment), it has done so for two reasons that are directly relevant to this manual. First, no effective mechanisms existed to channel and resolve the conflict. Second, the people involved (lay people *and* professionals) lacked the experience necessary to handle their disagreements.

If there is a minimal level of conflict in a neighborhood, then establishing an involvement mechanism may be relatively costless. If there is already substantial conflict, then the presence of the mechanism can only help with an already difficult situation. But what about conflicts that develop—and escalate—after the group's establishment? What should the principal do about those? The answer is the same with or without a mechanism for community involvement. In large part, of course, it depends on the issue. The answer to the question "Who's right?" determines a great deal about the principal's response. But absent that information, the first reaction of most principals would be to mediate while staying relatively uninvolved. If mediation fails, if the stakes escalate, and if the principal joins in, then it is with the same risks as are always involved in conflict situations. When conflict is unavoidable, the principal's decision to become involved or not is a personal one. But the *outcome* of that conflict may depend on how carefully an involvement group was designed and supported by the principal.

The opposite side of the coin from visible conflict is neighborhood apathy. The political culture of some communities emphasizes respect for tradition and deference to authority. Such communities often appear to be very allegiant and quiet about educational matters until some grievance precipitates a change. Principals who work with these communities will need to build knowledgeable involvement prior to crises. Other communities are so alienated from their schools—and vice versa—that there is little if any involvement. A more common pattern is the situation in which the opportunities for involvement offered by the school to parents and other citizens are so trivial and so tangential that they do not elicit any significant response. Principals who use advisory committees to rubberstamp decisions that have already been made, who consistently override advice, or who never ask parents about policy questions central to teaching and learning should not conclude that their neighborhoods are apathetic. It is much more likely that the citizens have made a reasonable response to an unrewarding opportunity.

Principals are in the middle of what happens between schools and communities. What are the likely personal consequences of increased involvement for them? Principals who believe their current stock of power to be inadequate to the demands of their jobs might rather increase their control of the school affairs instead of sharing it. But there is a general and irresistible societal trend toward more democratic participation by urban citizens in schools along with health, social-welfare, and housing institutions. The reality of community and client participation is quite simply a new boundary on all professional decisions. Those decisions are right now circled by participants with whom the principal has to share control. Teacher unions, factions within the staff, other building administrators, and numerous bureaucratic superiors are already thoroughly involved in the control of the school. Thus most principals recognize that autonomy or the idea of solely personal control is an illusion. The neighborhood group may stabilize and systematize what is already a reality, but whether it does or not, the group is an opportunity for the principal to capitalize on involvement for the purpose of achieving the school's goals. The remainder of this handbook describes how neighborhood involvement can be realized. The mechanisms described have been designed specifically to cope with, and to make creative use of, some disagreement and to overcome apathy and reluctance on the part of urban neighborhood residents.

Who Should be Involved

An accurate reflection of opinions, strengths, and needs is one of the most useful things a neighborhood group can provide the principal. The group's ability to do that will depend on how it was selected. The importance of elections will be stressed here, but elections are not something that the principal either can or should control. On the other hand, the principal is a directly concerned individual who bears a good deal of the responsibility for the quality of school/community relations. The purpose of this manual is to give the principals the kind of information they need to play an active leadership role. The principal's influence will be substantial. And, of course, the principal's responsibility not to misuse that influence—by setting up a committee of cronies, for example—is also substantial. Thus the principal may wish to restrict his or her role in the selection process to calling attention to a number of desirable attributes of involvement and perhaps to suggesting ways they may be achieved.

It is desirable that the group be broadly representative; it should reflect all segments of the neighborhood, or it will not be seen as a legitimately representative group. Second, it should give the school access to both the existing and the potential contributions of the neighborhood. That means that in addition to people who are already active in the school or who are already involved in public affairs, people whose potential exceeds their experience should be encouraged to take part. There should be some young people and some people who have not yet become known through the neighborhood. Other social-welfare agencies, churches, and social groups, may help to identify these people. Involving them can demonstrate the group's intention to include *all* points of view; it can provide training for additional people; and it can ensure a pool of qualified indigenous leaders who will provide continuity to the group over time.

Community involvement can originate in response to a particular event or as a part of a conscious effort. Where involvement begins in response to a dramatic event or crisis such as a budget reduction or a personnel controversy, that crisis can be used as a basis for mobilizing a more general and lasting effort. Because the dramatic event will already have focused attention on the schools, the task becomes one of balancing the points of view presented and ensuring that the involvement does not dissolve when the crisis is past. It helps a lot if the principal can feel that the total burden of resolving the crisis, the total responsibility for finding a solution, is not solely hers or his. An attitude of openness, an expectation that others can and will come forward, helps make their participation a reality. The experience gained by the early, crisis-stimulated participants can contribute to the later success of the group. Involvement that originates in crisis situations can provide the basis for more stable interaction; but for that to happen, it is necessary that participation be expanded and the group's concerns be widened to include more than the original incident or event. The principal should keep in mind that different people are interested in different things. Adding issues and topics to the agenda of a group increases the number of people who may wish to be involved.

Community involvement may also be developed without a precipitating event. It can be a response to a government mandate, or it can be planned and initiated by educators or other concerned people. However, when it is initiated by professionals, especially by professionals who do not live in the neighborhood, then it is extremely important that neighborhood residents be encouraged to participate as soon as possible. Without that early participation, relevant information is greatly reduced and so is the crucial identification of the community with the involvement mechanism. The third way an involvement mechanism can come into being is as a logical extension of an existing group. Advisory groups or parents' associations have sometimes provided a successful foundation for more authoritative involvement. The advantages of building on these groups is the ready availability of experienced people. On the other hand, because the purposes and requirements of control sharing are different from those of mere advice and traditional public relations, the features of the existing group (composition, topical focus, etc.) should be carefully reviewed and modified as necessary according to the topics dealt with here.

Member Selection

How do people become members of school-related groups? The most common way is simply by volunteering. People who show an interest in school affairs make themselves available or are asked to serve on such groups. Although the fact of volunteering guarantees some motivation, it does not guarantee that a group composed of volunteers can speak for the neighborhood. Because the poorest people are least likely to have the time or inclination to volunteer, volunteerism will not represent their interests. In the case of a continuing group that is expanded, the members of the existing group often select either their successors or additional members. Unfortunately, because people tend to choose those others who are most like themselves, this self-perpetuating procedure freezes an earlier balance of views, and, in a very short period of time, the group may lose its ability to reflect the total interests of the neighborhood.

Three alternate selection methods should be considered: (1) appointment, (2) election, and (3) a combination of appointment and election. The same questions arise in all instances—who is to do the selection and on what basis? For a building principal to appoint those with whom control is shared is not recommended for several reasons having to do with the possibility of abuse, the probable lack of neighborhood confidence in the appointees, and the simple fact that the procedure is incompatible with the democratic principle of self-governance. It might be possible to allow the Parent-Teacher Associations, block associations, tenant associations, etc., to appoint a number of members. However, because such appointments will be objectionable to people on grounds largely similar to administrator appointments, it is not recommended. Appointment should be used only in unusual circumstances, for example, in the selection of a temporary group charged with initiating more systematic involvement. Even there, extreme caution should be used so that these screening groups or election committees are perceived as being fairly representative of the community. Including some manifestation of religion, ethnicity, attitude toward the school, attitude toward a variety of relevant political and social issues, plus other situationally relevant characteristics—*and* displaying appropriate combinations of all of those characteristics—all within a group of perhaps a dozen people is a fantastic task. The inevitable result will be that some, perhaps many, people will feel left out. Thus it is much better to give people the opportunity to decide for themselves whom they want to represent them.

Elections are the preferable method of selection because they begin the process of involvement on the broadest possible basis and help ensure the acceptability of its results. The proper conduct of an election, even on a neighborhood scale, requires considerable planning. An election committee may be formed to help plan and conduct the election. The following points are a general guide to election procedure. They may, of course, be modified to fit particular situations.

1. *Any adult* living in the school's geographic attendance area should be eligible to vote. In the ordinary course of things, parents will be the most interested and will dominate the election, but other citizens should have the opportunity to vote as well. Membership, and certainly *not* dues-paying membership, in a school association should not be required in order to vote.
2. *Any adult* living in the attendance area should be eligible to run for office except those people who are currently employed by the local school.

Note: The special case of paraprofessionals and teachers: Many paraprofessionals are employed exactly because of their knowledge of the community and their ability to bridge the gap between it and the school. It may be difficult for them to agree that a characteristic that qualifies them for taking part in one capacity should prevent them from taking part in another. They may resent what may seem to be a denial of a democratic privilege to run for a school office. The same argument can be made by any teacher who lives in the same community. There are, nonetheless, two compelling arguments against their eligibility for membership on the shared-control group. First, if the group is indeed to share control in the sense of significant policy determination, then it would be a conflict of interest to have the school's employees determining policy that is also governing them. Think, for example, of the difficulties that would arise in personnel selection and in program evaluation. The second objection is that the school's employees are already influential participants in policy determination. Simply because they implement policy, they will also inevitably influence it. In addition, professional unions and associations are zealous guardians of the interest of teachers, and to some extent, of paraprofessionals. Allowing teachers and other school employees to serve on this mechanism of community involvement would move away from a new balance of interests and back in the direction of professional dominance which the mechanism is designed *inter alia* to remedy.

3. *Notice of the impending election* should be prominently displayed, especially outside the school, well in advance of the closing date for nominations. Leaflets, newspapers, group and club announcements, and telephone chains may also be used. Careful attention will need to be given at this point, as at all others throughout this process, to make any information available in all of the languages used by the area's residents.

4. *A nominating petition*, but with a small number of required signatures, say, 25, should be used to place a name on the ballot. People should not be allowed to sign more petitions than some fraction, say, one half, of the available seats up for election.

5. *Candidates' nights* and other opportunities to make views known should be arranged. Attendance will be improved if these are held along with other school activities, especially where those activities involve a lot of children as performers.

6. All candidates should run *at large* and simply for membership, not for predesignated positions like chairperson. This allows the group, once elected, to determine for itself its own organization and leadership. Most attendance areas are small enough to do away with the need to have people selected on any smaller geographic or other basis—grade level, for example. For high schools, where attendance areas cover more than one neighborhood and it seems desirable to elect group members from smaller areas, extreme caution should be used in dividing up those areas. Drawing lines around and between areas virtually guarantees the election of particular points of view; the group that results could easily be unfairly representative. On the other hand, electing everyone at large—that is, from the whole geographic area, not from parts—can end up the same way. A minority of say 20 percent of those

voting—who might have been able to send a representative to the group if their area had been designated as an election district—may, under the at-large procedure, simply never be able to select anyone. The dilemma is a real one; which method is more fair depends on particular local conditions.

7. *The election should be scheduled* at a time that will be most convenient to most people, a weekday afternoon and evening, preferably including the night of a school "Open House". Turnout will be small, so it may be helpful to consider holding the election over a 36-hour period, or running it at the same time that people are voting in another city, state, or federal election.

8. *The place of voting* should be the school. Where, as in the case of a bussed-in population, there are two attendance areas, there should be centrally located, easily accessible places to vote in both areas.

9. *Absentee ballots* should be provided as long as they arrive in time to be counted with regular ballots. Whether it is necessary to provide for absentee ballots is something that should be decided locally according to available resources and probable need. The same holds true of several of the other features suggested here.

10. The ballot itself should be *secret*, reproduced in all relevant languages, and the order in which the names appear should be determined by chance.

11. Voters must supply a *proof of current residence* (but without a minimum time limit for residence) and should either be checked off a prepared list or added to an alphabetized list at the time of voting. Voters should sign the list as they vote. (These records are confidential and should be retained as such by the principal or the election committee.)

12. The election will not be valid unless a *specified minimum turn-out* of eligible voters is achieved (perhaps 5 percent of the attendance area population or 20 percent of the parents).

13. The ballot *count should be public* and prompt.

14. People with the *highest number of votes* will be elected.

15. New elections should be *held every year* either in the fall or the spring. A spring election has the advantage of allowing some time for informing the new members prior to their taking office. A fall election may get a higher turn-out, especially of residents who are new to the attendance area. Because of graduation and family mobility, a school's parent clientele turns over quite rapidly. The yearly election of at least one third of the membership provides replacement members and can keep the group representative of the neighborhood.

Elections can maximize the amount of self-determination exercised by a neighborhood. But they do not necessarily guarantee that the membership of the group will meet every desired characteristic. The procedures suggested here are exactly that, suggestions that need to be reviewed in light of local circumstances. If it seems likely that an election will produce unfair results or inaccurate representation, then the principal and the community will want to consider ways to augment the selection process. One way to ensure the fairness of the election procedure itself is to have the election conducted by an outside agency—for example, a city board of elections. That is, however, likely to be more costly than it is worth. Neighborhood-based elections can be run properly by an impartial election committee that is aware of the need for procedural safeguards of the sort described here.

Another method of securing a broadly representative group is to create a "delegate assembly." Delegate assemblies have representatives who are chosen by their organizations and sent to the assembly as representatives of those particular groups. Delegate assemblies have worked well as coordinating devices on a city-wide basis for community-action programs. Block associations, tenant groups, social-welfare agencies and councils, grade-level organizations, and others might, for example, appoint some delegates to a school-based control-sharing group. (However, the need for representation of all parts of the community, including the less organized people, should be carefully considered. A delegate assembly, by itself, is unlikely to deliver satisfactory representation.)

It is also possible to combine the delegate assembly procedure with an at-large election. For example, half of the places in a group may be filled from organizations in the neighborhood. The other half of the places would be filled by an election. While this combination might increase representation, it might also effectively double the influence of existing groups. In addition to getting to choose their own representatives through the delegate assembly procedure, those groups may be able to use their organizational resources to unfairly influence the election.

The principal needs to keep in mind that the methods for selecting the group's members will strongly influence the sort of group that emerges. The principal has the responsibility and the opportunity to influence some aspects of this process. There is a fine line between, on the one hand, encouraging and assisting neighborhood involvement, and on the other, unduly determining its outcome. The chances of crossing that line can be reduced if the principal acts openly, carefully, and in cooperation with the community.

An election can minimize but not eliminate recriminations about the social class, racial, and ethnic make-up of the group. A properly conducted election provides a forum for all points of view—supportive and critical—to be expressed and then allows that expression to be reflected in the composition of the group. If grade levels are relevant (for example, the parents of younger and of older children sometimes have important disagreements), then grade levels should be reflected in the group. If groups feel strongly about innovation (for or against) or particular teaching practices, then they should have a voice in the group. Antischool, or antiadministration forces too have a right to compete for the support of the neighborhood. A succession of elections can help people get their complaints acted upon and ensure that the school is responsive to them.

The prospect of conflict is not a happy one for school administrators even though (or perhaps because) they deal with so much of it. The possibility that elections—or lay governance of any sort—will encourage factions and blocs and controversy makes many administrators wary of community involvement. Yet most administrators recognize that their neighborhoods are not homogeneous and that controversy is never very far from the surface. Even at the level of the neighborhood school, there are important differences that need careful and respectful attention. If the goals suggested earlier are to be realized, then treating community involvement in all its facets as a matter for systematic attention *over time* is clearly recommended. It should be stressed that involvement is a continuing process; representative groups working in technical areas like education take time to become established, knowledgeable, and accomplished participants. Principals working with such groups should be at least as patient with that group's training and education as they were with the long process of their own professional preparation.

What Should They Do?

From everyone's point of view, this is the paramount question about community involvement. It has two aspects: *how much* control is to be shared, and control *over what.* When the subject of sharing control comes up, many principals tend to think of it in absolute terms; yet no principal has absolute authority or total power over the things that happen within his or her school. Neither total professional control nor total community control is a possibility. Most decisions are compromises worked out between different positions. Many decisions are strongly influenced by an estimate of the anticipated reaction of different groups. How will the teachers react? What about the paraprofessionals? Can this be made more acceptable to those who favor open classrooms? Every time a principal modifies a decision to take someone else's views into account, control is *being shared.*

The informal sharing of power is one aspect of this. Principals often seek out and defer to the judgment of others on specific matters of education policy. They also avoid making some judgments that they know will be unacceptable to powerful factions or groups within the school. The net effect of these informal realities is to locate policy determination between the principal and several "others"—especially teachers. But there are formal restraints as well. School principals operate within a net of contractual obligations (especially about personnel matters), legislative mandates (the state school code will cover parts of virtually every aspect of the school), central office regulations, special program regulations, and constitutional requirements. All of those boundaries are better known to administrators than to lay people, and they will be the source of constant friction unless a concerted effort is made to outline to the community the impact of these restraints on the autonomy of the local school and its local control-sharing group. That task is the principal's responsibility.

Thus schools are already conglomerations of legal checks and balances and informal alliances of teachers, paraprofessionals, headquarters, grade level, and program groups, existing parent groups, and others—all striving to take part in "professional" decisions. But the difference between the current informal reality of shared control and the creation of a neighborhood group for the same purpose is not a small thing. The group will have important consequences for the principal. However, from one point of view, the group is a formalization and extension of what is already an unsystematic reality for most urban principals. Because that is the case, principals are already in possession of some ways to make up their minds about how much control they feel should be shared.

What sorts of concerns do principals usually have about this matter? What standards are appropriately used to determine their position? It is always difficult to make these decisions in the abstract, without the guidance specific facts give. Yet, the initial decision about a community-involvement mechanism will usually have to be made in a sort of "have or have-not" lump. Should the principal become committed to a control-sharing mechanism or not? The stormy history of decentralization in some cities, the relative lack of experience with control-sharing groups at the neighborhood level, and the natural striving toward independence common to all professionals are sources of real apprehension. That apprehension will have to be weighed against the prospects for increased goal achievement along with whatever situational factors exist (for example, a mandate from the central board or from a federal agency).

The principal will also need to consider some other things in making the initial, overall judgment. What are the prospects for accurate representation of neighborhood needs and interests? Will the group's involvement help achieve the school's goals; and, if so, how much will it help? How much power will the group have—that is, when the principal and the group disagree, whose judgment will prevail? The problem of legal authority is closely linked to the question of power. The statutes governing most school systems make the building principal "the responsible head of the school." Legally, the principal is responsible for what happens in the school even though de facto control over school matters may be widely shared. What about situations in which decisions are made at least in part by other people and the principal dissents. If something goes wrong, the principal is responsible, not the other participants. Principals have reason to be concerned about this imbalance between their control of decisions and their responsibility for results. (The imbalance occurs not just between neighborhoods and principals but also between unions and principals.) The long-term resolution may be to find ways for lay groups at the neighborhood level to share decision-making responsibility (or accountability) in the same proportion that they share control. The election of the group should help with that in that one of the consequences of bad judgment or unresponsiveness may be not being returned to the group. But we will probably have to find other ways to hold group members at least as accountable for their actions as are school board members. Those developments rest on changes in state education law that will be too slow in arriving to do school principals much immediate good with this difficult problem. In the short run, principals will have to rely on their own persuasive powers and on their faith in the judgment of neighborhood people.

The question remains—in a dispute, can the neighborhood group overrule the principal? When push comes to shove, who must yield to whom? In almost every case, the neighborhood's ability to "control" things, which really means to influence, to participate, or to share control, will rest on the same sort of basis as does the principal's—the ability to persuade other people that something is right or needs to be done. The amount of control is decided by the ability to attract supporters and to exploit advantages. In practically every instance, the result of shared control will be shared influence over the outcome, and that outcome will be a *compromise*. But, if it is not, if no compromise is possible, if differences are irreconcilable, then because of the legal position of the principal, the principal can invoke that authority to prevail. Of course, the resort to legal authority is not without cost; its price can be hostility, disillusionment, and sometimes, a job.

Each principal will want to think through the way these factors enter the particular situation. The initial consideration may determine the principal's overall orientation to neighborhood involvement, but involvement is made up of more precise things as well. For example, in what areas of the school's policy should the neighborhood group participate? Should its participation be the same in each area?

There are five general areas of school policy: (1) curriculum, (2) budget, (3) teacher personnel, (4) administrative personnel, and (5) student affairs. In each area, the role to be played by the neighborhood group will depend on a series of factors that must be assessed by the principal in cooperation with the group and with reference to the local situation. Again, speaking generally, these are:

A. the interests and abilities of the shared-control group itself;
B. other possible actors (teachers' unions, the central board, community-action groups, etc.);
C. legal restraints (federal, state, and local laws, regulations, guidelines, contracts, etc.);
D. the estimated effects of the involvement on achieving the school's goals; and
E. the availability of the means and opportunity to influence decisions.

Participation in school policy determination means participation in the overall direction, not the specific administration of the school. The distinction is a favorite adage of the textbooks, but practicing administrators know how difficult it is to observe and maintain. Routine administrative decisions sometimes amount to policy in that they seriously affect many students (for example, the handling of records or the choice of testing materials) while "policy" announcements often have no measurable impact on what really happens in a given building. In addition, parent concerns are stimulated by specific incidents and getting something done about them inevitably crosses into administrative, not policy, concerns. Three points should be made. First, the tug of war between "policy" and "administration" goes on all the time whether or not there is a mechanism of shared control. An effective mechanism can ameliorate it. Second, shared control must not be confined to such a small area or to such specific questions that it fails to affect what the school as a whole does. Third, the line between involvement in policy and in daily operations is a difficult but important one to establish. Sincere efforts to involve neighborhoods at the policy level can attract participation where it is most important while still maintaining the principal's ability to make day-to-day operating decisions.

1. *Curriculum.* The process and materials through which teaching and learning are conducted are often regarded as the province of experts, and expert knowledge is certainly a necessary input for this area. But lay people can be useful in determining community preferences, stimulating or supervising evaluations, reviewing current or proposed parts of the curriculum, and making recommendations and pushing for their adoption. The principal will need to decide whether to encourage the neighborhood group to become involved in the spectrum of curriculum activities, and, if so, on what basis within the school (for all grades or only some? for all curricular topics or only some? which grades? which topics?). The neighborhood group itself should also make decisions about its interests and priorities. Having successful experiences with participation early in its development can motivate groups to greater achievement. If it can be arranged, a focus on an important, yet somewhat limited and feasible problem, is a good way for a group to begin. As the group gains experience, more difficult problems can be tackled. Lay people who interest themselves in technical matters usually need some assistance in dealing with professionals (especially where the professionals use their own jargon and expertise for partisan purposes). In the curriculum area, for example, the efforts of the neighborhood group should be coordinated with those of teachers and headquarters specialists who can gain a better idea of the strengths and interests of neighborhoods by working with them. When a neighborhood group has been in existence for a couple of years, it will have become more familiar with state textbook laws, the whims of the national publishing industry, a variety of different ways to perform educational evaluations, and other topics that can enhance its involvement. As the expertise on both sides grows, the prospects for a creative school/community partnership increase.

2. *Budget.* Budget policy determines how resources are allocated in the school; a related set of questions deals with how schools are paid for at the

district level. The neighborhood should be represented in district-wide decisions, it may wish to argue and lobby for more support, it may wish to participate in city-wide coalitions for state aid, but there is little else that it can do directly in the area of finance. The amount of money allotted to an individual school is usually determined by a formula that is beyond the principal's control. This kind of prior restraint on the principal's autonomy is often misunderstood but can be cleared up through shared involvement in the budget process. Resource allocation *within* the school is another matter.

Some schools use a neighborhood parent group as a review board to consider that school's budget before it is sent on to the central office. Sometimes this review is organized on a school-wide, grade-level, or classroom basis. Unless there is ample time for the community groups to ask for, receive, and consider additional information, and unless the budget is presented in a manner that relates it to the neighborhood's concerns, these budget "reviews" are little more than an opportunity to approve what has already been decided. Control sharing in the resource-allocation process at the building level requires more extensive participation. In the budget process, as in other policy areas, there are two dimensions to community involvement: the range of topics dealt with and the effect of involvement. For example, the neighborhood's recommendations may be purely advisory in nature (the principal may retain the final say), or they may be binding, with the principal being required to incorporate the community's ideas into the budget. Or the effect of the group's involvement may be somewhere in between those poles. The precise amount of the group's involvement, like its topical distribution, will be determined by circumstances. That is a process of mutual negotiation and experimentation, but the principal should keep in mind the cardinal rule that involvement succeeds when it is significant. In those cases in which the community's role is only advisory and the principal retains the final authority, the need to respect community opinion and to keep the community informed will be increased exactly because of the expectations created by a mechanism of shared control. Budget questions are very likely to go to the heart of the teaching and learning process. What teachers and materials go to which children? What are the priorities for new money requests, and how are they to be determined? How can programs be evaluated, and who should establish performance standards? Involvement can range over a variety of activities: establishing budget priorities, recommending budget categories and expenditures, and/or approving the final allocation of the school's scarce resources. The group's role can also vary from advice, to exhortation, to endorsement, to recommendation, to veto, and so on, according to the various stages of the budget process.

That process has been properly called "the lifeblood of organizations." Neighborhood participation in it implies a familiarity with existing needs and programs and their costs and a familiarity with alternate programs. The knowledge base required to do that is likely to be a significant *short-term* obstacle to effective participation. Neighborhood involvement will be most successful when a nucleus of group members have established considerable familiarity with the process. Because of turnover within the group, this sort of training should be a constant concern of the principal.[a] Some of the best learning is by doing. Neighborhood groups should plunge into the budget process early in the cycle of budget development. It is also important that budget documents and forms themselves be related not to bureaucratically determined categories of expenditure (line items such as "instructional salaries," etc.) but rather to the narrative justification for those expenditures (that is, program items such as "two teacher aides for specified duties x, y, z per kindergarten classroom," etc.).

School principals sometimes complain that no one understands the problems they face. Because the things that need to be done far outstrip the resources available to do them, the budget process is an opportunity to describe some fundamental constraints on the neighborhood school. Participation in that process can be realistic training for the group. A constant lament at the building level is the extent to which budget allocations are determined "downtown." Communities need to recognize that reality if they are to help in changing it. Many schools that have involved community groups in all the frustrations of budgeting have discovered that the process turns parents into informed and effective allies in the struggle for more money and more discretion in its use.

3. *Personnel.* The issues involved in neighborhood participation in personnel decisions are similar enough that the two areas of teaching staff and administrative staff may be considered together. Both rest on the ability of lay people to participate in decisions about professional competence—especially *estimated future* professional competence. That is a difficult task for anyone, but it must be recognized that the professional's work will be practiced upon the neighborhood's children and therefore should reflect the neighborhood's interest directly.

The situation is a clear example of why control should be shared rather than vested in any single group or individual. Administrators alone, teachers alone, lay people alone cannot make adequate decisions about matters that are so central to *all* their interests. Each *must* respect the other's strengths and competencies, and those strengths should be reflected in the procedures established for decisions in this area. The use of a personnel subcommittee is one common procedure. The subcommittee, which may work closely with administrators and teachers, can help review and establish personnel standards, interview new candidates, establish hiring criteria, etc. Sometimes such committees screen all new candidates and recommend a small number, say, three, from among whom

[a]Training in resource-allocation decisions, for any participants, has been a neglected area especially at the level of the school building. For a simulation exercise designed to equip school principals to make use of the resource-allocation, budget-development process as an instrument of program change, see Dale Mann, "Site Budgeting Simulation," *UCEA Urban Simulation: Wilson High School* (Columbus, Ohio: University Council for Educational Administration, 1975).

the principal makes a penultimate selection. Subcommittee personnel may take part in teacher evaluations with the principal. The subcommittee may also participate in decisions about promotion, transfer, and dismissal. In personnel matters, as in budget matters, the effect of involvement can take a number of forms. The subcommittee can have veto power over personnel decisions but lack the power to require the administration to do any particular thing. Alternatively, the subcommittee's decisions may be regarded as final (either formally or informally), or they can be treated as nonbinding recommendations. Obviously, this is an area in which the legal situation varies widely. The roles described here are listed as options for consideration as local circumstances warrant. Those local circumstances—especially the legal framework governing personnel matters— need to be clearly communicated to the group so that exaggerated expectations are avoided.

The personnel area is especially sensitive for neighborhood involvement. The hard-won rights of professionals are clearly at stake and jealously guarded. Just as clearly, the economic, social, and educational reasons for allowing qualified neighborhood residents access to those same positions, are also at stake. Fortunately for everyone involved, the "how much" and "in what" factors can be rather closely calibrated. In some aspects of personnel policy, it may be better to have very authoritative involvement (binding decisions) but only over a limited portion of the policy area. Thus it might be impossible to tenure a teacher without the concurrence of the shared-control group, yet that group's role in promotions may be strictly advisory. The point is that "how much" and "in what" can be purposefully regulated to achieve a proper balance of interests. Obviously, arranging community involvement in the personnel area will require patience, energy, and good will on the part of everyone involved. The process of working out a satisfactory arrangement is likely to be stormy and educational.

Here again, principals will need to pay special attention to teachers. Shared control gives the community a role in school policy determination that will threaten some teachers. Because teachers carry out the school's face-to-face interaction with the community, their cooperation is essential. It will be helpful to point out the many ways teacher interests continue to be protected (by their own associations and unions, by their daily participation in the school's affairs, by laws and regulations, by tenure, and especially, by their own diligent performance as educators). Whenever possible and appropriate, teachers should be invited to participate in tasks with the shared-control group.

4. *Student Concerns.* The last major area of school policy is that dealing with student-related concerns, especially discipline. Members of the group can help to review, plan, and establish policies and procedures in this area. Again, the precise role played by the group can range from advice to policy-making. As with other areas, the potential contributions from the neighborhood must be balanced against the possibility of favoritism or other undesirable influences. A properly conducted member-selection process for the neighborhood group

should ensure a broad representation of interests. That representation, combined with the experience of the group members and the assistance of the principal should minimize the dangers of abuse. (For schools that deal with older students, especially high schools, some student representation on subcommittees or task forces in this area is mandatory.)

Even in response to a crisis, community involvement does not emerge suddenly and blanket all areas of school policy. Rather, it develops in a more or less cumulative fashion. Interest in personnel policies may give way to interest in budget development and be followed by a concern with the potential of open classrooms. A group's concentration on the lines around its school's attendance area may turn into a focus on the kind of facilities available to its children. The principal's task is to encourage the accumulation of experience and to assist its transfer from one area to another. Because community involvement develops over time and through different policy areas, it is neither necessary nor desirable to attempt to decide, at one point in time, the total distribution of control in all policy areas, in all situations. However, that does *not* mean that the principal should not have a comprehensive and detailed plan. Uncertainty and poor preparation are two of the most certain ways to arouse charges of bad faith from neighborhoods. The principal's commitment to involvement and the overall guidelines within which the principal believes it should proceed must be clearly and *publicly* stated. Those guidelines can then be applied to particular contingencies, or they can be revised as events dictate.

The sharing of control means exactly that. However, realism suggests that the principal's pivotal location and other responsibilities will reinforce his or her influence in this process, especially where there is not already an established base. The relative dominance of the principal is unavoidable and from many points of view desirable, but it may also distract from some of the essential purposes and prerequisites of involvement. The amount of neighborhood involvement necessary to elicit, for example, increased support for the school, is quite high. Relatively large numbers of people need to be quite extensively involved before the sum total of that involvement can add to the reservoir of support. The influence of the professional should be carefully monitored and regulated (both by the professional and by the community) so that it does not stifle neighborhood initiative and development. We have made the point several times that community involvement is not a take-it-or-leave-it proposition. The amount and focus of shared control can be regulated. It can also be manipulated. This manual outlines the working features of successful involvement, and it is always possible to use that knowledge to sabotage or dilute participation. But misusing involvement means that nothing about the school will be improved and, in fact, the likelihood of a rapid slide into school/community hostility will be greatly increased. Again, involvement is successful when it is significant. Communities have learned to tell the difference between authentically shared control and public relations manipulation.

Communications Responsibilities

The obvious purpose of communicating from the neighborhood to the school is to get all relevant points of view before the school's decision-makers. However, there is no necessary relation between the amount of squeaking and the amount of grease that is actually needed. A representative neighborhood group will want to be sure that it is active enough in soliciting neighborhood opinions to reach those people who have something to say but who might not otherwise have a chance to express themselves. The group will also need to decide how receptive it will be to individual grievances as distinct from those that may affect groups as a whole. The danger in accepting individual grievances is that the group may be viewed as only the spokesman for special pleading. Concentrating too heavily on individual as opposed to more widely shared concerns can carry the group away from its policy orientation. On the other hand, one basic way groups establish their own credibility and build support is by assisting individuals with their legitimate problems. The balance to be struck is between being responsive to needy individuals and maintaining an effective presence for the school as a whole. In a similar fashion, the group will also need to determine the extent to which it should be concerned with problems that are district-wide and city-wide as opposed to strictly local matters.

In general, the involvement mechanism should provide for the following things.

1. A central phone number and mailing address should be publicized to receive neighborhood opinions. The phone numbers and addresses of the group's leadership should also be public.

2. Subcommittee and task force meetings should be held in various non-school locations around the neighborhood, and the scheduled rotation of those meetings should be announced well in advance. Meetings should be held at different times of day to allow everyone an opportunity to attend. Over the course of a year, meetings should have occurred at all appropriate times and places in the attendance area.

3. Meetings themselves should be summarized and reported—including statements from the neighborhood—through appropriate media including local newspapers. (Again, this should be done with attention to the languages spoken by the school's constituencies.)

4. Wherever the issue is important enough to justify the effort, neighborhood attitudes should be tapped in a systematic fashion. A postcard survey, an informal door-to-door canvass, or a table at the school can be used for this purpose with simple questionnaires prepared to find out how people feel about particular school issues. Efforts of this sort may be especially important for a newly established group to gain visibility and also to validate the group's own sense of priorities.

5. Members of the group should be encouraged constantly to seek out the

opinions and interests of neighborhood people beyond their immediate circle of contacts. At open houses and other education-related events, teachers and principals should make an effort to introduce group members to people whom they have not yet met. (And of course, the group members should return the favor, introducing community people to the school's staff.)

6. In all encounters with their fellow citizens, members of the group should be certain to register whatever shades of opinion—both favorable and unfavorable—are expressed. Because the group exists to encourage, register, (and to refine) neighborhood input, people should be actively solicited to express their opinions and desires.

Communicating from the school back to the community probably accounts for most of the work of most of the community groups now operating in schools. The function is an important one, even if, given the purposes of a shared-control group, certain cautions may be advisable. A broadly based group of citizens, drawn from all parts of the community can be a marvelous resource in telling the public what the school is doing, and in building support for its programs. The intention is fine, but great care must be exercised so that the group's independence is not compromised. If the group becomes merely the publicity agent or bake sale organizer for the school, then its unique ability to serve as a vehicle for broadly based, policy-relevant participation will be seriously lessened. The group needs to judge for itself the communications tasks it will undertake on the school's behalf. Because, as the group grows in experience, it will also have had a greater hand in school decisions, its defense and interpretation of school policy can be expected to grow naturally.

How Should the Group be Organized?

In administration, as in architecture, form follows function. The decisions already made about what the group is to do, how intensely and comprehensively it should be involved, etc., will have a bearing on how it should be structured. Structure deals with aspects such as size, leadership, and decision-making procedure through which the group conducts its business.

A representative group acting on behalf of the community has an obligation to make its decisions in a democratic fashion. In relatively closely knit groups (those which share goals, respect, and experience), decisions often seem to "emerge" through consensus, which is desirable where this level of agreement occurs naturally and where it is not done by overriding people's interests. However, some groups, especially newly established ones, are not that cohesive. Even the most closely knit groups sometimes deal with issues that are so volatile and deeply felt that consensus would be an unrealistic expectation. In such cases, decisions may be made by majority votes among the members. Where votes are used to determine the group's decisions, it will be necessary to consider in advance what proportion of the group constitutes a quorum. A small proportion may lead to allegations about the lack of representation. A large required quorum, two thirds, for example, may cripple action where attendance is low, or it may allow a faction to block action by simply not attending. In this, as in other situations, the premium will be on good judgment and good faith in local circumstances. The group may wish to require "extraordinary majorities" (for example, two thirds of those present and voting beyond the quorum) for its most important decisions such as proposals about personnel, or the budget, or revision of the group itself. The matter of voting can be simplified if subcommittees are used to develop and refine alternatives prior to the group's action.

A note of caution about voting. Although majority decisions are basic to our sense of fair play, the principal should remember that votes can lead to an emotional as well as a numerical division. Instead of unifying the group, votes may create clearly visible sets of winners and losers. That may or may not be a problem, and it may or may not be avoidable. Again, the success of the group will rest on its own judgment and the support of the principal.

Groups making important decisions often encounter procedural wrangles about who can speak and for how long, what is and isn't relevant to the decision, how and when the decision itself can be made, etc. The standard reference for these occasions is *Robert's Rules Of Order*, but the details and formality required by *Robert's Rules* sometimes make it unacceptable to groups. More informal procedural guides, based on group dynamics research can be found in the National Training Laboratories—National Education Association Selected Readings Series (1961), especially No. 1, "Group Development," and No. 2, "Leadership in Action." Whatever procedural guides are used, they must be established by the group early in its career because the rules of the game must be known before the game begins. This establishment usually occurs when the group adopts a set of by-laws to govern its operations. The by-laws should clearly state (a) the group's purpose and the limits on its activities, (b) the rights and responsibilities of its members, and (c) the procedures for the group's operation. Wide circulation of clearly written by-laws can head off later misunderstandings. (Sample by-laws are available in Appendix 7B.)

A basic choice facing most group members is determining how they should relate to their constituents. When both they and their constituents are agreed on a course of action, there is no problem. However, if the two disagree, the question of who prevails will be of utmost importance. Basically, the community representative has three choices:

1. the "delegate" who does what the constituent wants even though the delegate may personally disagree;
2. the "trustee" who does what his or her own best judgment indicates rather than what the constituent wants; or
3. the "politico" who decides every question on its merits.

Each position has a great deal to recommend it. Moreover, the dilemma of choosing the "correct" position has been around since the beginning of representative government. This is one of the areas in which there are a few hints but no totally right answers. The best guides seem to be: (a) to recognize the difficulties inherent in this situation; (b) to be especially sensitive in the early days of the group's existence to neighborhood opinions about the proper relation between representatives and constituents; and (c) to maintain the integrity of the group's election process, so that, whatever style of representation is chosen, the group's members will remain basically accountable to the neighborhood. The group's members should keep in mind that many people feel that the only way they are represented is if their representatives do exactly what they, the people, want done. Communities can become disillusioned and angry very suddenly if, out of conscience, the representative disagrees and acts on that disagreement. When it arises, the choice between conscience and constituency can be a profound problem. Whether or not the group's representatives should be bound to follow whatever the neighborhood wants (the delegate style) or whether the constituents must accept their representatives' actions even when they disagree with those actions (the trustee style) is a choice that probably cannot be made in the absence of specific contextual information. It is also a choice that must be made by all of the participants themselves, and if necessary, through trial, error, and conflict.

The best size for a group can be described in terms of upper and lower limits as related to the group's purposes. The lower limit for group size will be determined by the need to ensure adequate representation for all points of view—including especially minority points of view. Very small groups, say, five or six members, may be charged with being a clique or an élite. In addition, very small groups will probably not allow most interested people a reasonable opportunity to participate either currently or in the near future. Finally, a group that is too small places too great a burden on its members. On a part-time basis, community people will not have the time to become knowledgeable participants and to sustain that participation in each of the major areas of school policy.

The upper limit of a group will be largely determined by the same factors. For example, beyond a certain point, a group can become unwieldy; it will begin to require so many subcommittees and executive sessions and other group management devices that the sense of shared participation may be damaged. Exactly where that upper limit may be is related to the preferences that group members have for conducting their own business; according to member interests and purposes, some groups may wish to operate as a "committee-of-the-whole," but it is more likely that the group will want to use a variety of specialized subcommittees. Election to the group should confer some status and responsibility on its members. If everyone who wants to can become a member, then the sense of responsibility and status that should be attached to membership will be spread so thinly that the group will be meaningless. In very large groups, it is difficult to know just who is responsible and who is to be held accountable for what decisions. Moreover, when every interested person is already a member of the group, there are no critics or alternates waiting to replace those members who fail to maintain the confidence of the community.

These considerations point to a group of between nine and fifteen members. The group should have an uneven number of members to minimize the chances of stalemate when it is divided.

A neighborhood involvement group needs to be in continuous existence and its activities need to be timed to *anticipate* the school calendar. For newly established groups, terms of office should be staggered so that about a third of the group is scheduled for selection each year. Scheduled expirations plus the inevitable vacancies due to resignations and family mobility will mean that about half the seats will be up for re-election each year. The terms of office for members of a newly established group can be determined at the first meeting, with one-, two-, and three-year terms allotted by some chance method. A procedure for replacing members between elections will be necessary. Some members will move out of the neighborhood, others will resign for personal reasons, and still others may be removed by the group for failure to attend meetings. (Three absences within a year result in automatic removal from some groups.) The group should, by majority vote, appoint a replacement to serve until the next regularly scheduled election.

The frequency of the group's meetings will be related to the calendar of school decisions, but, in any case, the entire group will need to meet on a monthly basis. For the group as a whole, meetings should be scheduled on the same day and time throughout the year (e.g., "the second Wednesday of each month at 7:30"). Whenever possible, an agenda of items to be considered should be included in mailed notices of upcoming meetings. An agenda should also be posted conspicuously in several locations around the neighborhood. Many decisions about such key matters as personnel and budget occur every year at the same time because of routine reporting requirements to district and state officials. A calendar of these anticipated deadlines should be prepared with the assistance of the principal and headquarters officials. The neighborhood group can then plan its own involvement (committee work, information sessions, etc.) so that its participation is informed and timely. The most effective schedule of activities will not coincide with peaks of popular involvement such as the opening of school—by then, most key decisions will already have been made.

It is clear that a group that has the increased involvement of the neighborhood as its purpose should conduct its business in meetings that are open to the public. On the other hand, some matters will require confidential fact-finding and deliberation. Such closed meetings should only be used when they are absolutely necessary. If all business is determined in executive sessions or private meetings prior to an open meeting, the public meetings will be empty performances that will discourage those nonmembers who might otherwise attend.

The larger the group, the greater the need for internal specialization. The virtues of having specific people knowledgeable about particular aspects of school policy should be balanced against the need to develop the expertise of the group as a whole. Many groups establish in their by-laws a series of topical subcommittees which then report to the whole group. The group may wish to appoint subcommittees (or more simply, to ask particular individuals to concentrate) on the five areas of school policy previously identified.

Leadership is one of those obviously desirable but usually elusive characteristics. It is essential that the group's leadership be indigenous to the neighborhood. Whether that leadership develops depends heavily on the attitude and action of the principal. But principals also need to be concerned that they are not too helpful. In assisting the group or in helping to make it function more efficiently, the principal may block its independence and initiative. Leadership develops, if it develops at all, through responsible engagement with real issues. The risk of failing is the price of growth.

Group characteristics should change as the nature of the problems changes. It must be possible to modify group features that have not proven successful. Any feature of the by-laws or charter of the group should be open to amendments by two thirds of the group's entire membership.

How to Help

There are many ways the principal can help the group succeed. Principals scarcely need more things to do or more responsibility, yet this entire manual focuses on their role. In one sense, there are no apologies for that. Relations between urban schools and communities are in great need of improvement, and that improvement is instrumental enough in its contribution to other school goals to justify more of the principal's attention than it ordinarily gets. Still, principals are busy people, and personal responsibility for every one of the tasks outlined here would distract them from other important jobs. The range of options included in this handbook is purposefully comprehensive. Principals and communities will adopt some features but not others. Also, many of these tasks can and should be performed by other school staff. Delegation to teachers, for example, can reap the same benefits of their support for this program as can be expected from community involvement as a whole. The evidence indicates that successful involvement breeds more successful involvement. Once a mechanism of shared control has been established, the principal should find it a resourceful partner that bears some of the decision-making burdens now too narrowly distributed.

The simple opportunity to participate is the first requisite. The group's existence helps, but is not enough to ensure the fulfillment of this requirement. Announcing the formation of a neighborhood group and electing it is only the beginning. Neighborhood involvement, at the control-sharing level, is not a standard operating procedure in big cities. The principal will need to be continually supportive of the group and its work at a high level to attract substantial neighborhood participation. The neighborhood must see its involvement as potentially important and potentially effective. People can tell the difference between authentic groups that offer real participatory opportunities and symbolic groups that are not intended to change anything. Decision-making about education is a complicated and demanding task. One of the most certain ways to prevent neighborhoods from rising to that challenge is to prematurely cut down the size or the relevance of the task. A trivialized opportunity then yields disappointing results. Because teachers and parents take cues from the principal, the principal's actions and attitudes are critical. If the cues indicate solid expectations, trust, and patience, the group's chances for success will be materially improved.

In addition to the existence of a structural opportunity for involvement, it is apparent that group members must have the resources to take part. The people who are least represented in school decision-making—the poor—have to spend almost all of their time and energy struggling to survive. Anything left over is likely to go to family responsibilities or to other, nonpublic uses. To succeed, the neighborhood group must take that reality into account. The first way to deal with this has already been discussed—provide an opportunity that makes the act of involvement worth the effort. The second way is to encourage meetings to be held at times and places convenient to group members. The third way is to provide members with a modest stipend or honorarium on an annual basis. The stipend, which might be as little as $5 or $10 per meeting, can be used to pay for transportation and babysitting services. It may also help to offset some of the income (from second jobs and overtime) that some group members will be giving up to attend meetings. Where the money stipend might cause problems, services in kind (especially child care) may be arranged. For principals who are used to having to meet union requirements that professional teachers be paid for "extra" duties, the recommendation that neighborhood group members receive a small amount for their services should not be a shocking one. The amounts involved are certainly no incentive for exploitation, but they can make possible participation (and its associated benefits) that would not otherwise be available.

Successful groups are willing to mobilize all their resources. It does a neighborhood little good to have residents who feel strongly about the schools, who have concrete proposals to make, and who have influence to spend if those feelings are not expressed, the proposals are not pushed, or the influence is not applied. The rate at which neighborhoods mobilize to exploit their resources is one of the keys to success. The main responsibility for this belongs within the neighborhood representatives themselves, but the principal can help in several ways. First, the principal's cooperation can demonstrate to the community that its mobilization makes a difference. By helping the group achieve some early successes, the principal can help diminish the feeling of helplessness that blocks action. The principal can also encourage the staff to help. If teachers are knowledgeable about and supportive of the neighborhood group and if they are encouraged (or required) to make home visits and other community contacts, they can help the community get together. If the school has social workers or a school community agent assigned to it (or if the principal can influence workers from other city agencies in the neighborhood to help), they can be enlisted in the same effort.

The principal may be even more directly helpful in the area of material resources. Successful groups need to be able to communicate with their constituents. They need money for miscellaneous expenses. The principal can help by making the school's duplicating machines, phones, space, and other facilities available to authorized parent and community representatives. The principal may also wish to consider assigning administrative staff or releasing teacher time to help with particular tasks. The most useful contribution in this category comes from the group having money to support its own operation. That kind of money is rare in school budgets but not impossible to find. An established group may be able, perhaps with the principal's assistance, to get support from the central board, a foundation, a government agency, or local civic or business groups. To the extent that the principal shares the goals of the group, then it is to the principal's self-interest to help the group succeed because its success will be reflected in educational achievement, responsiveness, and support for the school. That realization should reinforce the principal's motivation to help the group find the limited amount of money necessary to support its operation. (See the sample budgets in Appendix 7A.)

Without adequate information the most carefully constructed group cannot succeed. Much of the information the group will need to consider is available in the school. Budget records, program evaluations, achievement test scores, and so on should be given to the group. Of course, proper safeguards should be used—for example, the confidentiality of individual student and employee records should be maintained. The interpretation of school records (e.g., performance comparisons among different schools, the identification of trends) is a sensitive matter. However, without relevant data, the group's decisions cannot be properly informed, nor can the group become more sophisticated in its assistance to the school.

School administrators have a lot of respect for the amount of training and expertise necessary to support high-quality education decisions. That sort of knowledge can be built up by participating in the group, but it is a slow process that can be helped along by training and by staff assistance. All orientation or training should be as carefully planned as any other lesson. Orientation sessions may be brief (20-minute?) exposures to the major areas of school policy. It may be possible to combine some early group meetings with these sessions. Training sessions are more extensive and will need to be scheduled separately. The use of outside experts (from the central office, from local colleges or universities, or from other already established neighborhood groups) should be considered. It is often useful for group members to play specific roles or to simulate decisions in which they will later participate. Both orientation and training sessions should be backed up with written materials. If, over the course of a year, these materials cover all facets of the school, they can be collected and made available to interested people, especially to new group members as a comprehensive introduction to the school's decision-making. The principal should also explore the possibility that the parents may wish to conduct orientation sessions for the professional staff. Knowledge about the community is difficult to gain for teachers who do not reside in the neighborhood; parents and teachers could both profit by such interaction.

The second way in which the group's substantive knowledge can be increased is through staff assistance. The most successful groups are those that have independent, professional help, for example, through child advocates, or through community-development specialists. Unfortunately, that sort of help is not very often found at the neighborhood school level. The principal might explore the possibility of teachers receiving in-service training credit in return for community work. Neighborhood groups can also take advantage of the efforts of city-wide watchdog and special interest groups in education. The possibility of using interns or other students from graduate schools of education should be explored.

A Note on the Distribution of Resources

One of the principal's chief responsibilities is to be certain that the school's resources are impartially available. The more time, energy, access to staff help, and so on that any individual has, the more likely it is that that individual can pursue his or her own points of view. It is inevitable that some people *within the group* will have more of the resources necessary to succeed than will others. "Resources" is a neutral word, but "advantages" is not. When time, energy, and substantive knowledge are applied to a particular position about what the neighborhood school should or should not be doing, then it is clear that those resources are also partisan weapons. Thus they should be as impartially available to all participants as can be arranged.

The closest, most frequent, and most important interaction is that which occurs between the school staff, especially the teachers, and the community. Whether teachers will have a responsive or a disdainful and indifferent orientation to their neighborhood clientele may determine a great deal about the success of neighborhood involvement. The teachers' apprehensions that lay people will cut into professional prerogatives should be understandable to principals. One way to allay those apprehensions is through careful, public planning of the involvement mechanism *with* the participation of key teachers.

Every task that can be jointly undertaken between teachers and neighborhood residents should contribute to mutual understanding. Thus the citizens' group should be careful to invite, encourage, and utilize teacher participation wherever it is appropriate. Additionally, the principal's own actions should demonstrate that the neighborhood is a respected partner in decisions about teaching and learning.

The amount of attention that the neighborhood group gets from the local communications media is the last factor considered here. The visibility of the group will help it succeed. Its ability to represent all parts of the neighborhood will be enhanced if local newspapers, radio, and TV stations publicize the group's activities. Of course, the neighborhood school is unlikely to attract much attention even from the local commercial stations, but most cities have noncommercial UHF channels (sometimes municipally sponsored) that can be used to publicize the work of the neighborhood group. The central office of most city systems will also have TV and radio public relations specialists who are supposed to help school groups. These media opportunities can dramatically expand the group's visibility, but the old stand-bys of school community relations such as newsletters, fliers, and public meetings should not be overlooked. In all of these instances, the initiative and influence of the principal (with headquarters specialists in public relations, for example) can be an important assist to the group.

Appendix 7A:
Sample Budgets

Budget A: Low Option

Note: Budget *A* is probably the most realistic for urban schools without outside support for this purpose. It relies heavily on contributed space and services from school personnel.

Salary
> None; School/community agent services provided through delegation and released time from a number of school employees and coordination with other social welfare agencies in neighborhood.

Stipends
> *Group members*; minimal stipends to cover out-of-pocket transportation costs. Group child care provided at place of meeting.　　$ 200

Facilities
> Meeting space (contributed); school openings (meetings to coincide to the maximum possible extent with other times school is open) five special after-hours meetings at $50 each　　250

Supplies　　250

Phone
> Contributed

Duplicating　　500

Mailings
> Seven mailings to average of 500 households = 3,500 at 1.7¢ each*　　60

Election conduct
> A. Duplicating (see above)
> B. Paid advertising　　500
> C. Supervision (contributed)
> D. School openings (2)　　100

Consulting and Training
> Contributed by district and school staff　　————

> Total: Low Option　　$1,860

---

*Shared-control groups would be eligible for a nonprofit organization indicia entitling them to the reduced rate. Mail must be organized by zip code, delivered to post office, and paid in advance.

Budget B: High Option

Salary
School/community agent (acts as staff to shared-control group, assists in school/home linkage, etc.) $12,000

Personnel benefits (20% of salary) 2,400
Overhead support (50% of salary) 6,000
$20,400

Stipends
Group members 12 members (avg.), 18 meetings per year (8 subcommittees, 10 full group meetings) = 216 meetings at $15 each 3,240

Facilities
Meeting space (contributed). Cost for 10 after-hours school openings at $50 each 500

Supplies 1,000

Phone 500

Duplicating 3,000

Mailing
Five bimonthly reports plus two mailings in connection with elections = 7 mailings to average of 500 households = 3,500 at 8¢ each 280

Election conduct
A. Duplicating: see above
B. Paid advertising in local media 500
C. Supervision of election 100
D. School openings (2) 100

Consulting and Training
Four special sessions, one in each of school policy areas plus preparation of written materials 1,000

Total: High Option $30,620

Appendix 7B:
Sample By-Laws*

Note: The by-laws of the group should be written and available to all interested individuals.

I. Officers
    There will be a chairman and a secretary elected annually by the group at its first meeting after school opens in the fall.

II. Member Selection (See "Handbook.")

III. Subcommittees
    A. Subcommittees may be established and discharged by a majority of the group. They may be temporary or permanent, depending on their tasks.
    B. Each subcommittee shall elect its own chairman and secretary. Other people may be invited to meet with the subcommittee, e.g., students, teachers, administrators, etc.
    C. Permanent subcommittees may be established in the most important policy areas.

IV. Program
    The group will plan a program and agenda for the year's meetings. The plan should include specific details of who is to achieve what by what time.

V. Meetings
    A. The annual program will indicate the time and place of regular meetings for the year (and to the extent possible, the topics of each meeting).
    B. Meetings should occur on a monthly basis.
    C. Special meetings may be called, or regular meetings may be canceled by a majority vote of the whole group.
    D. Decision procedures (e.g., voting, parliamentary operation, etc.) will be established within the first two meetings and will govern the group's procedures in any case of dissent.
    E. Regular and subcommittee meetings will be publicly announced in advance and will be open to the public.
    F. A written record of each meeting will be kept by the secretary, and bi-monthly reports will be disseminated through appropriate channels to the neighborhood.

---

*These by-laws have been extensively revised from Richard K. Hofstrander and Lloyd J. Phipps, "Advisory Councils for Education: A Handbook," Rurban Educational Development Laboratory (Champaign-Urbana: College of Education, University of Illinois, 1971); ERIC ED 057213.

G. All meetings shall include an opportunity for nonmembers to make known their views on items relevant to the business of the shared-control group.

VI. Responsibilities of Members

Each member is expected to prepare for, and participate in all regular meetings and to serve on subcommittees when requested.

Bibliography

Bibliography

Abrams, Joan Dianne. "Relationships Among Responses of Elementary School Principals in the New York City Public School System to School Decentralization, Their Perceptions Concerning Teacher Professionalism and Their Public Control Orientation." Ph.D. dissertation, New York University, 1971.

Agger, Robert E., and Marshall Goldstein. *Who Will Rule the Schools: A Cultural Class Crisis.* Belmont: Wadsworth, 1971.

Aleshire, Robert A. "Power to the People: An Assessment of the Community Action and Model Cities Experience." *Public Administration Review.* 32 (September, 1972, special issue) pp. 428-443.

Alinsky, Saul. "Organizing Low-Income Neighborhoods for Political Action" in *Urban School Administration* ed. by McKelvey and Swanson. Beverly Hills, Calif.: Sage Publications, Inc., 1969, pp. 37-48.

Altshuler, Alan. *Community Control: The Black Demand for Participation in Large American Cities.* New York: Pegasus, 1970.

Andrews, Richard L., and Ernest G.S. Noack. "The Satisfaction of Parents with their Community Schools as a Measure of Effectiveness of the Decentralization of a School System." American Education Research Association, Annual Meetings, New York, February, 1971.

Arnstein, Sherry R. "Eight Rungs on the Ladder of Citizen Participation" in *Citizen Participation: Effecting Community Change* ed. by Edgar S. Cahn and Barry A. Passett. New York: Praeger, 1971, pp. 69-91.

Austin, David. "Resident Participation: Political Mobilization or Organizational Cooptation?" *Public Administration Review.* (September, 1972, special issue) pp. 409-420.

Averch, Harvey A., Stephen J. Carroll, Theodore S. Donaldson, Herbert J. Kiesling, and John Pincus. *How Effective is Schooling.* Santa Monica: The Rand Corp., March, 1972, R956-PCSF/RC.

Bell, Wendell and Maryanne Force. "Urban Neighborhood Types and Participation in Formal Association." *American Sociological Review.* (February, 1956) pp. 25-33.

Bernstein, Abraham. *The Education of Urban Populations.* New York: Random House, 1967.

Berube, Maurice. "Educational Achievement and Community Control." *Community Issues.* 1, n. 1 (November, 1968).

Bloom, Benjamin Samuel. *Compensatory Education for Cultural Deprivation.* A report based on working papers contributed by participants in a Conference of Education and Cultural Deprivation. New York: Holt, Rinehart, Winston, 1967.

Bloomberg, Warner, and Morris Sunshine. *Suburban Power Structures and Public Education.* Syracuse: Syracuse University Press, 1963.

Bloomberg, Warner, and John Kincaid. "Parent Participation: Practical Policy or Another Panacea." *The Urban Review.* 2, n. 7 (June, 1968) pp. 5-11.

Board of Education of the City of New York. "Guidelines to Decentralization for the Period Ending June 30, 1969: Prepared for the Use of Local School Boards and Local (District) Superintendents." Brooklyn, N.Y.: Board of Education, December, 1968.

Board of Examiners. "Preliminary Notice: Next Examination for License as Principal of a Day Elementary School." Brooklyn, N.Y.: Board of Education of the City of New York, 1970.

Brandeis University. "Community Representation in 20 Cities" in *Citizen Participation* ed. by Edgar Cahn and Barry A. Passett. New York: Praeger, 1971.

Brookover, Wilbur B., *et al. Self-Concept of Ability and School Achievement (II).* East Lansing: Bureau of Educational Research Services, Michigan State University, 1965.

Brownell, Clifford Lee, Leo Gans, and Tufie Z. Maroon. *Public Relations in Education.* New York: McGraw-Hill, 1955.

Burke, Edmund M. "Citizen Participation Strategies." *Journal of American Institute of Planners.* (September, 1968).

Cahn, Edgar S. and Jean Camper Cahn. "Maximum Feasible Participation: A General Overview" in *Citizen Participation: Effecting Community Change* ed. by Edgar S. Cahn and Barry A. Passett. New York: Praeger, 1971.

Carter, Richard, and Steven Chaffee. *Between Citizens and Schools. Vol. II.* Stanford, Calif.: Institute for Communications Research, Stanford University, 1966: ERIC ED 017 058.

Carter, Richard F., Bradley S. Greenberg, and Alvin Haimson. *Informal Communications about Schools. Vol. I.* Stanford, Calif.: Institute for Communications Research, Stanford University, 1966: ERIC ED 017 058.

Carter, Richard F., and W. Lee Ruggels. *Vol. IV: The Process of School-Community Relations.* Stanford, Calif.: Institute for Communications Research, Stanford University, 1966: ERIC ED 017 058.

Carter, Richard F., W. Lee Ruggels, and Richard Olson. *Structure of School Community Relations. Vol. III.* Stanford, Calif.: Institute for Communications Research, Stanford University, 1966: ERIC ED 017 058.

Carter, Richard F., and W.R. Odell. *The Structure and Process of School Community Relations. Vol. V: A Summary.* Stanford, Calif.: Institute for Communications Research, Stanford University, 1966: ERIC ED 017 058.

Carter, Richard F., and John Sutthoff. *Voters and Their Schools.* Stanford, Calif.: Institute for Communications Research, Stanford University, 1960.

Carver, Fred D., and Thomas T. Sergiovanni, eds. *Organizations and Human Behavior: Focus on Schools.* New York: McGraw-Hill, 1969.

Clark, Kenneth. *A Relevant War Against Poverty: A Study of Community Action Programs and Observable Social Change.* New York: Metropolitan Applied Research Center, Inc., 1968.

Cloward, Richard A., and James A. Jones. "Social Class: Educational Attitudes and Participation" in *Education in Depressed Areas* ed. by A. Harry Passow. New York: Teachers College Press, 1963, pp. 190-216.

Cohen, Wilbur J. "Education and Learning." *The Annals of the American Academy of Political and Social Science.* 378 (September, 1967), pp. 79-101.

Coleman, James S. *Equality of Educational Opportunity.* Washington, D.C.: U.S. Office of Education. USGPO, 1966.

Conway, James A., Robert E. Jennings, and Mike M. Milstein, *Understanding Communities.* Englewood Cliffs, New Jersey: Prentice-Hall, 1974.

Crain, Robert L., Elihu Katz, and Donald Rosenthal. *The Politics of Community Conflict: The Flouridation Decision.* New York: Bobbs-Merrill, 1969.

Cunningham, James V. "Citizen Participation in Public Affairs." *Public Administration Review.* 32 (October, 1972, special issue), pp. 589-602.

Cunningham, Luvern. *Governing Schools: New Approaches to Old Issues.* Columbus, Ohio: Merril, 1971.

Deutsch, Martin. "The Disadvantaged Child and the Learning Process" in *Education in Depressed Areas* ed. by Harry A. Passow. New York: Teachers College Press, 1963, pp. 163-180.

_____, ed. *The Disadvantaged Child.* New York: Basic Books, 1967.

Dewey, John. *The Public and Its Problems.* Chicago: Sage Books, The Swallow Press, Inc., 1954.

Dubey, Sumati N. "Community Action Programs and Citizen Participation: Issues and Confusions." *Social Work.* 15 (January, 1970).

Easton, David. *A Framework for Political Analysis.* Englewood Cliffs, N.J.: Prentice-Hall, 1965.

Edelman, Murray. "The Political Lanugage of the Helping Professions." *Politics and Society.* 4, n. 3 (1974), pp. 295-310.

Eisinger, Peter K. "Control Sharing in the City." *American Behavioral Scientist.* 15, n. 1 (September/October, 1971), pp. 36-51.

Falkson, Joseph, and Marc Grainer. "Neighborhood School Politics and Constituency Organizations." *The School Review.* 81, n. 1 (November, 1972), pp. 35-62.

Fantini, Mario, Marilyn Gittell, and Richard Magat. *Community Control and the Urban School.* New York: Praeger, 1970.

Fein, Leonard J. *The Ecology of the Public Schools.* New York: Pegasus, 1971.

Friedman, R.S., B.W. Klein, and J.H. Romani. "Administrative Agencies and the Publics They Serve." *Public Administration Review.* 26 (September, 1966), pp. 192-204.

Gallup, George. "How the Nation Views the Public Schools." Princeton, N.J.: Gallup International, 1969.

Gamson, William A. "Stable Unrepresentation in American Society." *American Behavioral Scientist.* 12 (November/December, 1968), pp. 250-260.

_____. "Rancorous Conflict in Community Politics" in *The Search for Community Power* ed. by Willis D. Hawley and Frederick M. Wirt. Englewood Cliffs, N.J.: Prentice-Hall, 1968, pp. 164-175.

Getzels, Jacob W., and Egon G. Guba. "Role, Role Conflict, and Effectiveness." *American Sociological Review.* XIX (1954).

Gilbert, Neil. *Clients or Constituents.* San Francisco: Jossey-Bass, 1970.

Gittell, Marilyn. "Urban School Reform in the 70's" in *Confrontation at Ocean-Hill Brownsville* ed. by Maurice R. Berube and Marilyn Gittell. New York: Praeger, 1969, pp. 327-334.

———. "The Balance of Power and the Community School" in *Community Control of Schools* ed. by Henry M. Levin. Washington, D.C.: The Brookings Institution, 1970, pp. 115-137.

Gittell, Marilyn, Maurice R. Berube, Frances Gottfreid, Marcia Guttentag, and Adele Spier. *Demonstration for Social Change: An Experiment in Local Control.* New York: Institute for Community Studies, Queens College of the City University of New York, 1971.

Gittell, Marilyn, and T. Edward Hollander, *Six Urban School Districts: A Comparative Study of Institutional Response.* New York: Praeger, 1968.

Goldstein, Marshall, and Robert Cahill. "Mass Media and Community Politics" in *The Politics of Education in the Local Community* ed. Robert S. Cahill and Stephen P. Hencley. Danville, Ill.: The Interstate Printers and Publishers, Inc., 1964, pp. 163-188.

Haider, Donald. "The Political Economy of Decentralization." *American Behavioral Scientist.* 15, n. 1 (September/October, 1971), pp. 108-129.

Havelock, Ronald G. *Planning for Innovation through Dissemination and Utilization of Knowledge.* Ann Arbor, Mich.: Institute for Social Research CRUSK, 1971.

Hess, Robert D., Marianne Bloch, Joan Costello, Ruby T. Knowles, and Dorothy Largay. "Parent Involvement in Early Childhood Education" in *Day Care: Resources for Decisions* ed. by Edith Grotberg. Washington, D.C.: Office of Economic Opportunity, reprinted by the Day Care and Child Development Council of America, Inc., no date, pp. 265-298.

Hess, Robert D., and Virginia C. Shipman. "Maternal Attitudes Toward the School and the Role of Pupils: Some Social Comparisons." Paper prepared for the Fifth Work Conference on Curriculum and Teaching in Depressed Urban Areas, New York, Teachers College, Columbia University, 1966 (mimeographed).

Hollister, Robert. "Citizen Participation in Health Planning." *Planning for Health Services and Facilities and Its Relation to City and Regional Planning Activities.* Cambridge: Joint Center for Urban Studies of MIT and Harvard University, June, 1968.

Howe, Harold. "Should Educators or Boards Control our Public Schools." *Nation's Schools.* 78 (December, 1966), pp. 30-31, 58-60.

Hughes, John, and Anne O. Hughes. *Equal Education: A New National Strategy.* Bloomington: Indiana University Press, 1972.

Iannaccone, Laurence, and Frank Lutz. *Politics, Power and Policy: The Governing of Local School Districts.* Columbus, Ohio: Merrill, 1970.

Isbister, Russell L., and G. Robert Koopman, "Citizen Participation in School Affairs." *Vital Issues in American Education* ed. Alice and Lester D. Crow. New York: Bantam, 1964.

Jennings, M. Kent. "Parental Grievances and School Politics." ERIC ED 010 0900, June, 1966.

_____. "Parental Grievances and School Politics" rev. ed. *Public Opinion Quarterly*. 32, n. 3 (Fall, 1968), pp. 363-378.

Jennings, M. Kent, and Harmon Zeigler. "Response Styles and Politics: The Case of School Boards." *Midwest Journal of Political Science*. V. XV, n. 2 (May, 1971), pp. 290-321.

Jencks, Christopher. "The Coleman Report and the Conventional Wisdom" in *On Equality of Educational Opportunity* ed. Frederick Mosteller and Daniel Moynihan. New York: Vintage, 1972, pp. 3-69.

Kindred, Leslie W., and Associates. *How to Tell the School Story*. Englewood Cliffs, N.J.: Prentice-Hall, 1960.

Kirst, Michael W., ed. *The Politics of Education*. Berkeley, Calif.: McCutchan, 1970.

Kleinfeld, Judith. " 'Sense of Fate Control' and Community Control of Schools." *Education and Urban Society*. III n. 3 (May, 1971), pp. 277-300.

Kotler, Milton. *Neighborhood Governance*. Indianapolis and New York: The Bobbs-Merrill Co., 1969.

Knezevich, Stephen. *Administration of Public Education*. New York: Harper and Brothers, 1962.

Kramer, Ralph M. *Participation of the Poor: Comparative Case Studies in the War on Poverty*. Englewood Cliffs, N.J.: Prentice-Hall, 1969.

La Noue, George, and Bruce L.R. Smith. *The Politics of School Decentralization*. Lexington: Lexington Books, 1973.

Lauter, Paul, and Florence Howe. "The School Mess." *The New York Review of Books*. (February 1, 1968), pp. 16-21.

Leiberman, Myron. *The Future of Public Education*. Chicago: Phoenix, 1960.

Lipsky, Michael. *Protest in City Politics: Rent Strikes, Housing, and the Power of the Poor*. Chicago: Rand McNally, 1970.

Lopate, Carol, Erwin Flaxman, Effie Bynum, and Edmund Gordon. "Some Effects of Parent and Community Participation on Public Education." New York: ERIC Information Retrieval Center on the Disadvantaged, Teachers College, February, 1969. ERIC ED 027 359.

Lopate, Carol, Erwin Flaxman, Effie M. Bynum, and Edmund Gordon. "Decentralization and Community Participation in Public Education." *Review of Educational Research*. 40, n. 1 (February, 1970), pp. 135-150.

Lurie, Ellen. *How to Change the Schools*. New York: Vintage, 1970.

Luttbeg, Norman R., and Richard W. Griffin. "Public Reactions to Misrepresentation: The Case of Educational Politics." Florida State University, no date (mimeographed).

Lyke, Robert F. "Political Issues in School Decentralization" in *The Politics of*

Education at the Local, State and Federal Levels ed. Michael W. Kirst. Berkeley, Calif.: McCutchan, 1970.

McCaffrey, Michael D. "Politics in the Schools." *Educational Administration Quarterly*, v. 7, n. 3 (Autumn, 1971), pp. 51-63.

McCloskey, Gordon. *Education and Public Understanding*, 2d. ed. New York: Harper and Row, 1967.

Maccoby, E.E., T.M. Newcomb, and E.E. Hartley, eds. *Readings in Social Psychology* 3rd. ed. New York: Holt, Rinehart, 1958.

McLaughlin, Milbrey Wallin. "Parent Involvement in Compensatory Education Programs." Cambridge: Center for Educational Policy Research, Harvard University, 1971.

Mann, Dale. "Administrator/Community/School Relationships in New York State." New York: New York State Commission on the Quality, Cost and Financing of Elementary and Secondary Education, 1972.

_____. "Public Understanding and Education Decision-Making." *Educational Administration Quarterly*. 10, n. 2 (Spring, 1974): pp. 1-18.

_____. "Representational Role Orientations of New York City Elementary School Principals." New York: Columbia University, unpublished Ph.D. dissertation, 1971.

_____. "Shared Control in Urban Neighborhood Schools: An Interpretive Essay and Bibliography." NIE, ERIC ED 083 355, September, 1973.

Massotti, Louis. "Patterns of White and NonWhite School Referenda Participation in Cleveland 1960-1964" in *Educating an Urban Population* ed. Marilyn Gittell. Beverly Hills, Calif.: Sage, 1967, pp. 240-256.

Mayor's Advisory Panel on Decentralization of the New York City Schools, McGeorge Bundy, Chairman. *Reconnection for Learning: A Community School System for New York City*. New York: Mayor's Advisory Panel, November, 1967.

Meranto, Phillip. *School Politics in the Metropolis*. Columbus, Ohio: Merrill, 1970.

Milbrath, Lester. *Political Participation: How and Why People Get Involved in Politics*. Chicago: Rand McNally, 1965.

Miller, S.M., and Martin Rein. "Participation, Poverty, and Administration" in *Public Administration Review*. 29, n. 1 (January/February, 1969), pp. 15-24.

Minar, David. "Community Politics and School Boards" in *The American School Board Journal*. (March, 1967), pp. 33-37.

Moehlman, Arthur B., and James A. van Zwoll. *School Public Relations*. New York: Appleton-Century-Crofts, 1957.

Mogulof, Melvin B. "Citizen Participation: A Review and Commentary on Federal Policies and Practices." Washington, D.C.: The Urban Institute, 1970 (mimeographed).

_____. "Coalition to Adversary: Citizen Participation in Three Federal Programs." *Journal of American Institute of Planners*. (July, 1969), pp. 225-232.

Mosher, Frederick C. *Governmental Reorganizations: Cases and Commentary.* Indianapolis: Bobbs-Merrill, 1967.

Mowry, Charles E. "Non-Technical Report: Investigation of the Effects of Parent Participation in Head Start." Denver, Col.: Midco Educational Associates, Inc., prepared for OCD, HEW-OS-72-45, November, 1972.

Nunnery, Michael Y., and Ralph B. Kimbrough. *Politics, Power, Polls, and School Elections.* Berkeley, Calif.: McCutchan, 1971.

Pateman, Carole. *Participation and Democratic Theory.* London: Cambridge University Press, 1970.

Pelz, Edith B. "Discussion, Decision Commitment and Consensus in 'Group Decision'." *Human Relations.* 8 (1955), pp. 252-274.

Peterson, Paul E. "Participation of the Poor." *American Political Science Review.* LXIV, n. 2 (June, 1970), pp. 491-507.

Pitkin, Hannah F. *The Concept of Representation.* Berkeley, Calif.: University of California Press, 1967.

Pomper, Gerald M., Richard W. Boyd, Richard A. Brody, Benjamin Page, and John H. Kessel. "Issue Voting." *American Political Science Review.* LXVI, n. 2 (June, 1972), pp. 415-428.

Prewitt, Kenneth. *The Recruitment of Political Leaders: A Study of Citizen-Politicians.* Indianapolis: Bobbs-Merrill, 1970.

_____. "Political Ambitions, Volunteerism, and Electoral Accountability." *American Political Science Review.* LXIV, n. 1 (March, 1970), pp. 5-17.

Prewitt, Kenneth, and Heinz Eulau. "Political Matrix and Political Representation: Prolegomenon to a New Departure from an Old Problem." *American Political Science Review.* LXIII, n. 2 (June, 1969), pp. 412-427.

Provus, Malcolm. "In Search of Community." *Phi Delta Kappan.* 54, n. 10 (June, 1973), pp. 658-661.

Raffel, Jeffrey A. "Responsiveness in Urban Schools: A Study of School System Adaptation to Parental Preferences in an Urban Environment." Unpublished Ph.D. dissertation, Massachusetts Institute of Technology, 1972.

Rankin, Paul T., Jr. "The Relationship Between Parent Behavior and Achievement of the Inner City School Children." Paper presented at the 1967 Annual Meeting of the American Educational Research Association, New York, February, 1967.

Ravitch, Diane. "Community Control Revisited." *Commentary.* 53, n. 2 (February, 1972), pp. 69-74.

Redford, Emmette S. *Democracy in the Administrative State.* New York: Oxford, 1969.

Rempson, Joe L. "School-Parent Programs in Depressed Urban Neighborhoods" in *The Urban Rs: Race Relations as the Problem in Urban Education* ed. by Robert A. Dentler, Bernard Mackler, and Mary Ellen Warshauer. New York: Praeger, 1967, pp. 130-157.

Rosenthal, Robert, and Lenore Jacobson. *Pygmalion in the Classroom.* New York: Holt, Rinehart, and Winston, 1968.

Salisbury, Robert H. "Schools and Politics in the Big City." *Harvard Educational Review.* 37, n. 3 (Summer, 1967), pp. 408-424.

Savitch, Harold. "Powerlessness in an Urban Ghetto: The Case of Political Biases and Differential Access in New York City." *Polity.* V, n. 1 (Fall, 1972), pp. 19-56.

Sayre, Wallace. "Additional Observations on the Study of Administration." *Teachers College Record.* 60 (November, 1958).

Schmandt, Henry. "Municipal Decentralization: An Overview." *Public Administration Review.* XXXII (October, 1972, special issue), pp. 571-588.

Stearns, Marian Sherman, and Susan Peterson, with Anne H. Rosenfeld and Meredith L. Robinson. "Parent Involvement in Compensatory Education Programs: Definitions and Findings." Menlo Park, Educational Policy Research Center, Stanford Research Institute, mimeographed, March 16, 1973.

Stelzer, Leigh. "School Board Receptivity." *Education and Urban Society.* V, n. 1 (November 1972), pp. 69-90.

Strange, John H. "The Impact of Citizen Participation on Public Administration." *Public Administration Review.* 32 (September, 1972, special issue), pp. 457-470.

Swanson, G.E., *et al. Readings in Social Psychology.* New York: Holt, Rinehart, Winston, 1952.

The Urban Education Task Force Report, Wilson C. Riles, Chairman. New York: Praeger, 1970.

U.S. Department of Health, Education and Welfare, National Center for Education Statistics, W. Vance Grant and C. George Lind. *Digest of Educational Statistics.* Washington, D.C.: Government Printing Office, 1975.

U.S. Commission on Civil Rights. "Public Knowledge and Busing Opposition: An Interpretation of a New National Survey." Washington, D.C., March 11, 1973, mimeographed.

U.S. Office of Education. "Parental Involvement in Title I ESEA, Why? What? How?" Washington, D.C.: DHEW Publication No. OE 72-109, 1972.

_____ . "Memorandum to Chief State School Officers: Advisory Statement on Development of Policy on Parental Involvement in Title I. ESEA Projects." Washington, D.C.: USOE/DHEW, October 30, 1970.

Vanecko, James J. "Community Mobilization and Institutional Change: The Influence of the Community Action Program in Large Cities." *Social Science Quarterly.* (December, 1969), pp. 609-630.

Verba, Sidney. "Democratic Participation" in *Social Intelligence for America's Future: Explorations in Societal Problems* ed. by B.M. Gross. Boston: Allyn and Bacon, 1969, pp. 126-162.

Wahlke, John, Heinz Eulau, William Buchanan, and Leroy Ferguson. *The Legislative System: Explorations in Legislative Behavior.* New York: Wiley, 1962.

Wilson, James D. "Research for School Board Members: School-Community

Relations." No. 7-D, "Community Support for Education: Elections Involving School Issues." ERIC ED 034 083, 1969.

Wirt, Frederick M., and Michael W. Kirst. *The Political Web of American Schools.* Boston: Little, Brown, 1972.

Wolf, S.L. "The Identification and Measurement of Environmental Process Variables Related to Intelligence." Ph.D. dissertation, University of Chicago, 1964.

Yates, Douglas. "Neighborhood Government." *Policy Sciences.* 3, n. 2 (July, 1972), pp. 209-218.

Yin, Robert K., William A. Lucas, Peter I. Szanton, and James A. Spindler. "Citizen Participation in DHEW Programs." Washington, D.C.: The Rand Corporation, R-1196-HEW, Xerox, January, 1973. The final report (April, 1973) is available under the title referred to above.

Zeigler, L. Harmon, M. Kent Jennings, and G. Wayne Peak. *Governing American Schools: Political Interaction in Local School Districts.* North Scituate, Mass.: Duxbury Press, 1974.

_____ . "Creating Responsive Schools." *Urban Review.* 6, n. 4 (1973).

Zurcher, Louis A. "The Poverty Board: Some Consequences of 'Maximum Feasible Participation' " *Journal of Social Issues.* 26, n. 3, pp. 85-107.

Index

Index

179

About the Author

Dale Mann is an associate professor in the Department of Educational Administration at Teachers College, Columbia University. He received the A.B. from the University of California and the Ph.D. in Political Science from Columbia University. During the Johnson Administration he served in the U.S. Office of Education and was a special analyst for education in the Bureau of the Budget. Mr. Mann is a consultant to the National Committee for Citizens in Education, has worked with several metropolitan school districts on community problems, and is a long-time consultant to the Rand Corporation. He has recently published *Policy Decision-Making in Education: An Introduction to Calculation and Control.*